digital storytelling

Listen deeply. Tell stories. This is the mantra of the Center for Digital Storytelling (CDS) in Berkeley, California, which since 1993 has worked with nearly 1,000 organizations around the world and trained more than 15,000 people in the art of digital storytelling.

In this revised and updated edition of the CDS's popular guide to digital storytelling, co-founder Joe Lambert details the history and methods of digital storytelling practices. Using a "7 Steps" approach, Lambert helps storytellers identify the fundamentals of dynamic digital storytelling—from seeing the story to assembling and sharing it. Readers of the fourth edition will also find new explorations of the applications of digital storytelling and updated appendices that provide resources for budding digital storytellers, including information about past and present CDS-affiliated projects, and place-based storytelling, a narrative-based approach to understanding experience and landscape. A companion website brings the entire storytelling process to life.

Over the years, the CDS's work has transformed the way that community activists, educators, health and human services agencies, business professionals, and artists think about story, media, culture, and the power of personal voice in creating change. For those who yearn to tell multimedia stories, *Digital Storytelling* is the place to begin.

Joe Lambert founded the Center for Digital Storytelling (formerly the San Francisco Digital Media Center) in 1994, with his wife Nina Mullen and colleague Dana Atchley. Together they developed a unique computer training and arts program around the Digital Storytelling Workshop. This process grew out of Joe's long running collaboration with Dana on the solo theatrical multimedia work *Next Exit*. Since then, Joe and his organization have traveled the world to spread the practice of digital storytelling.

More storytelling resources available online at: www.routledge.com/cw/lambert

digital storytelling

capturing lives, creating community

4th edition

joe lambert

Routledge
Taylor & Francis Group

NEW YORK AND LONDON

Published 2013
by Routledge
711 Third Avenue, New York, NY 10017

Simultaneously published in the UK
by Routledge
2 Park Square, Milton Park, Abingdon, Oxon OX14 4RN

First edition published in 2002 by Life on the Water, Inc.
Second edition published in 2006 by Life on the Water, Inc.
Third edition published in 2009 by Digital Diner Press

Routledge is an imprint of the Taylor & Francis Group, an informa business

Library of Congress Cataloging in Publication Data
Lambert, Joe.
Digital storytelling : capturing lives, creating community / Joe Lambert.
– 4th ed.
    p. cm.
  Includes bibliographical references and index.
  1. Storytelling. 2. Literature and technology. 3. Creative writing.
  4. Digital storytelling. I. Title.
  LB1042.L36 2012
  808.5´43–dc23   2012021164

ISBN: 978-0-415-62702-3 (hardcover)
ISBN: 978-0-415-62703-0 (paperback)
ISBN: 978-0-203-10232-9 (ebook)

Typeset in Minion and Optima
by HWA Text and Data Management, London

For Dana Atchley
Artist, Friend, Digital Storyteller.
Your final exit was beyond reason.
Your vision will live on.
See you on the flipside.

Contents

Foreword

Barbara Ganley

A decade ago, just about when Joe Lambert wrote the first edition of the indispensible *Digital Storytelling: Capturing Lives, Creating Community,* he and his colleague Emily Paulos ventured to Vermont to teach a Digital Storytelling workshop to faculty and staff at Middlebury College. How brave of those two to guide a bunch of academics out from their comfort zones of the rational domain of critical discourse into the deeply affective process of locating, articulating and communicating personal stories. Personal stories? In our own, recorded voices? We would share them? Use multimedia? Whatever for? How vulnerable we felt—would our stories be well-received? Would we be skilled enough using the tools? And…why, again, exactly were we doing this?

Joe, of course, knew what he was at.

He knew that grounding learning in our own lives would give it relevance and thus make it stick. He knew that the Digital Storytelling workshop setting would build community through giving voice to each of us equally and developing collective intelligence among us. And he knew that we teachers and librarians needed to start in our own stories. We couldn't just teach it, we had to do it.

Those three days changed my teaching. I experienced how deep storytelling—listening and being heard—helped us to relax into doing our best work. I saw how the digital stories themselves, as natural vehicles of reflection and understanding, convey learning. From then on, instead of diving right into the course content, my students focused first on the learning community. After reading Joe's book, they created digital stories of identity and learning and their journey to this subject matter: the story of their hands, their love of getting lost in the woods, their grandmother's arrival in the United States.

Ensuring from the get-go that we were all "somebodies," as Joe would put it, contributed mightily to the success of our work together. This turned out to be especially essential for students from marginalized communities who, ordinarily finding themselves with no voice or ownership of the classroom, often feel shut out. When we started in digital story, they felt they mattered, they belonged. In one student's words, "It is a medium that easily speaks to the multiple perspectives and simultaneous existences of hyphenated identities."

Before then, I hadn't known how much my students needed to tell their own stories, that they had never been asked to consider their stories as important markers, doors, and conduits. To record their voices. To share their images. To put them all together into a coherent, pleasing, emphatically twenty-first-century whole. And to see what happened when their stories bumped up into one another. No matter what they were studying.

Digital Storytelling, woven through the semester, improved engagement, connection, creative and critical thinking, and communication. Furthermore, it took students out of themselves and into the community. They fanned out into our rural county to mentor youth in using Digital Storytelling to participate in shaping their towns' future. Several went on to win a grant for a Digital Storytelling project in Ireland, to win college-wide writing prizes for their stories, to submit their stories with graduate school applications, and even to start a nonprofit in India bringing Digital Storytelling to schools.

I hadn't known that a classroom could be so electric, students so on fire. We had begun the journey, as Richard K. Miller urges, to move beyond focusing on worlds ending; we set about to create better worlds. What I also didn't know was that ten years later, these revelations would send me out of the classroom for good and into community engagement work. If my students could feel a new connection to their studies, a new interest in community because of the storytelling, what might happen through weaving storytelling into change efforts in geographic communities? With Joe's book by my side, I went to find out.

What Joe teaches us so convincingly in this new edition is that a healthy community—no matter the setting—is grounded in belonging, in understanding, in plurality. As I've experienced through community-based storytelling efforts, people will get out of their chairs and into town. When relationships are built and strengthened through deep storytelling, people feel welcomed and valued, and civic participation is enhanced. Just as in the classroom. People feel better about their communities. And positive change can follow. There is nothing new in this.

What is new is the digital. We now communicate our stories widely, beyond our own hearths, out of time. Indeed, we're awash in such stories. Look at the popularity of radio's *StoryCorps* and *This American Life*. Look at the stories woven through *TEDtalks*, the performance-based gatherings such as *The Moth* and the Internet's www.Cowbird.com. Look at www.YoungWritersProject.org and www.Globalvoicesonline.org, look at small, localized story movements coming out of museums and libraries and open-access television and oral history centers across the planet. Medical, business, and law schools are paying attention to the power of stories in healing, and in developing ethical, effective business leaders. Citizen journalism, as seen in the Arab Spring and Occupy movements, is grounding the big moment in the mural of the individual experience. We're telling it as it is. As we experience it. We're forming communities around our stories.

Indeed, the Me-story has gone viral. And that's both good and bad. At its worst it has become the Me-Me-Me-story, manipulative or cynical, exploitative or narcissistic, superficial or vapid, a way to seduce us into buying or believing or giving. Splashed across screens.

At its best, the Me-story becomes the I-story: I share my experience as one small but essential piece of a large complex mosaic of stories—*Our* story. But it takes time. As creativity and psycholinguistics scholar Vera John-Steiner notes, successful collaborations "require sustained time and effort ... the shaping of a shared language, the pleasures and risks of honest dialogue, and the search for a common ground" (2000: 184). But it's hard to find the time when we must be agile, shifting approach, tool, and interaction as needed. We're on the move. Everything is uncertain. We treat public spaces as private; we're reluctant to get out of our cars, tear ourselves from our mobile tethers to look at each other, to take on the slow endeavor of building relationships across and between affinity groups, of making the lasting connections that underlie a democratic society. But Joe understands that if we have any hope to restore the health of our communities in this time of convulsive change, we'd better find the time.

That this fourth edition should appear just now gives me hope. Its comprehensiveness, its balance between vision, example and guide, speaks to Joe's responsiveness to change, and to the building of a digital storytelling movement across education, community-change, and health sectors. This book will help us in our community work to give deep storytelling its due, with the tools and media of our time, wherever community is important, wherever we need to be "somebodies" instead of "nobodies." There could be no more important moment to tell stories as a means to bear witness to our world and to change it for the better. There could be no more important moment for Joe to write the new edition of his book.

We need this book. We need it now. We need Joe's unmistakably warm, wry, passionate voice showing us that we matter, we heal, we belong, we take responsibility, we act.

—Barbara Ganley,
Founder and Director,
Community-Expressions.com
June, 2012

Acknowledgments

On behalf of my collaborators at the Center for Digital Storytelling, I would like to graciously thank a number of people for their contributions to the development of the *Digital Storytelling: Capturing Lives, Creating Community*. To start with, I would like to thank the thousands of students who have shared their lives and stories with us and inspire the work of our Center. My colleagues and I have the greatest job in the world, and in every workshop we expand our circle of friends. We must recognize that this book itself has seeds in two projects. In 1996 we were given support by Apple Computer, under the guidance of Ralph Rogers and Kelli Richards, to create the original *Digital Storytelling Cookbook*. Then in 1998, the Institute for the Future, led by our friends Kathi Vian and Bob Johansen, gave us support for *Digital Storytelling: The Creative Application of Digital Technology to the Ancient Art of Storytelling*.

The original work in 2002 on this particular book was made possible principally as a collaboration with Emily Paulos, the Managing Director at CDS. Her support and guidance has remained vital to the ongoing process of evolving this text. I want to thank all the staff at CDS, Daniel Weinshenker, Andrea Spagat, Stefani Sese, Allison Myers, Rob Kershaw, Amy Hill, Zoe Jacobson, and former staff Caleb Paull and Thenmozhi Soundararajan, and our numerous other collaborators. My work is driven by the efforts of this family of co-workers, and I thank all of them for their commitment to the general development of the practice of Digital Storytelling. For his help on the prior edition, and in the last review of this edition, I give a high five to the Ithaca Kid, Patrick Castrenze. I want to give thanks to Erica Wetter and Margo Irvin of Routledge for their work on this edition, moving up from a self-published book, to an "official" publication is a great step for us, and we appreciate the vote of confidence this represents in our work.

Over the years Digital Storytelling has evolved beyond our studios and our workshops with practices in numerous contexts. We look back to recognize the importance of our collaboration with countless organizations and individuals. Some of the names include Warren Hegg and the Digital Clubhouse Network, Glynda Hull at UC Berkeley, Ana Serrano and the Canadian Film Centre in Toronto, Daniel Meadows and the team at Capture Wales from the BBC, Helen Simondson and the Australian Centre for the Moving Image, Geska Helena Andersson, Simon Stromberg, Grete Jamissen, Nikolene Lohmann, and Kaos Pilots in Scandanavia; Pip

Hardy, Tony Sumner, Clodagh Miskelly, Alex Henry, Barrie Stephenson, and others around the UK, Neus Marin and the colleages of Neapolis in Spain, Sabine Felber in Berlin, and our partners MediaShots in Portugal, and Burcu Simsek in Turkey. Larry Johnson and the entire network of the New Media Consortium, the developing work of Aline Gubrium and her associates at the University of Massachusetts (Amherst) to create our New England Center, Sai Ling Chan-Sew and our partners at the Community Behavioral Health in San Francisco, Sonke Gender Justice in South Africa, Downtown Aurora Visual Arts, and more recently Mary Ann McNair in Denver, Jessica Reynolds at Volunteer Toronto, and Liz Norville and her work on Seattle Refugee Youth, and countless others.

I would like to thank the following individuals for permission to reproduce illustrations in the text: Zahid Al-Amin (Interlude 5); Ray Baylor (Interlude 4); Rosalie Blakey Wardell (portrait of Dana Atchley); Roberto Gerli (images on pp. 113–15, Chapter 9 images 7–13); Monte Hallis (Interlude 1); Rob Kershaw (images on pp. 108–11, Chapter 9 images 1-6); Wynne Maggi (Interlude 2); Elizabeth Ross (Interlude 3); Thenmozhi Soundarajan and Thiakavalhy Soundarajan (storyboard in Chapter 8).

Finally, as a book of ideas, inspired by the Digital Storytelling workshop, grew out of my collaboration with Nina Mullen and Dana Atchley. Nina Mullen spent nine years at my side developing our centers in San Francisco and Berkeley, and traveling the world teaching. As my life partner, she has been through this saga, and her support, and the support of our amazing children, Massimo and Amalina, has sustained me in this work. Dana Atchley and I took the original trip on *Next Exit* twenty-six years ago. His exit in 2000 was unbearably heartbreaking. His spirit sits over my left shoulder, keeping me laughing at my own self-serious perspectives. He would have enjoyed how this road trip has continued.

Introduction

As I write these words the sun is shining in Berkeley, California. Springtime. Good time to start anew.

If you are new to this subject, and this approach to media practice, you might be expecting a textbook. Well, this is not exactly a textbook, although the prior editions have been used in this way for the last decade. These are thoughts, both contextual, practical, and speculative, that have grown out of my work in media. The principal topic is the gathering of personal stories into short little nuggets of media called Digital Stories, through a methodology called Digital Storytelling.

Twenty years ago my non-profit organization, the Center for Digital Storytelling (CDS) began work in this field. Digital Storytelling has evolved to become an international movement of deeply committed folks working with story in virtually every field of human endeavor. Our experience in managing over 200 small- to large-scale projects, leading over a 1,000 workshops, and assisting more than 15,000 individuals to complete films informs this writing, as does the work of more than 1,000 other professionals working in the field. You can learn more about CDS at www.storycenter.org.

But you are probably more interested in how to use this book. In the first four chapters, I attempt to establish the context for our work in Digital Storytelling. I present some of the larger reasons why I believe this movement came to be, the specific history of my organization, how to think about story ideas, and how the CDS model of Digital Storytelling relates to other media practices that have been also described as digital storytelling. In the middle of the book, Chapters 5–9, you find the how-to section of the book, describing both how to make a digital story, how to manage the workshop process from the facilitative, and some thoughts on an approach to design in the form. And in Chapters 10–15, we address how the work is applied, starting with a discussion of the public/private issues of a workshop-based practice, then turning to a broad catalog of applications and finally interviewing several practitioners in the fields of public health, education, community development, and health care.

The book is meant to be helpful for first-time students exploring this genre of media, as well as educators, activists, artists, and human service professionals wanting to lead Digital Storytelling processes with local communities. The book makes general arguments but always lands in practical help for someone trying to make their first digital story.

But how should you understand this book? To start with, despite an emphasis on helping people to make a media document, this is not a book about writing and producing media work for broad distribution. We are discussing forms of personal storytelling as an expressive form for anybody, from students in a middle school to retirees in a nursing home. In this sense, it is not about authoring multimedia stories as a profession. I still hope would-be professionals or committed amateurs find some useful thoughts here as well.

This is not a book about becoming an author, but authorship is certainly a central topic of this book. And also how authorship creates agency in life and social interactions. Being the author of your own life, of the way you move through the world, is a fundamental idea in democracy. We want to help everyone use the power of storytelling to project their authority, to expand their sense of being celebrated, of becoming at whatever level, a celebrity within their community.

At the same time, I have a deep mistrust of celebrity, of authority, of specialization and expertise, and the most cutting "-ism" of all, elitism. Elitism separates those of us that get to trade on their rank, and those that may not, would not, or simply cannot. I believe that our collective future is based on re-negotiating the distinctions of privilege and rank in our world. As long as authors are allowed to act like authoritarians, taking more than their share of resource, and presuming they know what is best for other people's stories, we are not going to get out of the mess we find ourselves in at the moment. Of course, we should continue to value those that climb ladders – who distinguish themselves through various achievements; the ability to out-perform, out-maneuver, and out-play others because of sacrifice, focus and determination – as important ... as worthy of celebration. But we should also learn new ways to celebrate those that simply overcome ... whatever their barriers, whatever their challenges. We need to cherish that which is in all of us to step over and around the obstacle in front of us, and move forward with our lives. If that is simply crossing a border with a family and surviving, getting a GED and learning to drive a bus, making your way past a history of family or community violence to find yourself as a peer leader, then your story counts, your rank matters, and your authority deserves our attention.

As I travel around the world, often to universities or other kinds of places of relative privilege, I am drawn to people who are using story to negotiate these distinctions in rank and opportunity (not by accident, these same people are drawn to this work). People who, though perhaps successful as media storytellers themselves, see in every single person a tremendous potential for sharing insight, for wisdom, for teaching us a bit more about what it means to be human. The majority of people who will benefit from this book are those that are looking at ways to break down distinctions of privilege – from Service Learning students working in communities, to people joining in human rights and international development projects, to community organizers and local activists leading campaigns for justice.

Somebodies and Nobodies

One morning at the end of January (of 2012) I woke up with a startle. I was sitting at a desk, listening to the crickets that feed my daughter's gecko chirping nearby.

What startled me up and started me writing feverishly was the convergence of several thoughts that seemed connected to the large project of this book. The previous night my daughter had another homework crisis. She is on the cusp of being defined as a special needs reader/writer, and she is going through massive sadness in recognition of the event. I have this strong sense the pain comes from that falling from grace, from believing yourself as a child as being a naturally and completely whole and flourishing person, to a sense of less than, dissected, left out, not fully a body. A nobody.

As it happens I had started a book called *All Rise: Somebodies, Nobodies and the Politics of Dignity* by my fellow Berkeley resident, Robert Fuller. The book is a summation of his thoughts on rank, and what he calls rankism, not just elitism, but the broader category of differences based on the distribution of power in our societies.

What struck me is how a third-grader is prepared for her entry into rank, into a sense of either being advanced, or being left behind. I understood how completely dedicated the dominant system is to this premise. The students are racing to college; some will win, some will lose. Those that lose will be nobodies, and conversely, to be somebody you had better win. This creates monsters out of both categories. Selfish investment bankers and raging gangbangers. Educational reform is the endless attempt at making this unpalatable system seem bearable.

The converse to ranked privilege is solidarity. Solidarity excludes the possibility of actual difference between anybody. Anybodies then become anathema to systems of exploitation, of rank, of privilege. That could be "anybody" becomes a clearer way of expressing a sense of sameness as opposed to difference. If I am anybody, I am already somebody, and I can never be a nobody.

Healthy Bodies, Healthy Stories

This winter, I also spent time with Dr. Richard Jackson at UCLA. We talked about storytelling and healthy communities. Positive psychology, and self-esteem, are always the staples of healthy living. We need to nourish all the seeds that sit within us that make us feel good about ourselves. As our work has become more and more about surfacing those stories of survivors from traumas big and small, I have come to appreciate how much storytelling is also about mucking around in the seedbed, digging up the crap that holds us down, so that the biological process of story can flourish. The real person inside us descends into our bodies as we face diminishment in our lives. We eat ourselves big, we stress and strain ourselves hard to build a shell around those losses.

I have come to a deeper appreciation of the relationship between story and health. That the stretching, massaging, and meditating our way out of our predicaments as individuals and as societies needs to be combined with the process of telling and re-telling stories good and bad about our lives, not just at on therapist's sofa, but as acts of art and creativity. We need to stop and listen to each other's stories as daily ritual, as life process.

Which is why listening is the hallmark quality of positive social engagement. Listening, making space for the silenced, making room for the nobodies in mind to find their somebody at heart so they feel like anybody else, makes us dignified. It allows us to check our status at the door.

If we are to create, to use Fuller's language – a Dignitarian society, it starts with the signifying process of story.

Storytelling in the Social Media Moment

This work in Digital Storytelling began a few months after William Jefferson Clinton was elected President. I am aware the freshman college student that might be reading this book was not yet born. We started before computers were broadly used to make media, before the World Wide Web, before the emergence of search engines, blogging, ipods, podcasts, smartphones and tablets. And long before social media and YouTube. Personal computers have traveled a great distance, once the tools of business people and designers, we live with computers as the most common appliances. Communication technology is the landscape of our imagination, and an average middle-class kid born in 1993, has never experienced anything other than the ubiquity of tools that allows them to shoot, sample, and share media.

In the twenty-first century, the companies that make this possible, Apple, Microsoft, Google, and Facebook, are not only are bigger than most media companies, they are bigger than most oil companies. Yet we have not become a world of media producers, the ease of production and distribution does not mean all of us see ourselves as authors. We simply watch more of everything – the internet-capable device *is* our television set, and many of us can walk around the world with a screen in our hand, almost never disconnected to a stream of media.

But among a quickly growing number of consumers, as in a large number of the nearly billion Facebook members and 100 million Twitterers, leisure time has become increasingly interactive, where some amount of creative participation is part of the fun. More people than ever are sharing their own media, social media engagement now represents over 20 percent of total internet use, many millions of hours are being spent by people uploading pictures, tagging links with comments, writing little blurbs, and yes, once in awhile uploading a video they made themselves.

Many more people, and communities, are waking up to the power of their own voice in the media, and are finding the means to express themselves, for themselves and their communities through the new media. Change is constant, from iPhone apps to produce and edit digital stories, to intensely creative social media projects like cowbird (www.cowbird.com), we can imagine a thousand new ways to lure us into sharing our stories. We are just beginning to see how our shared creativity will become our main ways of entertaining each other.

This book suggests how we can take our deeply felt attraction to media, which has done so much to silence our own voices, and find our way back to the campfire. Through digital storytelling, we all can become storytellers again.

I hope you find it useful, and I always invite my readers to email me, joe@storycenter.org if they have any questions, thoughts or stories to share.

1

The Work of Story

Why tell stories? This is the basic question to ask at the beginning of a book about storytelling. Stories are what we do as humans to make sense of the world. We are perpetual storytellers, reviewing events in the form of re-lived scenes, nuggets of context and character, actions that lead to realizations. But the brain you are using to listen to me talk about stories and storytelling is very different than the brain you have when you hear me tell a story.

Here is a story.

We had this sofa chair. Brown Naugahyde. An embossed weave stamped into the plastic, and a cigarette hole burned into the arm. I loved that chair.

I remember my dad sitting in that chair one afternoon. A book in hand, glasses perched on his nose. Cigarette in the ash tray.

He raised his head and looked at me.

"Remember that story I told you about the guy in San Antonio. The painter?"

"Yeh 'sure" I answered.

I had remembered the story. Natividad – A character in my father's stories of union organizing in San Antonio, Texas – A Mexican-American artist. One story told about he had painted something critical of the local Catholic bishop on the wall of cathedral. He then sat across the street to watch the nuns try desperately to wash the paint off the wall. Another story was about Natividad's studio up above a storefront near downtown. The staircase was no wider than two and half feet. Despite having to lug his canvas up and down the narrow stairs, the artist had chosen the place precisely. No cop in San Antonio could fit his rump in there to chase him.

My dad would laugh and laugh. And I would laugh with him. These stories made my father happy – ingenuous ways to make those redneck authorities in Texas squirm.

"What about him, dad?"

"Nothing," my dad just smiled. "I was just thinking about him is all."

He took a puff of his cigarette. His eyes returned to the book.

When I am explaining an idea to you, I want to be clearly understood. I want very little distance between my intended meaning, and your perceived meaning. To accomplish this, I need to be precise. I need the ideas to be substantiated by argument, where each example, each concept, builds upon the other, toward a coherent conclusion.

But when I tell a story, reflecting on moment in time, and reflecting on that reflection, I am not so concerned about interpretation. Perhaps I imagine my meaning is evident. While I might hope you would read something similar to me about what this story tells about the source of my political views, I am not trying to convince you to share them. I want you to relate my experience to your own.

Much more important is that my feeling is evident. Unconsciously, I am sure I tell stories that I hope would endear me to you; or at least create an emotional connection between us. An intimacy. When I am in conversation and drop into telling a story, something changes about my choice of words, about the way I describe interactions, impersonating the characters, pulling out the details, feeling, even as I recite my memories, how the actual events worked upon my psyche, how they changed me.

The Biology of Story

> What gives real memory [organic and biological instead of an image of a computer-like brain] its richness and its character, not to mention its mystery and fragility, is its contingency. It exists in time, changing as the body changes. Indeed, the very act of recalling a memory appears to restart the entire process of consolidation, including the generation of proteins to form new synaptic terminals. Once we bring an explicit long term memory back into working memory, it becomes short-term memory again. When we reconsolidate it, it gains a new set of connections ; a new context.
>
> (Carr 2010: 191)

My exploration of story has always coincided with an interest in cognition and memory. Over these many years I find myself lost in some popular press discussion of the advancements in neuroscience, and the evolving discipline of neuropsychology, specifically the biology of our sense of self and the role biochemistry has in emotion and identity.

We have many ways of thinking of story from a biological sense. The hunter/hunting party returns from the hunt and explains how to catch the next big meal. The mother shares her birthing story with a teenage daughter, and explains the process by which she kept the child alive through a long cold winter. Story becomes a teaching tool for survival. And one could argue that the human race stills uses story for this reason, to put the stakes of survival, and the emotions that come with it, as the basis for attentive consideration of a remembered event. Many of the stories we have in our work in public health are life and death cautionary tales, about the results of our own unfortunate or disastrous choices, or those by a person exerting power over us and with those for whom we have primary relationship and attachment.

We now know the general pattern of brain activity that causes short-term memory to become long-term memory. We know that sensory experience is mostly forgotten, moments after we hear, see, touch, smell, taste it. Based on the research of psychologist Brenda Milner, we learned that to remember, we move sensory information from a slower part of our brain that senses back to the fast-working hippocampus. The hippocampus is integral to a complex process of consolidation of the memory over days, weeks, and years. The process, as far as we can tell, requires rehearsal, reviewing the experience again and again in our minds. The new neural pathway that is forged in the cortex through this process becomes long-term memory. The more we rehearse, in our conscious mind, but also in our dreams and subconscious, the deeper the pathway, the more the memory is sustained (Kandel 2006: 129–33)

We all think of this as the essence of learning, you repeat something again and again until it sticks. This works for both physical activities, playing an instrument, using a fine tool, as well as mental activity; multiplication tables or following directions. Practice makes perfect. Repetition creates retention.

As it turns out if we have an affective relationship to the sensory information – if that information is connected to the part of our brains that processes our emotions – then the pathways become even stronger. The memories associated with our most important life lessons are inevitably those with either strong emotional encoding at the moment, as in traumas or events involving those close to us. When we describe these events, and their meaning to our lives, we inevitably drop out of argumentation and into story. Story in this sense, works biologically to insure the total recall of those events which define we have ingrained as of greatest emotional importance to us.

In re-telling, we set the scene of the learning not only to help the listener have a rich context for the meaning, but also to simply return us to the sensory and emotive environment that burned the memory into our neurons. As we remember the scene, we actually are linking back to the sparking neural pathways that were formed in the strong associative memory (Rappoport 2006, Siegel 2012).

The Hollywood Century and the American Myth

Myth is an imaginal story or statement that addresses existential human issues, and that has behavioral consequences. This is in line with Joseph Campbell's proposal that myths are "motivated from a single psychophysiological source – namely the human imagination." Myths often, but not always, employ symbol and metaphor; they are usually, but not always, expressed in verbal narrative. Myths can be cultural, institutional, familial, or personal in nature; a "mythology" is the interwoven (and sometimes contradictory) collection of myths held by a culture, institution, family, or individual. Unlike such related terms as "scripts," "attitudes," "beliefs," or "worldviews," the word "myth" is able to encompass the unconscious as well as the conscious dimensions of the concept.'

(Krippner n.d.)

Life and death, moments of clarity, decisive events that change us; these are not just the subjects of life recalled, these are the essence of our oral traditions of myth and folktale, our literatures, and in the last century, the immersive medias of the screen and recorded sound.

We first know story through our experience, but the stories told us become part of our tribe, our community, our culture and are formed into myth and archetype.

We see our own lives in the plots of the journey, the romance, the mystery. We see our identity and those of our most important relationships in the characters of the hero, the lover, the seeker, the wizard, the sidekick, the beast. We know them as they reappear in our sacred texts; the Bible, the Quran, the life of Siddhartha the Buddha, Anansi the Spider, as well as our epic and children's narratives, the Odyssey, King Arthur, and the Brothers Grimm. We know how they work in Westerns, sci-fi, detective stories, and romantic comedies.

Myths have always served our coming to term with developmental processes – our place in the world, selfhood, partnering, parenting, death – the stories that held us, that spoke to us, gave us patterns that we could be assured of in considering the choices and changes that are part of our lives. But in the recent centuries, the myths that bound us as tribes, as cultures, that gave us the particulars of our definitions of good and evil, speak to the process of dissembling identity as we left the farm for the factory.

Much of the twentieth-century literary and media history was to assist in the development of how societies and individuals could process the vast exit from the agricultural life to the city. As human experience changed, we searched the old myths for patterns to help explain our feelings of dislocation. We also created new myths and archetypes. The machinery of mass media was put to the project through all the genres of storytelling. With Disney and others, they borrowed directly from the folktale to contemporize children's stories to the experience of modern existential alienation, showing us hipster heros and wise-cracking damsels battling corporatist monsters and dictatorial tyrants. The Western showed us how to bring frontier ethics into our chaotic urban experience, mapping the pastoral ideal of self-sufficiency and familial integrity onto a suburban ideal of the single family dwelling, and the sense of embattlement with the savage and wilderness with the relationship between civilized suburb and the lawless inner city. Science fiction, for instance, provided a way to take our fear of sweeping technological innovation and overlay the mythos of the hero's confrontation with the evil genie let loose upon the world. Crime and mystery narratives gave us ways to examine the psychology of social dysfunction through a mythic presentation of the detective as shaman. And romantic narratives helped us to explore difference, juxtaposing characters of different class, situation and culture, negotiating the chaos of prejudice and simmering fears of the other that exploded as cities crammed a multiplicity of tribes into close proximity.

Implicit in these mass-media mythologies was a sense of both nation-state signification and a new universalism, the American century could also be defined as the Hollywood century. The US imperial mythic landscape also served American-exceptionalism in the battle with the totalitarian Other. Our stories were more than reassuring forms of entertainment assisting with our social transitions, they brought with them the values of democracy and a particular sort of individualism that was perceived as the inevitable ethos of all the planet's peoples and societies. As presented by our dominant medias, the American ideal continues to be an unquestioned pinnacle of human progress.

And as has been true with all dominant ideologies inside a culture, we took on the characters as our own. Rather than the collectivist ethos, we saw ourselves as individually responsible for our fate. We saw the signifying success of our own specialized career, our own successful family, single family house, two cars, and endless stuff to continually validate our status. And as an empire, we exported (and continue to export) those expectations as far as we as we could/can reach.

Our Ordinary Stories Become Extraordinary Journeys

Inherent in the individualism of citizen democracy is that every story matters. In practice twentieth-century media culture also can be seen as the triumph of the ordinary person. Traditional cultures took individual experience and mythologized the hunt into the hero's journey or the animist characterizations of mysterious forces in nature. Feudal societies privileged the lives of kings, gods and saints, magi and warrior-heroes. Industrial culture gave us the lifestyles of the rich and famous. But the forces of industrial class struggle and the democratic impulses it created stressed that even the most plebian character had a powerful story to tell. Charles Dickens, Mark Twain and other of their contemporaries created stories about the people, in which the people became their own heroes. The newly literate laboring classes could see themselves in the stories, and a tradition of working-class storytelling has continued through their literary progeny. In Western industrial culture these traditions emerged. At the same time, a feminist literary tradition, a tradition of representations of the racially oppressed, stories of outcasts and marginalized peoples, of the silenced and invisible, of all kinds emerged as well. By the 1920s and 1930s these stories became increasingly written not as outsider celebrations of the ordinary by authors of the "Other" but by working-class men and women, storytellers who lived racial, class, and gender oppression themselves.

People had the idea that their stories mattered, but in form and attitude, the narration of these lives did not necessarily take on self-mythology. The natural orientation of many, if not all of these stories, was heroic melodrama (in those countries where the success of social revolutions created an "official" social realist proletarian culture, simplistically drawn melodrama were all the stories were allowed to become.) The storylines were simple, an evil oppressor tortures the masses. Heroes rise from the mass, and through a mix of individual smarts and their leadership of collective action, the oppressed conquers the oppressor. Transformation occurs, but not the kind of transformation that reveals new insight, or advances depth of understanding. The power to take the actual life and make a document for personal, and community, ongoing transformation, needed another impetus.

Precisely as the industrial landscape created a proletarian literature, psychology and the other social sciences gave us concepts about the relationship between the individual and society that suggested the role of myth, and therefore story, was hard-wired to our subconscious.

Sigmund Freud and the large cohort of specialists delving into the science of our minds and behavior learned very quickly that what we thought we knew about ourselves wasn't the half of it. Maybe not even the tenth of it. Our conscious minds are in fact slaves to our subconscious in ways we could not, and still cannot, easily grasp. It is not easy to understate what this insight did to Western storytelling. Just as our instinct for fairness and social reform was telling us to value individual stories, we also learned that as individuals we were essentially puppets of our developmental bodies.

Our mammalian urges for safety, food and reproduction, were driving as much of our decision making as were the cognitive faculties we associated with our rationality.

Perhaps this is the point. Freud's insights fit nicely into the collapse of religious-based dogma about human "uniqueness" in the face of the Darwinian certainty of our mammalian ancestry. Darwin made Freud possible. What makes a story a contemporary story is that it substitutes god-given fate for subconscious personal history. There not because of god's will, but because of good (or bad) will generated by context, parenting, and the luck of biochemistry.

In literature, almost all the Western canon was informed by psychology. Having been trained in theatrical literature, as much as I focused on the social playwrights of the twentieth century – Bernard Shaw, Bertolt Brecht, Clifford Odets, Arthur Miller – I was also privileged to study the psychological realism of August Strindberg, Henrik Ibsen, Anton Chekhov, Eugene O'Neill and Tennessee Williams. All these authors inhabited their stages with characters driven by demons within the family history. And while they were critiqued by the social realists as hopelessly individualist, it was clear by the postwar period, that even proletarian characters needed complex personal lives from which we could read their journey as both against the "system" as well as their demons; think of Marlon Brando's character in *On the Waterfront*.

Freud's colleague Carl Jung, and then later contributors like Joseph Campbell and others, helped create a sense that we all had a "personal mythology." We learned we have a hero's journey myth in all our lives. A journey that allows us to confront demons, come to terms with ego, and place ourselves as victors over our demons and deficits.

This concept of personal mythology became more frequently used in the 1960s and 1970s to suggest a framework for psychological intervention and individual transformation. We should know our myths both about ourselves, and that we tell about the world we inhabit, and if they do not suit our healthy existence, we should seek to change and/or reframe them.

And many of the practitioners of the concept of personal mythology found that the recounting and shaping of personal stories was precisely what enabled resiliency from earlier traumas.

For those psychological practitioners and theoreticians concerned with a more inclusive democracy, it was not difficult to see how coping with the demons of systemic oppression; family dysfunction, violence, sexual abuse, substance abuse, low self-esteem, learning disorders and disabilities, general lack of agency, etc meant the project of understanding and re-framing the myths of the oppressed was central to the social project. As Patti Labelle sang, "Free your mind, the rest will follow."

Story Work in the Age of Media Ubiquity

While we do not question the psychological benefit derived by story work, ours has *not* been a fundamentally psychological endeavor for personal transformation. People come to our trainings to express themselves creatively. The Center for Digital Storytelling is self-described as an arts organization, focused first on creativity. Our storytellers' aspirations are limited, based on the time we have to engage them. We are not dedicated to long-term reclamation of individual lives. We do not have any examples of facilitators working with individuals for several years, compiling one story after another to allow for a complete re-vision of a person's operational myth, and the little myths that left them stuck in their healing process, as one would expect with psychological treatments.

At CDS, we became aware that one small story in the form of film has totemic power for the storyteller. The story allows some shifts in perspective about the events in our lives, and we believe that those shifts are particularly useful to work in identity. The process of identity construction in the twenty-first century will be as accelerated, fluid, and dislocating as has been virtually all aspects of our current economic and social experience within our societies.

Storywork, whether through the contemporary narrative-oriented traditions of counseling and psychotherapy, or through various arts practices similar to ours, (PhotoVoice, expressive arts, drama and movement therapy with a textual or story-component, creative writing therapies, journaling, etc) is as important to our emotional survival as our strategies for healthcare and recovery, diet, and sustainable use of energy/resources are necessary for our physical survival.

The work of digital storytelling is to support the continued construction of a healthy, individual identity. We share this goal with all educators, social service providers, and agents of social change.

As media workers, we recognize the particular dysfunctions caused by dominant media. Part of what accelerates social dislocations is our ubiquitous screen culture. This culture is driven by massively centralized engines of entertainment, information technology, and telecommunications industries. All three work to read the pulse of society and serve us with content and form that we seem to desire, but all inevitably replicate their worldview into the products and services. They are counting on the shaping of our desires and fears, they need to connect to our intimate selves in order to sustain our attention, but their real goal is to shape our identities as *Homo consumerus*.

And we resist as we can. But the effort to unplug, or at least take perspective, is making us crazy. The project of human survival and success as a species will be as much about keeping people from going completely bananas in the face of media ubiquity, as it will be charting the policy path to sustainability. We are losing ourselves in the face of massive change in the way we inter-relate. We are seeking adaptive reactions. We are finding many ways to unplug and retreat to pre-information technology, lifestyles, and ideologies. And while these approaches many be ingenuous, they do not seem to be equal to the task. We need to wean ourselves from screen culture twitch, and the jittery, deficit-disordered, deeply insecure, fragmentary identities that come with it. This will not occur because of total abstinence, but by ascribing more humanistic possibilities to these tools. We need to claim the screen machines not as a fuel for our addictions, but as a tool to make ourselves whole.

Reframing Our Personal Myths

Our old myths gave us solidity. They gave us a meta-reference to our understanding of good and evil. They still play this role, but they are only part of the massive chatter that nurtures and sustains us now. If I grow up as a Pakistani-German living in Dusseldorf, or an Aymara Bolivian living in São Paulo, Brazil, or a Sri Lankan in South Korea, I negotiate both rooted identity and my global identity on a minute-by-minute basis. But even if I am a relatively homogenous suburban WASP in the Simi Valley of Los Angeles, I can have a hip-hop side of me, as well as a curious attraction to an esoteric form of Thai spirituality. Which are my operational myths, WASPish conservator of Western tradition, hip-hop gangsta questioning authority or Buddhist monk retreating from the noise? In the end, they are my own, and whether they evolve in stages, or manage to integrate into a single mash-up identity, the creative process of narrating a story, with image, voice and sound, becomes a way to mark these changes and make sense of them.

But what does that look like? How does the process of story turn into personal mythology.

Another version of the story :

> I see him there. Sitting, book in hand, glasses perched on his nose. Cigarette in the ash tray. His ghost looks up "Remember that story I told you about the guy in San Antonio. The painter?"
>
> What do I do with those memories? Of course I remember. All his stories. The hundred ways he outfoxed authority, the endless quixotic adventure of a union organizer in Texas. They filled my childhood with romance of having fun while fighting the good fight.
>
> And I remember his ulcers, his addictions, and the final heart attack that stole him from me at 17. I remember his sadness, his longing, what drove him to keep fighting, drove him out into the world, also took him away from those he loved dearly. He did not process attachments. Never sad, rarely angry. His body broke down, even if he never did.
>
> I spent a life trying to be like him. To be a peaceable warrior with a smile on my face. To make some sacrifices for the causes I believed in. To endure the stress and strain. But for the sake of my own children, I also learned to cry. To let go of the cause just enough to be present for them. To be present for myself.
>
> His ghost is still there. He is still speaking to me.

The expression of the myth of my father, can serve as inspiration to social action, or as cautionary tale. My story becomes a remapping of the meaning of these primary relationships to serve whom I need to be now. The story become a way to find, if not a re-statement of rooted identity, at least a new center of gravity.

Looking back at the many thousands of stories I have heard, the vast majority end as texts that address these kinds of re-negotiations. Our storytellers take the current moment's anxieties and fears, hopes and aspirations, to reframe a story about a core relationship. The retelling of an incident of trauma, or a situation of achievement, or even a seemingly mundane interaction is made to service the establishment of new equilibrium – a homeostasis – in the storyteller's sense of self. That equilibrium may not be stable, but the story becomes a successful marker, a lingering positive feeling. You have returned to some critical part of your past, a part that hung like a shadow over your identity, and you have begun to make sense of that experience.

As suggested, story has many jobs, as a learning modality through memory, as a way to address our connection to the changing world around us, as a form of reflection against the flood of ubiquitous access to infinite information, as the vehicle to encourage our social agency, and finally, as a process by which we best make sense of our lives and our identity.

What story cannot do is completely simplify the messiness of living. Story is essentially an exercise in controlled ambiguity. And given the co-constructed nature of meaning between us as storytellers, and those who are willing to listen to our words, this is story's greatest gift.

We can feel whole about impermanence. We can bear to be ourselves.

2

Stories in Our Lives

A story can be as short as explaining how you misplaced your keys this morning, or as long as multi-volume autobiography. Many people have entered our workshops with ideas appropriate for a television mini-series instead of two–three minute digital story. In the coming chapters we will talk about shaping a content and form of your story, but before you consider crafting a tale you need to decide what story you want to tell.

Everyday, with virtually no effort, you tell stories to other people. At the water cooler, the dinner table, walking your child to school, you find yourself reciting an event from memory to make a point, to give a "case" where the attitudes and actions of the characters provides insight to your audience. These casual storytelling experiences well up out of us as naturally. But ask most of us to jump on stage, or pick up a pen, or turn on a camera or microphone, and tell a story, and our minds tend to go blank. Authorship from our own life experience suddenly forces the questions about what role the story will have in our lives, right now, or in the near future.

If you are someone trying to sell a story, as a writer, filmmaker, dramatist, you as often as not ask yourself what stories compel me and where might I find a profoundly dramatic story. You want a subject filled with high consequence, compelling characters, exciting challenges, plot twists, and an ending that provokes insight. So you go looking for the equivalent of the trapped miner story in Chile, or some other miraculous event with people facing tragedy and escaping at the last moment.

We see versions of these "trapped miner" stories every night via entertainment and news. In my observations of countless storytellers, I have found that people have learned to equate the idea of a good story with high drama. If they have not had major drama in their lives, then they have no story. Frankly, even it their lives were filled with loss and setback, inside their stories it seemed more mundane than dramatic.

In the practice of community work and storytelling, we are talking about a story that emerges from a small audience, within a safe environment, that is as close to private as family, as close to personal as diary. This is an essentially private media. A media document may find a broader public forum, but the purpose of the artifcat may simply help you to process your dreams and aspirations. It may be public, but it starts first with the authentic voice in your head saying this story will help me, will heal me, will help me survive.

You may have your own life and death tale, and you may have been waiting for this moment to tell it. As likely as not, you, or your students, or your story circle, are not so sure.

As we will discuss below, there are rooted primary relationship stories; partners, parents, grandparents, siblings, children, and of course, pets. There are natural challenge/achievement points in education, work, sport, and vocational interest. There are journeys and vacations. There are reflections on loss and memorializations. All these are solid choices, but so are quirky explorations of what you ate at lunch yesterday and what it tells about you.

Why is it sometimes so hard to decide upon a story from our lives? Here are four possible reasons.

Infoglut

Last July 22nd, around noon, what were you doing? Unless the day had extraordinary meaning, you are clueless. Where was I in July? On that day what might I have been doing? Who was I with? What was I eating for lunch? Was there a conversation? Is there any evidence in my calendar? My cell phone? Could I call someone with a better memory than me to ask?

Our brain unconsciously processes some 10 billion sensory inputs a day, 40,000 separate conscious thoughts. We are biologically incapable of holding what comes in, but we are superbly capable of focusing our attention to hold onto certain parts of our experience. In the end, our ability to learn is a subconscious and conscious letting go. We forget to remember. Our minds construct a sense of memory immediately after being part of an experience and unless we have a dramatic experience, or have a particular reason to quickly and consistently return to the story of the experience, it slowly diminishes in our memory. Retrieval of a given story or experience becomes more difficult the farther away we are in time from the original story or event.

Added to our natural tendency to keep thinking thought after thought is how we are bombarded with millions of non-digestible and non-memorable story fragments every time we pick up a phone, bump into a friend, watch TV, listen to the radio, read a book or a newspaper, or browse the Web. We simply cannot process this input, and then find a way to process our own experience and invent stories. So our experience becomes a jumble of fragments, that we can tweet and facebook about, but inhibit our ability to construct a coherent story to retain, let alone recite.

Turning memory into a story, as a witnessing of an event, can be coaxed out of us, as we imagine, with the detective's interrogation. Parts of the memory are perhaps intact, but as we have learned from the science of forensic psychology, eyewitness accounts can be useless. We generally construct descriptions out of the whirlpool of memory and recite it to ourselves until it becomes so vivid we believe we were a camera on the scene. It becomes our truth, shaped precisely by what we think we are being asked to tell.

All writing teachers when asking people to write an autobiographical reflection, suggest you worry less about whether the richness in detail you provide is factual, and more that it feels true, that it affects the response in sensations and response that you feel inside you as being true to the moment.

The memory bank is overloaded, but we have a selective ability to make sense of experience, to provide the cause for the effect of a decision made in a scene, and stories emerge precisely in that space.

De-storification

In oral culture, we learn completely through story. At the core of literary text and screen/electronic culture, stories are the fundamental tools of retaining knowledge as well. But what separates the literate culture in text and screen from the oral-centric cultures of story-exchange, is the unit of remembrance is held intact as a story that we are expected to not only interpret but retain. To know the songs of your community, to have the ability to explain how the harvest must be tended, how to birth babies, and care for elders, how to negotiate with outsiders, is built into stories. The collection of stories becomes your epistemology.

In traditional culture, stories are the units of knowledge to live by, and the ability to call them out and perform them is cherished. While many of the stories are in the form of folktale and myth, equally many are cherished family stories of recent ancestors, or tales spun out of people's own lives.

Historically, we lacked the instantaneous gratification of the book or the turning on of a machine with speakers and a screen to entertain ourselves. We had no choice but to entertain each other, at the dinner table or around a fireplace at night. Some part of our story muscle atrophied with mass culture; what is unpracticed is soon lost. Many cultures still value the family oracle or storyteller, but on the whole, the art of conversational storytelling has diminished or disappeared from our lives.

Author Richard Stone has described our culture as de-storied, as in de-forested, and that the various efforts at reclaiming story and storytelling are a process of re-storification. Our mainstream culture has "clear cut" our ability to make and hold stories, folktales, and even song lyrics. We can no longer see how our daily lives provide us with rich content for meaning making through creating and sharing stories.

Only people who develop effective filtering, indexing, and repackaging tools in their minds can manage to successfully and consistently articulate meaning that reconstructs a coherent story. We think of the skilled professionals in any given field as having developed this process for their specialty. They can tell appropriate stories – the memory of cases for a trial lawyer, for example – based on having systematized a portion of their memories. But most skilled professionals have difficulty using examples outside of their respective fields of knowledge and expertise, from their personal life or non-professional experience.

Those who can integrate narrative from one silo of context to another are described as storytellers.

The Editor

Having worked in various novice storytelling settings, we at CDS are experienced with people telling us that they have no story to tell. Along with language arts educators and psychologists, we are aware that most of us carry around a little voice, an editor, that tells us that what we have to say is not entertaining or substantial enough to be heard. That editor is a composite figure of everyone in our lives that has diminished our sense of creative ability, from family members, to teachers, to employers, to society as a whole.

We live in a culture where expert storymaking is a highly valued and rewarded craft. Once we fall behind in developing our natural storytelling abilities to the fullest extent, it takes a much longer commitment and concentration to reclaim those abilities. As adults, time spent in these creative endeavors is generally considered frivolous and marginal by our society, and so few pursue them. Those of us who have assisted people in trying to reclaim their voice know that it requires a tremendous sensitivity to successfully bring people to a point where they trust that the stories they do tell are vital, emotionally powerful, and unique. Were it not that we, as human beings, have a deep intuitive sense of the power of story, it's a wonder that we have a popular storytelling tradition at all.

The Good Consumer Habit

Our awareness of the residual impact of mass media has grown tremendously over the past fifty years. It appears that prolonged exposure to mass media messages over time is not quite as bad as we thought, we are not just sheep as media consumers. We are active consumers, and watching and participating in media can light up our imagination and create new pathways of awareness. We can and do make active commentary about what we see and participate in. We tell stories about our favorite TV show episodes or films that convolve with our own stories in vastly creative ways.

But it is equally clear there has been some impact on our sense of agency. At the simple level, in a culture where we spend four to eight hours a day entertaining ourselves with screens, we simply have a bit less time to be creative. At perhaps a more foreboding level, people who see themselves defined by consumption, not just in absorbing story, but by the whole culture of shopping to make meaning, are less able to surface a sense of unique voice and individuality. If the brands tell us who we are, why bother working it out for ourselves. If identity is an off-the-rack item, why bother manufacturing a story of ourselves out of whole cloth.

As a parent, as I am sure it was for my parents, observing the way play is interrupted by media consumption is disturbing. Imagination, so many parents believe, is so deeply tied to creative activity—original artmaking, crafts, music, and making up and telling stories—that the passive consumption of media must negate the successful development of a full imagination The truth is we hold both spaces, the connection to our deep impulse as humans to make stuff and make stuff up, and our desire to be entertained and reflective in a different way.

Mainstream media also has an impact on how we compose our stories. In our workshops, storytellers often end up replicating the tropes they have consumed in television and film. Teenagers want to add fictional violence and aggression into the stories about their lives. Adults turn emotionally complex stories and unresolved issues into uplifting "chicken soup for the soul" testimonials. These choices say less about what the person knows from their own experience and cultural perspective, and more about how they expect media to function—as high-impact action drama, or happily resolved melodrama.

We have joked for years at CDS that we are using the tools of television to end our addiction to television. Making a short film using video-editing software for the first time changes your perspective about what you have been watching forever, in the same way that learning to write changes the way you read. It does not make you a great author, but it makes it makes the form apparent, and manipulative power of immersive media less mysterious. The truth is that the shift from TV to ever more engaging games and social media has changed the dialog completely, from the fear of media turning us into passive zombies, to the fear of being unable to distinguish between screen and social reality at all. The good news is we still have within us the most fundamental act of agency – the one that comes from the off button.

Kinds of Personal Stories

There are all kinds of stories in our lives that we can develop into multimedia pieces. Here are a some examples of stories, and some question sets that arise for particular kinds of stories. Adapting any of the question sets by integrating the existing sets, or developing a separate set, is encouraged.

The Story About Someone Important

Character Stories

How we love, are inspired by, want to recognize, and find meaning in our relationships are all aspects of our lives that are deeply important to us. Perhaps the majority of the stories created in our workshops are about a relationship, and in the best stories they tell us more about ourselves than the details of our own life story.

Memorial Stories

Honoring and remembering people who have passed is an essential part of the grieving process. These stories are often the most difficult and painful to produce, but the results can be the most powerful.

- What is, or had been, your relationship to this person?
- How would you describe this person (physical appearance, character, etc.)?
- Is there an event/incident that best captures their character?
- What about the person do/did you most enjoy?
- What about the person drives you crazy?

- What lesson did the person give to you that you feel is most important?
- If you had something to say to the person but they never had a chance to hear you say it, what would it be?

The Story About an Event in My Life

Adventure Stories

One of the reasons we travel is to break away from the normalcy of our lives and create new vivid memories. All of us who travel know that the experience is usually an invitation to challenge ourselves, to change our perspective about our lives, and to reassess meaning. We often return from these experiences with personal realizations, and the process of recounting our travel stories is as much about sharing those realizations as sharing the sense of beauty or interest in the place visited.

Strangely enough, while almost everyone tells good travel stories, it is often difficult to make an effective multimedia piece from these stories. We rarely think about constructing a story with our photographs or videos in advance of a trip. And we do not want to take ourselves out of the most exhilarating moments by taking out a camera and recording. Before your next trip, think about creating a story outline based on an idea prior to your visit, as well as what sorts of images, video, or sounds would be useful to establish the story.

Accomplishment Stories

Accomplishment stories are about achieving a goal, like graduating from school, landing a major contract, or being on the winning team in a sporting event. These stories easily fit into the desire–struggle–realization structure of a classic story. They also tend to be documented, so you might find it easy to construct a multimedia story. Televised sporting events have taken up the accomplishment story as a staple, and it might be helpful for you to carefully examine an "Olympic moment" to see how they balance the acts of establishing information, interviews, and voiceover.

- What was the event (time, place, incident, or series of incidents)?
- What was your relationship to the event?
- With whom did you experience this event?
- Was there a defining moment in the event?
- How did you feel during this event (fear, exhilaration, sharpened awareness, joy …)?
- What did the event teach you?
- How did this event change your life?

The Story About a Place in My Life

Up until the twentieth century, ninety percent of the world's population died within a ten-mile radius of the home where they were born and raised. While this now might be difficult for us to imagine, our sense of place is still the basis of many profound stories. One of the earliest interactive storytelling websites, 1,000 Rooms, a German-based project, invited people to submit a single image of a room in their home and tell a story about their relationship with it. Hundreds of people responded with their own intimate stories. You may have a story about your current home, an ancestral home, a town, a park, a mountain or forest you love, a restaurant, store, or gathering place. Your insights into place give us insight about your sense of values and connection to community.

- How would you describe the place?
- With whom did you share this place?
- What general experiences do you relate to this place?
- Was there a defining experience at the place?
- What lessons about yourself do you draw from your relationship to this place?
- If you have returned to this place, how has it changed?

The Story About What I Do

For many people with professional careers, a life story is shaped by their job. Author and oral historian, Studs Terkel, collected a series of interviews in his book, *Working*, to demonstrate that we all have unique ways of perceiving and valuing what we do. And while jobs help to give some people a sense of identity, people also refer to their hobbies or social commitments when thinking about who they are.

A good story often comes from looking at the familiar in a new way and with a new meaning. The details of the tasks, the culture of the characters that inhabit our workplace, or our spiritual or philosophical relationship to our work or avocation can lead us into many stories.

- What is your profession or ongoing interest?
- What experiences, interests, and/or knowledge in your previous life prepared you for this activity?
- Was there an initial event that most affected your decision to pursue this interest?
- Who influenced or assisted you in shaping your career, interest, or skill in this area?
- How has your profession or interest affected your life as a whole (family, friends, where you live)?
- What has been the highlight of your vocation?

Other Personal Stories

Recovery Stories

Sharing the experience of overcoming a great challenge in life is a fundamental archetype in human story making. If you can transmit the range of experience from descent, to crisis, to realization, then you can always move an audience.

Love Stories

Romance, partnership, familial or fraternal love all naturally lend themselves to the desire–struggle–realization formula. We all want to know how someone met their partner, what it was like when the baby was born, or what our relationship is with our siblings and parents. We constantly test other people's experience in these fundamental relationships to affirm our own. These are also stories that tend to have plenty of existing documentation.

Discovery Stories

The process of learning is a rich field to mine for stories. The detective in us gets great pleasure in illustrating how we uncovered the facts to get at a truth, whether it is the pursuit of an intellectual passion, following the up and down events of a work project, or taking on a new hobby.

Dream Stories

You do not have to be Carl Jung to appreciate that the life of our dreams is filled with insights about what motivates and scares us. The writing down of a scene from a dream can present a perfect backdrop to exploring issues in your life in a provocative way.

Coming of Age Stories

While we associate these stories with adolescence, identity stories can come at any age, and any stage in life. What passage in your life deeply defines you? How did the experience shape your values and expectations about your place in life?

As you decide what story would best serve your needs, keep in mind that these categories are in no way sacrosanct, and they intersect in a number of ways. It is also probable that you will come up with your own additional categories or other ways of dissecting the stories in your mind.

Don't Just Sit There

One of the hardest, but most important thing to do is get started. Because many of these stories ask us to reveal things about ourselves that make us feel vulnerable, putting together a story can be a procrastinator's paradise. Just get up, start answering questions on a tape recorder, write things down, gather up the photos, review your videos, and bounce your ideas off of your friends and family.

Life is full of stories, but you may not have a lifetime to capture them as movies, so, go for it!

Interlude 1
The Legacy of Tanya

I never had a lot of friends, not really. The truth is that I didn't even know what one was. Growing up I was shy, and confused friendship with popularity.

Last year I met Tanya and we became the kind of friends that most friends are, acquaintances. She knew she had AIDS and would die soon, but facing death gave her more strength to live.

She had no place to leave her girls and wanted to find them a good home. Tanya also wanted to start an organization to help parents like herself die in peace knowing their children would be loved and cared for. She also needed a real friend.

Tanya got a lot of attention the minute she told her story, as if the world had been waiting for her. I stood by and watched in amazement.

A few months later she couldn't do much on her own, and for all her efforts she felt she had only accomplished one thing – she found a real friend, and it was me – I couldn't let her dreams die with her.

The other night, Tanya told me to lay my head down next to hers. She wanted to tell me a secret "Monte Fay, don't forget, all we've got is where we're going ..."

I couldn't believe she knew my middle name.

Tanya
—Monte Hallis, 1993
This digital story can be viewed at
http://www.youtube.com/watch?v=D0zA9q7qJZc&feature=plcp

Thoughts by Joe Lambert

At nearly every workshop I have taught, I have told the story of joining Dana and Patrick Milligan on the ride down to Los Angeles to participate in the first Digital Storytelling workshop. Dana performed his show, and the next night we gathered in a classroom to meet the students. We went around the room of eight participants, and it seemed promising.

I remember my first impression of Monte Hallis. She was my prototype of the Los Angeles woman: blond, professional, relaxed, and self-assertive. At a place like the American Film Institute, which to an old Texas boy like me seemed like a fairly fancy place, I expected to meet folks like her. Dana was sitting at a desk with one leg folded back, checking in with folks. Monte described the story of Tanya Shaw, a mother with

AIDS. Her story had inspired a number of people to take up the cause. Monte wanted to do a story about Tanya as a general profile. When Monte finished her description of her story idea, I remember Dana saying, "But what does the story have to do with you?" I cannot remember her answer, but I do remember when she came back the next morning, her story had changed. And she had a fire about finishing it.

Many years after the workshop, I spoke with Hallis and she told me she remembered staying up all that Saturday night to finish the work. The workshop went well on Sunday with lots of great first stories. I returned to San Francisco, but Patrick and Dana stayed down for the showing on Tuesday at Harry Marks' Salon at the AFI. As they described it, the other students arrived, and movies were put on one after another. But no Monte.

She finally came in, and before her movie was shown, she put an empty chair before the large monitor. "I'm sorry I am late, but Tanya died." Monte's movie was then shown.

I would suppose, some 20 years after that moment, of the thousands we have assisted coming to fruition, few have meant as much to the maker as this meant to Monte. There have been many memorial pieces. I have made several memorial stories myself. But there was something clear and something precise in the making of this tribute that continues to inspire storytellers today.

Of the many dedications that we could offer for our work, one would certainly be to Tanya Shaw. By her example of sharing her story to organize others, even in the face of death, we are all taught a valuable lesson about dignity.

Monte and I are Facebook friends, and I was happy to see both of Tanya's kids are friends of hers as well.

3

A Road Traveled

The Evolution of the Digital Storytelling Practice

I grew up in Texas. And all we had were horizons. And the line of a freeway stretching way out to nowhere. I have always enjoyed journey metaphors in stories, *The Wizard of Oz* and *Lord of the Rings* pretty much own me as stories. In most of the histories of CDS and our work in Digital Storytelling, our story started as a buddy story. The opening scene shows a New England WASP gonzo media artist and a Texan-in-Exile radical theater guy standing around scratching their heads over the script of a performance piece, *Next Exit*.

I like that story, because it privileges me. But it is not the truth, anymore than the stories of all the folks that have come to the practice would tell of their own initiation. It is a piece of the narrative puzzle.

In the journey myths I enjoy, you do not find your calling, your calling finds you. You make a choice, with no more ambition than the hope someone will want to play with you, and a few years later you are surprised that many folks have come to the playground, and gone off playing their own version of your game. Whatever I found to get me started, each of those that followed found something new as well. That makes us all founders. The greatest achievement of this effort has been how many different types of people and organizations have come to own the idea of Digital Storytelling as their own.

And whatever my personal story and perspective might be, it now pales to the story that our community has become. We are now part of a global movement, a little niche of a media practice that prides itself on gathering committed souls who cherish the opportunity to help people with their stories. The perspectives they brought to the practice, and the approaches they take to the work, are now being mapped by the writings of many scholars and practitioners. Writing the history of this work is no longer the task of a single chapter in a single volume by a single author, but is worthy of countless retellings, from hundreds of perspectives.

But let me share my version. I start with a perspective on my roots as a social justice activist, then discuss how my work in theater led to the founding of the San Francisco Digital Media Center and our work in Digital Storytelling. I will finish by discussing how we moved from a predominantly arts non-profit to a greater emphasis on education, health, and human services. As with many journey narratives, the shifts in focus were as much about luck as intention. I met many friends and collaborators on the road, as I headed out to where I heard a call for help.

I am still pleasantly surprised where the road leads me.

Story, Folk Songs, and the American Tradition of Celebrating Lives Lived

When I was a kid, my parents liked to host parties at our little house in Dallas, Texas. Over the years, lots of people showed up at our house: the local politicos and labor movement people, and sojourning activists and artists that found our home to be a small oasis of liberal friendliness in the desert of 1950s Texas conservatism. My favorite people were the folksingers.

The bardic tradition was resurrected in the name of social urgency in 20th-century America. Joe Hill and the Wobblies found that by rewriting commentary to the tune of Salvation Army hymns they could capture the lives and issues of working people as a form of social protest. Blues, always a reportage of life and living, found a broader audience, and captured new meaning in the context of the struggle by African-Americans against Jim Crow that came center stage in post-WWII American politics. Woody Guthrie lifted the Western ballad, traditional tunes for European folk culture adapted to the frontier experience, and told the stories of dustbowl desperation and New Deal optimism.

As it happens my parents were closely tied to all these movements. Both of my parents connected to the New Deal promise of expanded civil and human rights, working in electoral campaigns for unions and countless social justice campaigns all their lives. My father, born in West Virginia and influenced by the great coal mining struggles of Appalachia, became a lifelong activist and union organizer who crossed the South and Southwest working the needle trade factories. My mother, an aspiring model and radio personality, converted to left-wing causes and found herself using her theater skills as part of a troupe of theater workers performing Lee Hays, *One Bread, One Body*, to small tenant farmer communities in Arkansas. As a result of her friendship with Hays, my mother's WWII job was touring the Almanac Singers (Guthrie, Pete Seeger, Lee Hayes, and Millard Lampell) and other progressive artists for the Congress of Industrial Organizations. Both my father and mother would maintain ties to these communities of progressive cultural work and I grew up with all these songs filling my ears.

By the time I was born, my parents, already in their forties, had experienced the elation of the Popular Front and anti-fascist heyday in American left-wing history, and the profound sense of isolation and retreat of the McCarthy era. As survivors, they were hardened in some ways, and fragile in others. But people like my parents were able to build a bridge over the 1950s cultural lesions, from the New Deal and Woodstock nation. The folk music scene provided a vital line of continuity between these voices of the twentieth century's first fifty years, and the explosive cultural renovation that marked the second decade of the century's latter half.

Digital storytelling is rooted fundamentally in the notion of a democratized culture that was the hallmark of the folk music, reclaimed folk culture, and cultural activist traditions of the 1960s.

Inherently sympathetic to human experience, the voices of these folk-music storytellers looked for ways to capture their own and others' sense of the extraordinary in the ordinary comings and goings of life. Where a mainstream culture provided the glamorized and idealized lives of the movie-star-perfect people living in dramatic and exotic situations, the populist artist in the folk traditions sought out a way to celebrate the ordinary, the common person, and their daily battles to survive and overcome. This new folk culture spread as musicians worked to help find a guitar for each person in every living room, music hall, and outdoor gathering, and teach them eight chords, a set of licks, and set them off to record their own experience.

Most artistic disciplines became caught up in the democratization process of the era. In literature, new voices of women and people of color were strengthened in this greatly expanded notion of citizen-centered authorship and authority. In theater and dance, companies were formed to transform oral histories of poor and working class people into productions of broad impact and scope, and often involving the respondents in the production as performers, writers, and designers. In the visual arts, community muralism, youth arts, media interventions, and countless other riffs on the "Art for the People" idea came into being.

The legacy of this era informs educational, therapeutic, social service, professional, and civic processes in countless ways. The methods of capturing stories, reflecting on and analyzing how stories are told, and encouraging thoughtful insights about one's own experience all changed in the face of the social movements that shaped the public discourse during that time. Those of us who had taken on the professional task of encouraging the learning, growth, and stability of other people, realized that the sense of significance that resulted when a person "found their voice, and made their story heard" was fundamental to our healthy living.

We can live better as celebrated contributors.

And we can easily die from our perceived lack of significance to others, to our community, and to our society.

The Texan Gets Baptized in the Revolution

I found myself in San Francisco in 1976, bouncing around the debates of post-1960s revolutionary politics. One sector of that political movement was consumed with the debates surrounding race and social change. In the practice of criticism and self-criticism that was a currency of this kind of politics, I found large sectors of my Texas-white-boy identity being sheered away as part of transformative regeneration, as I moved toward creating a "new" Joe Lambert – one who was intricately aware of my own racism, sexism, subjectivity, and socioeconomically predetermined consciousness. In retrospect, while there was something naïve and a bit weird about this process of political correctness and multicultural immersion, there was also something liberating.

In his book, *The Politics of Authenticity: Liberalism, Christianity, and the New Left in America*, author Doug Rossinow, discusses how other activists emerging from the white-Southern, and more specifically, white Texan backgrounds in the 1960s tended to view their "conversions" to political rebelliousness as a transcendental moment. It wasn't that most of us had spiritual education (for myself, almost none) it was just that the languages of spiritual renewal were so prevalent in all aspects of the cultures around us, that using this language seemed to provide legitimacy to our crossing over to an outsider stance to the dominant culture. In deciding to link our perspective with the victims of American settlement and empire, and having shared some of the abundance created by that project, we felt fear and rupture. We were leaving home, both physically and psychologically. But we were also being baptized into a new world of possibility, and the potential for a fluid, expansive identity that connected us to the motion of history.

San Francisco's cultural environment made it easy to cross over. I learned Chinese and hung out with Asian-American activists in Chinatown and the Nihonmachi (Japantown). I danced to salsa, soul, and disco in the Latino Mission district. I went out to organize tenants in the housing projects of the predominantly African-American Hunter's Point. My references of identity – the stories that I connected with – were becoming less about people that looked like me and shared my background, and more about people that I thought were heroically struggling to remake a world beyond the legacies of oppression, racial mistrust, and class hierarchies. They just happened to be black, brown, red, and yellow, and as such, I became a bit more identified with the syntax, language, and story of those cultures in America.

Life and Life On The Water

From this perspective I entered the cultural field as a professional theater person, having trained in dramatic theory, literature, and writing, as well as the politics and sociology of art, at UC Berkeley. From 1983–1986, I worked for, and then directed the People's Theater Coalition (PTC), a non-profit organization that ran a theater, worked as an advocacy and networking service for almost twenty other local theaters, and for a couple of years, also ran a training academy. The wave of popular theater work in the 1970s had crested and broken on the beaches of the reality of the Reagan 1980s, and the PTC was in pieces as I took over.

I spent a couple of years holding on, and then reorganized my planning and development work to start a new operation in the Fall of 1986. With luck, I found three willing collaborators: Bill Talen, Ellen Sebastian, and Leonard Pitt – all successful experimentalists in various theatrical styles – to join me. We formed Life On The Water (LOH2O) in 1986, and opened our first season with Spalding Gray's *Swimming to Cambodia.*

Life On The Water had many things going for it. We emerged at a time when experimentation in theater, having belonged appropriately in marginal avant-garde, was somehow becoming mainstream. The 1980s began the United States' colonization of the "Culture of Cool." The trend to trend-hop in search of traces of authenticity meant that those on the margins suddenly had a place at the table of the national dialogue. This process was institutionalized in the socially democratic countries of the developed world, where the avant-garde became official culture in the1980s. However, in the States it was a hit-or-miss affair. Actors like Whoopi Goldberg, Willem Dafoe, John Malkovich, Anna Deveare Smith, and John Leguizamo, all coming from various experimental theater communities, could slip through the cracks and become Hollywood talent, while a whole host of other, extraordinarily talented performers could barely make ends meet. Careers of musical artists like Tracy Chapman, who was "Talkin' about Revolution," and scores of other artists in the rap/hip-hop movement also found mainstream acceptance right smack in the middle of the Reagan Conservative Restoration.

Our theater featured an eclectic mix of experimental and community-based artists. One week we would have the latest of the East Village hipsters, and the next, a local Chicano theater company. But perhaps we were best known as a home to solo performance – a quintessentially 1980s art-form. Contemporary solo theater had its roots in the performance art experiments in the 1960s visual arts communities, the community theater artists connecting with, and claiming, the folk tradition of "storytelling," and the collapse of the non-profit arts economy in the early 1980s. Solo was cheap to produce. Half of the productions at LOH2O were solo works.

Life On The Water, along with our sister theater, Climate, ran a national festival of solo performance, Solo Mio, from 1990 to 1995. It was in this context that I met and began my collaboration with Dana Atchley.

The Colorado Spaceman Exits in San Francisco

Dana Atchley wandered into Life On The Water just before we opened in 1986. Our theater was being remodeled, and we were on a budget of ten cents, and a timeline of the-day-before-yesterday. As such, a few days before the season opened the place still looked like a construction site. Dana stepped over a few 2×4s and introduced himself. At 45, he was approximately the same age as our season opener, Spalding Gray. And like Spalding, he had a mix of New England WASP carriage, with a twist of road wisdom and perspective. And despite quite different training and approach to performance, in retrospect, they both shared the self-anointed pioneer role of many baby boomers. They were enthralled with innovation.

Dana had a show, and/or idea of one, and wanted to know if we would be interested in collaborating. I agreed to go over and visit and have him give me a tour of his life's work. The show was called Next Exit, and it was exactly that: a guided tour of Dana's life. He presented his idea by opening up a large three-ring binder. There were only four pages of storyboards that described some of the stories and the layout of his stage. I looked up at him, and then back at the binder, and then back at him again, "Okay … uh, so what can we do?" I asked.

Dana explained that for the last twenty years he had been traveling around the country collecting roadside Americana – stories about offbeat Americans – as a sort of artistic practice. In the 1970s, his touring project was called Roadshow, and consisted of him singing, telling stories, and projecting slides of these oddities touring colleges, art schools, and community centers. In the 1980s he had taken on the role of commercial video producer, working for Showtime, Evening Magazine and French television, producing short "Video Postcards" in the context of licensing his content to commercial sources. Dana missed the stage, and wanted to build this show to get back into the arts after his seven-year hiatus.

Dana stayed close to our theater, assisting with some video documentation of one of our performances, and joining us at special events and openings. I explained the situation of fundraising, programming, and management of the project, just as I had to do with numerous other artists who wanted to be produced by our theater. As I left, I am sure I thought, he's too ambitious, and he needs to develop more of a project before we can search for support. I wish him luck. In all truthfulness, I didn't really think it would go anywhere.

The next time we met, the three-ring binder had fifty pages. He had three or four new pieces to show me that he had produced for the show. I agreed to write a few grants for the project, and somewhat as I expected, they were not funded. In the Spring of 1990, Dana said he would produce the work on his own, in his Mission District studio. I said I thought the work should be "workshopped," or given a test run in less than mainstage context, so I agreed to help with the show and to link it to our first Solo Mio Festival.

In September of 1990, Dana did a four-week run at his studio. At this point, the binder was full, and he had about 40 episodes organized into over an hour of performance time. The central metaphor was the campfire, with Dana entering the stage and sitting down next to a video monitor that he would "light," and would play a tape loop of a roaring campfire. Behind him was a large projected backdrop, usually a drive-in movie theater outline, inside of which the various video segments would screen. Dana would then both narrate and interact with the video segments as they advanced.

As this started, Dana was forced to rely on an operator/stage hand to assist him in starting and stopping the video deck. In his first performances, this naturally led to a mechanical performance as he slowed down or sped up his narration to remain in sync with the video segments in parts of the performance. This was less than satisfactory.

But even in these early performances, Dana's design choices and approaches to the subjects of *Next Exit* encouraged many people who watched the performance to think, "Yes, I have a story like this." His subject matter concerned five decades of his life. He had stories of his youth and included stories about camp, elementary school crushes, learning to drive, and his father's obsession with ham radio. Additionally, he had stories of his college days and coming of age as a young artist, his mentors, his travels, and his marriage and divorce. He also had stories detailing the beginning of his days as a traveling performer/experimental artist in the 1970s, and the many colorful characters he met on the road, as well as the loneliness he felt in spending time away from his children. And finally, he had stories of his days as a professional video producer covering hundreds of thousands of miles shooting an odd assortment of American attractions.

Dana was an Ivy-League-trained graphic artist, and had over a decade of work in video, but his design approach was, for the most part, transparent. He chose very approachable icons such as the road and the myth of the American highway, the campfire, the big painted skies of the American West, Americana, the family album, and home movies. He interpreted those icons through video segments that, while superbly produced, rarely called attention to their refinement. His own performance style was direct, informal, and conversational, which also tended to diminish the distance between him as performer and his audience.

Next Exit survived a couple of runs in his studio in 1990, but in 1991, with encouragement from me and others, he went back and rewrote the piece to make the performance more coherent, and to examine and re-tool the technologies he used for executing the evening. The 1991 performance run had him intertwining the themes of the evening effectively, and ending the performance on a more focused, and transcendent note. He also traded the video decks for laser discs that could be controlled by MIDI software on a computer, giving him increased flexibility in performance.

By 1992, the show began to travel around the Technology and Arts network of exhibitions, trade shows, and special events around California. As part of this process, Dana was introduced to the possibility of bringing his videos onto the computer through the great improvements in Apple's QuickTime technology. He met and began a long collaboration with Patrick Milligan, an interactive-authoring-design professional. Patrick adapted Dana's set backdrop design that had been accomplished with slide and video projectors, and created a computer-based interface with Macromedia's Director tool.

Computer art had generally been associated with conceptually "cool" and experimental expression, demonstrating what the "computer" could create as much as the point of view of the artist-creator. In this context, *Next Exit* was a sharp contrast. Populist, transparent, and emotionally direct, Dana's performance spoke directly to a large section of the new media audience that still liked to hear a good story that was well told.

An Exit Called Hollywood: 1993 at the American Film Institute

One of the great ironies of Dana Atchley's personal story was that in 1980 he was approached by a producer with Lorimar Productions (the people that brought you *Dallas*) with a made-for-TV offer on his life as a traveling artist collecting treasures of Americana. Dana signed an initial agreement for a relatively small amount of money. When the movie deal fell through, for various reasons, the fine print stipulated that the character he portrayed in *Roadshow*, the Ace of Space, was no longer his. He had sold his identity, and a small part of his soul, to the devil, and as he told it, spent his fortieth birthday in 1981 in the town of Nothing, Arizona. When you've seen Nothing, you've seen everything.

Thus, it confounded him a bit when he received a call in the autumn of 1992 from the American Film Institute in Los Angeles to be a featured performer at their upcoming National Video Festival. Dana was also asked to lead a workshop in their new Digital Media Computer Lab, having people make short, personal video-stories similar in style to the stories that he had been telling for years.

The backdrop for this event was what can only be called the Digital Tsunami of 1992 in California. The San Francisco Bay area happened to host a little place called Silicon Valley, and as such, the engineers had been letting artists play with their toys for three decades. When the potential of desktop computing reached the frontier of multimedia, still and moving image, and text and sound, there was a thunderous explosion of activity. Just before the dot-com boom, there was the interactive media mini-boom. Money seemed to appear out of nowhere, and artists jumped ship from photography, film/video, graphic design, radio and television to try and position themselves in the "second gold rush" that they perceived was taking place before their eyes.

In San Francisco, Dana invited me to an exhibition of work at a local professional meeting, the International Interactive Communications Society. Once there, I felt the electricity coursing through the room. The 100-person capacity of the room was overflowing. I invited the group to hold their next meeting at my 200-seat theater, and 400 people showed up four weeks later. I caught the very bug that was led by collaborators in the performing arts like Mark Petrakis and Randall Packer, and saw the need for the performing arts community to be in dialogue with this sector.

When Dana, Patrick, and I arrived in Los Angeles, in February of 1993, we felt confident that we would make a good impression. Dana's performance had improved, the technology was increasingly stable, and the audience was going to be folks that could easily spread the word about this show. Of course, the idea of spending a weekend learning digital video editing intrigued me particularly, because while I had worked closely with Dana in the video production, and had seen the toolsets demonstrated, I hadn't yet put any stories together myself.

In fact, the show had a nearly disastrous beginning. Dana had made some adjustments, and the computer and the projector seemed uninterested in working together. With some last minute work by Patrick, and with me laughing on the side, *Next Exit* was performed and it was a resounding success. In the audience sat Dana's future wife and collaborator Denise Aungst. So impressed was she, that she left making up her mind to marry him.

The workshop had similar affect. The story of that workshop is described in the First Interlude (pp. 23–4).

Inspirations and Transformations

Dana, Patrick, and I returned twice more to Los Angeles in 1993 to lead workshops at the AFI. Each time I felt something in the process that inexplicably moved me. I had experienced drama therapy, group art exchanges, and creative writing courses that were emotionally powerful, but the process of turning story into the medium of film in such a short amount of time (three days), defied my attempts at characterization. It was "like" many things, but it was also so unlike anything I had ever seen before. The sense of transformation of the material, and the resulting sense of accomplishment, went well beyond the familiar forms of creative activity I could reference. And even as the tools themselves frustrated me, I knew that this activity had a special power that could be shaped into a formal creative practice.

I came to understand that mixing digital photography and non-linear editing were tremendous play spaces for people. They could experiment and realize the transformations of these familiar objects – the photos, the movies, and the artifacts – in a way that enlivens their relationship to the objects. Because this creative play is grounded in important stories the workshop participants want to tell, it can become a truly transcendent experience.

Those of us that work with story know that in conversational storytelling around tables and public gatherings, stories lead to stories lead to stories. We can watch the patterns unfold as each story transforms the conversations, the meaning, and the exchange into deeper and more intimate communication. There is so much invisible power in this simple activity that people walk away from some gatherings feeling transformed, while having little-or-no-sense of the process that brought them there.

A critical component of our success in that first year were the inspiring stories that were shown leading into the workshop experience. In 1993, these were the design examples in Dana's show. But immediately, stories like Monte Hallis' Tanya (see First Interlude), for instance, became the example as it reflected the achievements of the two- and three-day process. As our catalogue of examples grew into the hundreds, and then the thousands, we have been able to show stories on innumerable subjects and contexts when necessitated by the occasion.

As a result of the AFI experience, numerous events unfolded within the year. We had closed down the theater operations of Life On The Water, reducing the organization from nineteen people to three. I moved Life On The Water to the studio adjacent to Dana Atchley's loft in the Mission and Dana and I organized what became a long-running series of informal salons called Joe's Digital Diner, which brought together leaders in the new media design field. Life On The Water took out a $50,000 loan to purchase six workstations and all of the necessary audio/visual equipment to offer digital storytelling classes. Then, we produced a six-week Thursday night run of Next Exit that was followed by six weeks of digital storytelling workshops in the Spring of 1994. At that point, we hired my wife, Nina Mullen, as the only other staff member. Life On The Water began doing business as the San Francisco Digital Media Center (SFDMC), and produced a calendar of classes conducted by a wide array of teachers, including the first HTML authoring class for the San Francisco community. We had surfed our way along the big wave of new media into a place at the center of the conversation.

From the Roadside Diner, The Circus Hits The Road

This little revolution opened up a world of possibilities for our new center, but the world did not stand still. We had a strong local program develop across the digital media arts, a youth program D*LAB started by a colleague Ron Light, and a continued number of collaborations with colleagues in the theater and visual arts communities. But it was clear within the first year that the whole world was entering the game of digital media arts training. When we opened in 1994, four other organizations in San Francisco, two universities, and two public media training centers offered a few courses in digital media, less than 12 months later some 15 additional organizations existed to train people in media, and whatever little market advantage we might have had, evaporated as large and small operations invested heavily in providing introductory, mid-level, and high-level professional training in all the new digital media toolsets.

What stuck was the emphasis on Digital Storytelling. People were quite interested in this new model of training. With the Digital Storytelling Festival in Crested Butte, Colorado, beginning in 1995, we had a national forum for discussing the idea, and we were beginning to get invites to travel to teach. By the 1996 festival we were asked by our corporate sponsor, Apple Computer, to write a manual for the festival workshop. That manual, the *Digital Storytelling Cookbook*, became our first curriculum, and the core of this textbook.

That same fall we ventured out to Santa Clara, California to assist with the beginning of a collaboratory underwritten by NASA to encourage corporate–civic cooperation in information technology. One entrepreneur, Warren Hegg, had proposed the creation of a Digital Clubhouse as a gathering place for various sectors of the local communities (youth, elders, women, entrepreneurs, disabled, people of color) to find common access to state-of-the-art software and hardware. Warren invited me to become the program director, and we brought, with some fanfare, our methods to the Digital Clubhouse Network, with the aspiration of expanding the model of the center to a national network of centers. While we only really made it as far as a New York City satellite, the experience of codifying the training-of-trainers deepened our methods, and suggested ways that our workshop model could move from a single center in San Francisco, to a branded methodology available to community organizations, schools, and professional organizations worldwide.

That period had Dana Atchley and the SFDMC heading in slightly different directions, ours in teaching and dissemination of a workshop model, Dana in finding projects for his production company. Dana was able to take the enthusiasm for his show and design perspective and pursue numerous commercial applications for his efforts; culminating in the Coca-Cola Company launching the Digital Storytelling theater at the Las Vegas World of Coke attraction in 1999. We did find a few shared projects growing out of our active collaboration with the Institute for the Future (IFTF), a leading scenario organization working with Fortune-50 companies and governments. The IFTF proposed our work as a mechanism to capture organizational knowledge, linking us to the very hot trend of knowledge management, sweeping large organizations at the time.

My image of the mid-1990s remains a blur. Every week seemed to bring a new opportunity, and every opportunity seemed to have high stakes and ambition. All around us people were turning ideas to profitable ventures, and the noise of this ambition, was exhilarating – and distracting as well. From my proximity to this noise, I had a sneaking suspicion that most of the dot-com was an ethically-challenged negotiation between fast-talking opportunists and fearful investors, neither of which knew the real value of their proposed products and services. It was a 24-7-365 casino, and certain days I felt like the only guy in town with a socialist, community-centered vision for new media. Some days that made me proud of my purity, but most days I felt like the last sucker at the poker game, clueless on how to exploit my vision into an initial public offering.

Digital Storytelling Goes to the University

Having our son Massimo in 1995, Nina and I were immediately in the process of considering home ownership, and it was already too late for an affordable home in San Francisco's now booming economy. We found a home in the East Bay, and with a couple of years of commuting back to San Francisco, we made up our mind that the operation needed to cross the Bay. By a bit of luck, Professor Glynda Hull had recently become the director of the College Writing Program at UC Berkeley and had sent some of her program staff to train with us in the Spring of 1998. That summer we jointly proposed relocating our efforts to UC Berkeley, and we closed down our San Francisco center. The San Francisco Digital Media Center became the Center for Digital Storytelling.

The two years at UC Berkeley re-defined our work from a more general purpose digital media center with a specialized offering of the Digital Storytelling workshop, to an organization completely dedicated to this form and practice. With one of the college writing faculty, Maggie Sokolik, I co-led a series of semester courses on Technology and Writing, and suddenly we were integrating our ideas into college curriculum. We found ourselves receiving an increasing number of invitations to assist other universities in the US and abroad in establishing Digital Storytelling projects on campus and in campus community partnerships. Academics on Cal made our work the subject of their dissertations, and other academics began to look at the model as having relevancy to any number of topics: multi-modal literacy, communication theory and practice, new forms of journalistic practice, and community-based research practices.

Having a shingle at UC Berkeley also meant we were generally taken more seriously by everyone. Foundations invited us to lead projects, corporations invited us to design materials, we were invited to lecture and lead workshops in places we could not have imagined. By the time we left Berkeley, we were no longer a mom-and-pop arts operation, we were establishing a new trend, a new movement in education, with staff and scaled projects across the US, and moving across the planet.

Death And Decision, Health and Healing

For many people the period of 2000–2001 was a major turning point. The dot-com cracked, Bush was elected by the fifth vote on the Supreme Court, and then the era-shattering events of 9-11. During that same period, my brother died suddenly, Dana went through a bone marrow transplant and died months later of complications, and my mother suffered a massive stroke which led to her death. Funerals all, it seemed, one after another, requiring us to re-think our lives, and our priorities.

By late 2001 it was clear that CDS was going to go through a challenging period of change, not just because the leadership was shaken, but because the ripple effect of all these changes were presented to the Digital Storytelling community as opportunities. Two of the most significant breakthroughs in the growth of the work happened during that time, our assistance in the launch of the British Broadcasting Corporation's "Capture Wales" program under the leadership of Daniel Meadows, and Melbourne's Australian Centre for Moving Image project under Helen Simondson. These projects shaped a world of our work to the present day. In turned out that the values we had held through the 1990s, out-of-sync as they were with the prevailing winds of go-go dot-com capitalism, suddenly made sense in the context of a new century.

Interest was growing rapidly, but we were not in the best shape to respond. We limped through 2001 and 2002 with just enough to keep us going. We used the period of re-structuring to publish the first edition of this textbook, and to attempt to launch the Digital Storytelling Association. But by 2003 we were in need of a break. A decade of work in, Nina and I, son Massimo and our new baby Amalina, left for Italy. We used the break to re-think the program, Nina and I ended our working partnership (allowing her to pursue her current career as a landscape designer), and Emily Paulos stepped up as the new co-director. Daniel Weinshenker was asked to be my teaching replacement for the sabbatical year, and returned to Denver committed to establishing a successful outpost.

Looking out at what had become a successful international movement inspired by our trainings, my and Emily's conception about what CDS could become began to shift. While projects large and small were popping up all around us, we were not benefiting from the feedback loop. We saw that we needed both a road to institutional solidity, as well as a clear path to program focus that would assure our stability through the next recession. In part because of this thinking, over a period of four years from 2002–2006, CDS changed it's primary emphasis, slowly moving away a focus of 70–80 percent of our work in K-12 or higher education, to 70–80% of our work in health and human services. The hiring of Amy Hill in 2005 as the third leadership partner, became the main catalyst for this shift, as she brought both the content perspective around the issues of gender-based violence through her Silence Speaks project (www.silencespeaks.org), but also the professionalism of a veteran human services provider, having us examine the ethical and professional development issues facing our work with new, and rigorous, perspectives.

CDS has grown steadily from that period, expanding our work to all continents, and giving us numerous mechanisms of engagement with countless partners and collaborators. While we have much more to learn, and much further to go on our journey to sustainable, healthy organizational adulthood, we feel like we are past our teenage years intact.

The Promise

Certainly when I think about CDS history, I am moved by the stories more than the organization required to get to the stories. I made a promise to myself in 1994 that I would pay off the $50,000 Wells Fargo loan come hell or high water, but my real promise was that I would never ever forget why I wanted to run an organization dedicated to this particular form of story work.

The hands of each of my parents sit lightly on my shoulders. They remind me that silences are all political. They remind me that overcoming silence, overcoming the sense of defeat and disenchantment that comes with oppressions social and personal, is a solemn commitment. They remind me that sometimes this comes with sacrifice. No one said the road would be smooth.

Each story, in each story circle, each finished digital story, is a bit more energy for this effort. The fuel for our journey was never material, or celebrity, we run on that wonderful feeling that comes over you when you hear someone surprised by their own voice.

As if they just found something amazing.

4

The World of Digital Storytelling

One cool September evening in Crested Butte, the fall of 1997, I remember sitting at a dinner table with Dana Atchley and a number of friends who had assembled at the annual Digital Storytelling Festival. Someone asked what makes a story, a digital story, and what makes a person, a digital storyteller. "Why define it," Dana said, "whoever wants to call themselves a digital storyteller, well that's fine with me." Dana was ecumenical about the community of Digital Storytelling, but I always felt, perhaps from my lefty days, that a movement without a theory, or at least a point of view, was not a movement.

Within our community, there remains a debate about whether the "brand" of Capital D, Capital S, Digital Storytelling, belongs to the genre and production methods very similar or precisely the same as described in this book. As a movement dedicated to de-centering authority, finding an authoritative self-definition has proved elusive. None of us wants to exclude other practices. But twenty years into the digital media revolution, does it mean anything to say, "digital storytelling is any story told with a computer?" In the twenty-first century, what storytelling is not intermediated by a digital device?

So what do we mean by Digital Storytelling?

As practitioners of a particular style of Digital Storytelling, we find it useful to define practices by creating a taxonomy based on three separate spectrums. The first is based on an approach to collaboration between facilitator and storyteller. The second explores the role of literary voice and the style that grows out of it. And the third spectrum is based on the form the stories take.

Defining the Digital Story

CDS digital stories are known for seven components. They are:

1   Self Revelatory – The stories feel as if the author is aware of a new insight that is being shared in the story, giving the story a sense of immediacy and discovery.
2   Personal or First Person Voice – The stories are personal reflections on a subject. They are known for conveying emotion in that the subject has deep meaning for the author.

3   They are about a lived experience of the author told, at least in part, as a description of a moment (or a series of moments) in time. They contain scenes.

4   Photos more than Moving Image – While many stories use moving image, the dominant approach is using still images, usually in small numbers, to create a relaxed visual pace against the narration.

5   Soundtrack – The typical story relies on a soundtrack of music or ambient sound to add meaning and impact to the story.

6   Length and Design – The workshop model created a necessity for brevity, but soon brevity became the nature of the artifact, a digital story is seen as something under five minutes, and ideally between two–three minutes. The duration serves the usefulness of the pieces in the age of internet-based distribution, but also presents an achievable goal for the beginning storyteller in the medium. The stories may use feature sets available in digital video editors, but they are taught as minimally, and so used as minimally, as possible. The emphasis is a raw, more direct feel, with pans and zooms to provide emphasis, dissolves to soften cuts, and once in a while the use of compositing or other special effects.

7   Intention – And this is less about form than function, but it can be said that the CDS workshop privileges self-expression and self-awareness over concerns of publication and audience. Process over product. The products may achieve a larger impact or audience, but the honoring of each individual's process of authorship, and resulting control over the context of the story being shown, is critical. The storyteller ideally owns the stories, in every sense. This perspective informs all choices about participation, ethics-in-process, as well as distribution.

These seven components could be said to define the style of CDS Digital storytelling, but the world of options for media expressions are much greater. Our approach evolved out of our perception of what would provide the shortest and most direct method to have someone invest in the power of their own story and complete an idea of an edit with a sense of "reasonable" satisfaction about their creative experience. As anyone who teaches knows, you cannot always control what any individual expects as a "reasonable" sense of quality, either in a learning experience, or in regards to the end product. We have found the elegance of this form lends itself to the range of pre-existing talents, technical newbies can make it as simple as a ten-image slideshow, where experienced editors can focus on a refined edit and an exploration within the limits. People with writing difficulties can spend a large amount of time on the script, and then complete a basic edit in a hurry if needed.

The Taxonomy of Media Practices

When we think about media, we generally see anything that we consume as passive, and anything we make as active. And if you come from a place like Berkeley, being passive is bad, being active is good. At an intuitive level we understand that reading and writing, looking at a picture, and taking a picture, watching a film, and making a film, are two distinct experiences. In one you are a reader, in the other an author. But researchers and theorists have known for years that consumption is endlessly

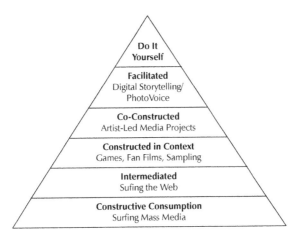

Media making can be thought as arising from a broad base of millions of consumers surfing television and the internet creating an "experience" unique to themselves, to gaming, to the beginnings of art making with collaborators and finally making work entirely yourself. This section addresses that spectrum of participatory media making.

creative, how each of us uses a story we are being presented to us in spoken words, text, recorded sound and screen, engages a broad range of choices that makes the experience a unique creative act.

Scholars and critics, such as USC's Henry Jenkins, have made a strong case that media consumption is fundamentally a creative act. While all of us have times of losing ourselves into a screen, generally, we do not just watch TV, we talk to it, get up and walk away from it, and at times throw things at it, and just turn it off. Being a fan of a TV show leads you to be creative, in simply revisiting the plot and punchlines of last night's sitcom, or putting on Spock ears at the Star Trek convention.

When we look at watching TV this way then we can say that the spectrum of digital storytelling creativity in media starts with channel surfing and ends with making your own TV with no help from anyone else. In these terms the creative experience is what you construct from changing channels, you devise your own version of a narrative. As you move across the spectrum, web surfing amplifies the complexity of this experiential narrative journey. In either case, there is a "whole" effect to the jumping from one page to another, watching part of a YouTube video, but then jumping to the next before the first is over. You are editing the material in front of you. Could an hour channel surfing or wandering the web be considered the construction of a digital story? In many ways, if you recorded it, and devised a way to read the pattern of choices as having meaning, yes, of course it could.

As we move to games, the constructive creative component is clear. Your agency as a storyteller is central to the experience. You choose to follow, in the roles inherent in the character you choose to inhabit, and your reaction to others in the game. Not surprisingly, this is where Digital Storytelling becomes a self-description for some game developers. While games may have started with PacMan and Mario Brothers, with little pretense at storytelling, with ever faster computers, tools for creation, and evolving aesthetics, a large section of game designers valued story and emotional engagement as critical to the growth of the gaming market. Presently, it could be argued, video games are approaching storytelling qualities equivalent to mass market film and television. Gamers now expect the narrative arc of the game to engage and inspire, for the players to learn something about life as well as the best solution to the game's puzzle.

In the last several years, we are seeing the same ethos of community engagement and personal transformation, inherent in our approach to Digital Storytelling, became part of the gaming world. The well-documented Farmville community via Facebook was able to raise over a million dollars for post-earthquake relief in Haiti. Non-profits like Games for Change are helping to forge large communities of developers dedicated to using the gaming platform for social good. We are certain to see more and more intersections between the community of CDS-style Digital Storytelling and game developers in the coming years.

Into this same category, I also put two other categories of creative expression. First, fan-based media, where fans construct their own versions of media related to the story, either using clips made available from a show, or constructed on their own media in the style or within the narrative world of the show. Like games, your own author's voice may be present, but it is restricted to some degree by the given context, and availability of artifacts, and plausibility of the characters within the genre. The other process, although more expansively available for creative voice, is sampling, the remixing or mashing up of elements of an existing media, with your own voice/ edit, that constructs new meaning. Mash-ups of content, from the making of your own slide show to a piece of popular music, to complete retelling of a narrative are now staples of YouTube, and represent a new found mechanism of expression, that draw people more deeply into the process of authorship.

As we move to the next section of the spectrum, we have large numbers of projects self-describing as Digital Storytelling that use all of the traditions of documentary engagement in the past eighty years. In this case, the author of the document brings the technical and artistic know-how to produce a complicated media artifact, as well as the resources to pay for the production and distribute it. As a result, it is understood it is the documentary artists' version of the story. But in order to honor the storytellers or subjects, they provide a mechanism to co-construct a narrative with as much engagement by the subjects/storytellers as they can manage. This could include discussions of who to interview, the nature of the questions, what to use to illustrate the narrative, even review by participants of some component of the edit (for example, the interview section that includes a given participant/storyteller.)

Here we are making a slight distinction between the historical ethos of documentary, as opposed to journalism. Old-school journalists might respect the sources/subjects (although often the degree of respect was balanced with what they felt was the need to "expose" the actions of their subjects), but the shape of the story was never considered up for discussion. Where some of the earliest documentarians took varying degrees of responsibility for the impact they had in presenting the story of another, and many, if perhaps not the majority, went to great lengths to see that the perspective of the subjects, an authentic voice presented in appropriate context, was preserved. At this point, this distinction may not apply. Documentary processes have perhaps moved more quickly toward complex participatory engagements, but contemporary journalism is also being built on participatory mechanisms where the public becomes the source of narratives, including video with written commentary, as we have seen in CNN's iStories and other media projects.

That these efforts are more and more often either self-describing, or being termed, Digital Storytelling, makes great sense, the difference between a documentary model and a participatory practice like Digital Storytelling represents small shades of distinction in actual implementation in the field. When issues of literacy of prospective storytellers, lack of time, demand for or presumed privilege to higher production or design quality, or simply a shared preference by expert documentarian/facilitator and storyteller to have the "expert tell the story," CDS facilitators always fall back on documentary mechanisms of interview, cut, review with subject/storyteller, and produce the final piece.

However, the distinction perhaps is that as practitioners based in the CDS model, we will always strive for the highest degree of agency for the storyteller that is possible, our fallback to documentary approaches is purely out of necessity, not preference.

What makes these distinctions important is how our cultures are changing in regards to authority and expertise in general. Those of us coming from journalistic or professional artistic training as storymakers, were trained to believe that it is precisely our ability to tell a story well, to make the story stand out based on broadly accepted criteria of creative success, that gives us the right, perhaps better described as the responsibility, to shape the final media product. But the ecology of meaning making through story has shifted in many ways. There is a general recognition that authorities that come with rank, technical expertise and specialization, do not include the right to speak for others' truths and experiences. Much of the work of democracy in the last forty years has been valorizing the concept of individual authority in their own life decisions. In virtually all human services and education fields, the idea of centering engagement with people being helped/taught/supported around their own needs, their own story, has become the dominant wisdom … even if in practice there is much left to be done.

Coming from a perspective of cultural democracy, our work continues to challenge perceptions of quality and of success in communication. In our view, the defense of creative control by the specialist creative class tends to ensure voice is not democratically distributed. Just as democratic mechanisms in art have given us participatory muralism, participatory music, dance and theater processes, we are seeking a broadly applicable method for participatory media production.

And as part of this approach we are recalibrating the bar for quality. My pleasure and the impact of a story on my psyche comes from many sources, but I tend to engage with a story based on how close I feel that story carries genuine meaning for the author. When stories are deeply felt, I listen. Much of what passes for expert storytelling is delivered out of a machine, a repetition of stories that the authors must continually reproduce in order to make a living from their craft. Inevitably, all but a few extraordinary people, can reinvest their souls in the artistic process, again and again, and germinate beauty that comes from an essentially powerful and new awareness about the subject. As audiences, we quickly we begin to recognize that authors have to recycle their core insights about human experience, and we can tell as audiences. This is known in the record industry as the second album syndrome. Most artists really do not have a second, or third (etc), album in them that can stir us as the first. This applies to all authors, despite the fact that the artists, and the industries that support them, want desperately to use the fame of the breakthrough to sell future releases.

Inherent in the participatory media perspective is that while this is a problem for people attempting to make a living as artists, it is not really a problem for us as audiences. It is pretty clear from Facebook we can enjoy entertaining each other as much as we enjoy surfing the experts' expressions.

So rather than watching a few authors share their stories, why not create mechanisms for millions of authors to take a crack at getting under our skin with their narratives.

I have said for years that I believe everyone has a solid twenty minutes of startlingly beautiful, engagingly original, time-stoppingly excellent material. Every human on the planet. Unlocking your own story could take a decade of dedicated creative practice, but it can also happen one afternoon, responding to the right prompt, the right question, and precisely the right moment. Many breakthrough songs happen just like that, a storm passes through the head of a person, and they write that feeling, those words, in more or less an exact dictation from the muse inside them. The hit is made. Showing up as a facilitator with the mindset that you might witness greatness makes it, well, the reason to show up.

And even if the stories are not the best an individual might have to offer, providing a way for us to learn the story behind a storyteller's effort, through context in presentation, then the story becomes that much more effective and meaningful. The trick then is assisting with the appropriate contextualization of a given storyteller's effort.

Facilitated approaches describe any environment where the storytellers understand that they are making the story with support, not completely do-it-yourself, but as close as is possible. Inherent in this perspective is that these processes are learning environments, people understand themselves as not just sharing a story, but learning a technique or technology, and following the process forward to a completed product. In our shared area of media production, these include Youth Media programs, Photovoice, participatory contexts like Storycorps, and local, personal and/or oral history projects that are community-based, and collaboratively run.

When we think about the range of these facilitated contexts, one thing the successful processes share is a consideration for all of the factors that provide optimal chemistry between the facilitators and the storytellers, and between each of the participant storytellers. As will be discussed in Chapter 6 on the story circle, the co-collaborative environment must be safe and comfortable for participants, and the perception of fairness, in valuing every person as contributing to everyone else's success, is critical.

In many of our workshops there is a significant spectrum of skills and talents related to the task. That people feel inadequate is assumed, but a successful co-collaborative student-centered process is predicated on having everyone set an individual achievable goal, and organizing each part of the experience to meet the participant's particular goal. Under these circumstance the facilitator/storyteller collaboration can flourish.

Workshop or classroom-based production processes share the challenge of participants having a relative buy-in around the concept of telling and producing their own stories. A documentary maker can focus on one participant at a time, interviewing and shooting whatever illustrative material. The participant with limited time is then free to go back to their lives. In participatory media, you are asking people to commit significant time and effort. If a storyteller has expressed an interest in the form, then the engagement is made easy, but we find that classroom teachers, and our facilitators sent into the field, often find themselves with a captive audience that had not self-selected into a process of sharing stories. In these settings, finding the tricks and techniques to develop engagement are critical to a successful collaboration.

As we move toward supporting the do-it-yourself tinkerer, working on ways to support makers through online tutorials and processes for sharing virtually, we are aware that we lose some of the essential dynamic of face-to-face collaboration. But larger and larger numbers of people are learning to edit on their own with the familiarity of iMovie, Windows Movie Maker and countless other pieces of software on PC and mobile platforms. They are finding ways to collaborate via countless channels as well, taking Digital Storytelling from its history as a enabling process to a broad self-generating movement of person-to-person exchange.

Approaches to Content in Digital Storytelling

Another way to understand our work is along a spectrum of literary voice. A commitment to first-person storytelling becomes another way to differentiate the CDS approach from other processes. CDS confronts all the same issues of other media processes in addressing the purpose of the products of the stories, we find ourselves working with storytellers that for any number of reasons choose to tell stories from perspectives where they are not speaking from the personal I, or the collective we.

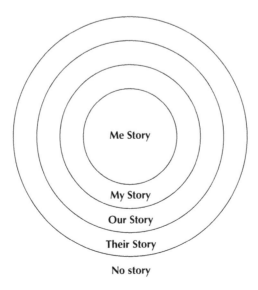

Me Story

The world of stories is rich with diaristic writing that holds our attention precisely when the person enters a highly self-centered reflection on what is going on inside their own bodies and minds. Even so, there is strong cultural taboo, especially among adults, against self-disclosure. CDS is often asked, do the stories have to be about me? And the answer is of course not. But they also could be, and the concern about self-reference as an indulgence can silence people. It might be more appropriate to mirror the question back as "shouldn't you know yourself first, before you attempt to understand others."

In countless creative story processes starting in early childhood and carried through to adolescence we are asked to tell stories that are purely self-definitional. They tell the story about how you became you, your identity as a person. Inevitably, these stories revolve around either the core context of your being (race, class, gender from stories about your family, friends, and community) or qualities of your specific engagement with the world around you (from stories about your favorite pets, places, games, sports, hobbies, interests, events, and vacations).

These identity stories are returned to at various stages of life, as a result of critical points of self-definition, whether they are emergent choices within a person, or events, positive or negative, that reshape one's identity. Going back to the incidents of direct personal experience, with trauma as an example, become ways for people to reframe the experience against whatever new tools of perspective that have become available.

Because of the intimacy, and emotional vulnerability of the "me" story, many people do not feel these are appropriate stories for public review. This is why these stories are not necessarily appropriate for school or work settings – after-school or creative settings with commitments to confidentiality in process are more appropriate, and more effective in surfacing authentic identity stories.

My Story

Writing in the first person is not usually about you. I speak about this subject, not always about what I am in relationship to the subject. The telling of the story as a purely confessional or self-centered perspective is typical with younger people, but as one gets older you see yourself in relationship to others, you see them seeing you, and you interpret them as characters. Stories become increasingly those of a witness, a witness of the actions of others in relationship to themselves.

The vast majority of first-person stories coming out of our workshops are these types of interpretive review of primary relationships, or events involving other people that had a critical impact on the lives of the teller. A story that looks at a mother's actions/behaviors in a new way, the story of a journey where the characters one meets, or befriends, change how one understands themselves and the world.

The "Me" or "My" stories is the easiest authentic story you can tell. It is either in your head, or you were there as a witness. Once you slip into first-person plural, second-person or third-person voices, you are challenged to add a deeper level of self awareness about your authorities to speak for others, or to interpret others experience through your own voice. In fiction, we give the author latitude to construct the internal causes of people's actions, in non-fiction, our antenna become much more sensitive to how people describe the action of another. We are looking for signs of the individual subjectivity within the author's descriptions, and many of us would prefer they drop back into the first-person voice to say, in essence, as I saw this event, or researched this person, allowing us to hear, appropriately, this is still only one storyteller's version of the story. Not a truth.

Our Story

First-person plural writing is usually proscribed by purpose. Am I speaking for myself, or am I speaking for an "us"? Is the story going to provide a window into my soul, or the soul of my community, my organization, my family? In addition, first-person storytelling in many cultural contexts is inconsistent with traditions and social protocol. We easily hear stories told in "we" form when these contexts are provided, and we sense that the author's connection to the community is an integral part of message.

The work of the storyteller is to make a moment of shared experience, how we built an organization, how we celebrate ritual, how we made progress in a campaign, as vivid observation. As one moves away from first-person voice, you tend to speak increasingly in generalities (as I am doing now), and the ability to describe an event, where we witnessed the experience, becomes awkward, because, in essence you are aware that we did not witness it, 100 sets eyes, ears and sensory apparatuses belonging to each individual in the group witnessed the events, and those witnesses probably saw different things. The politics of we, whether it is a community leader, or a presidential candidate, are filled with potential landmines, as you seek to represent consensus, but you may not actually have that authority of an existing consensus. Once again, then it is just your opinion on what we experienced, and therefore, what we take from our experience as insight.

Their Story

We move away from creative personal voice and toward expository and journalistic voice as we step into telling other people's stories. Writing non-fiction stories, biography, history, or narrative reflections on people or events beyond your direct experience, is a great art, and using someone else's story as homage and as a vehicle to insight about life process, is time-honored. When you have an in-depth, well-researched, or perhaps deeply personal, connection to the subject, we let you take us on your journey into their story.

But the trap is also set for your audience seeing the Da Vinci nose in your story. Mona Lisa's nose resembles the painter's quite strikingly, and most visual artists are aware that portraiture is inherently narcissistic for the painter, they show themselves through the idealization of the subject. Being self-aware of what you are projecting yourself on the subject is difficult, and many novice storytellers do not see how they have made the story of someone else essentially a reflection of their own story, their own concerns, fears, frustrations, and passions. Shifting back to the first person, relieves you of the attempt at objectivity, as you can freely admit at least part of the nose in question is the one on the your own face.

No Story

As Digital Storytelling has entered the classroom as a synonym for taking any subject, written in any style of discourse, and making a multimedia piece with it, it seems appropriate to question why the term story or storytelling has any reason to be attached to the work in question.

Third-person expository writing may have a strong narrative component, but it is usually strongly decontextualized from the author. In objectively providing information about a subject in the third person, we do not know if the author has any lived experience from which to draw from, and therefore any argumentation within the prose is suggested as a statement of known, verified, or verifiable, fact. At the point the writing switches to the context where the author was engaged in the assessment of facts, (the new journalism of Tom Wolfe, Truman Capote, Norman Mailer, every New Yorker essay), even if it is explaining the process by which they made their research, then they are moving back to story. Which is another way of saying that stories about how one wrote an essay is a story, where the essay, is, well, just an essay.

Approaches to Production Process in Digital Storytelling

We describe the form of Digital Storytelling above as having to do with a short video made in a workshop environment emphasizing existing still imagery over the moving image in the visual treatment. Other approaches to production, including within our own organization, shift the focus from a standard model to any number of other means and mechanisms of expression. We have engaged these approaches and styles of production (or seen other organizations engage these methods) to great effect.

Animation and Digital Storytelling

In working with youth from very young ages, the idea of drawing a background and animating a character within a background as a means to illustrate a story can be deeply satisfying for everyone. Numerous stories have been created with this approach to great effect within our workshop setting.

In the larger field of Digital Storytelling, the approach of linking professional animators with grassroots storytelling has been tried to great success. Early in our efforts, we met Dorelle Rabinowitz (www.dorelvis.com) and Kimberly Mercado when they helped create OurStories with the Oxygen Network of Oprah Winfrey. They produced several dozen stories on topics related to women and women's issues that combined the voice of the storyteller, some still images, and flash animation.

The approach was a remote process of gathering stories by email, followed by remote editing process in collaboration with the storyteller, and then having the storyteller record and send relevant images. The post-production and animation was done by the producer/animators. In a similar kind of collaboration, except in a semester long local collaboration, the Artmakers community arts organization in Hamilton, New Zealand (www.artmakers.co.nz) collaborated with animators from the Waikato University to make many powerful stories. Many low-entry tools exist for animation specific storytelling, but it is also quite possible to use video-editing tools with compositing and motion to create basic animation effects. Flash and Toon Boom Studio are probably the more stable approaches to 2D animation storytelling.

PhotoVoice – Photography to Digital Storytelling

In 1994, while living and teaching in Italy, I was visited by Anna Blackman and Tiffany Fairey of PhotoVoice (www.photovoice.org), to talk about the relationship between the PhotoVoice movement and the Digital Storytelling movement. We discovered a shared relationship to popular literacy and popular education perspectives that encouraged people to document their experience as a form of social engagement and social change. While PhotoVoice as a methodology has a specific heritage tied to the work in public health (see Caroline Wang and Mary Ann Burris's methods at *crossroads.ua.edu/media/pdf/PhotoVoice.pdf*), it has also become a catch-all for participatory media work based in photography, including the long-standing community-based work of Wendy Ewald, Josh Schachter, Jim Goldberg, Julian Germain, and organizations like the London-based Photovoice.org, Fotokids, Bridges to Understanding, Kids with Cameras, and the Rights Exposure Project.

While starting as a mechanism for local community and online exhibition, invariably these PhotoVoice projects have moved to multimedia. While the writing and story work may not be as central to these approaches in making short videos, the emphasis in strong narrative photography accomplishes much more affective impact than the typical digital story. Obviously much more work can be done to explore the collaboration between photography and the digital storytelling model.

Youth Media and Community Video Pedagogy

As we often reference, we stand on the shoulders of a generation of community media activists that engaged local folks in picking up the first Portapak video cameras going back to the 1970s. Processes like the FoxFire media pedagogy of the early 1970s and the work in Appalachia by Appalshop created deeply thoughtful approaches to generating media by, for, and about local community. Around the world, similar methods have found a mix of strongly artist led and strongly organizational method led facilitation practices. What we recognize in the more refined practices is a shared commitment to ethical engagement and political empowerment.

They also share with Digital Storytelling, PhotoVoice and other community-based perspectives on media work an implicit sense of social and political agency in approaches to subjects and issues in the lives of the storytellers and the communities in which they belong.

Audio Storytelling

Audio and radio-based processes have inspired a new generation of digital storytelling audio artists here in the United States.

StoryCorps (www.storycorps.org) is an independent media process focused on providing an environment for two intimates, father/son, life partners, grandfather/granddaughter, to sit and have a forty-five-minute recorded conversation. If need be, the conversations are prompted by an onsite producer. The storytellers receive a copy of their story, and the recordings become part of a permanent collection at the Library of Congress. But the success of the program exists to no small part because of the production of short excerpted segments of the conversations in five-minute segments that are presented nationally via National Public Radio, and available in collection online.

Authentically voiced storytelling also has a strong model in the astounding work of This American Life radio program in the US. While the pieces are created in a documentary style by professional producer/writers, the approach, like Storycorps, is to find a thread of ordinary experience, and shape it into powerful stories of insight and transformation.

The Moth is an informal storytelling salon that emerged in New York in the 1990s to encourage non-performers (although often highly experienced or literary communicators) to try their hand at first-person stand up performance. The salons became extraordinarily popular, and grew to a movement to encourage others to get on stage and share stories. Their popularity in the last decade has grown through the recording and dissemination of the stories in audio form via radio and the internet.

Also from the performance world, comes the broad movement of hip-hop and slam poetry, performance poetry and spoken word performance that have become audio and multimedia projects, and documentary projects in countless environments around the world. The various aesthetics of these movements influence all manner of contemporary creative expression and storytelling, and we have seen that influence in numerous digital storytelling projects.

Oral History/Ethnography/Local History

In 2006, I had the good fortune of traveling to Brazil to collaborate with the Museu da Pessoa, one of the most elaborately developed and successful oral history organizations in the world. I grew up familiar with oral history because of the numerous oral histories that were done with my parents as leaders of the labor movement in the South. So I knew my way around the oral history process, and I had a sense that this work had moved successfully into the digital domain. The museum's archive was enormous, and most of it available online. They were recognized in

Brazil not only for their work as archivists, but as new media designers, having won many awards for their publications in fixed and online media.

The museum's work, as well as countless other digital media projects that have evolved from the impetus to capture living memory of elders as historical record or of various generations of people as cultural record through ethnographic interviews, has become intimately tied to the international Digital Storytelling community. Each year since 2007, we have celebrated International Day for Sharing Life Stories on May 16, in honor of the birthday of Studs Terkel, the American journalist often credited with inspiring popular enthusiasm for oral histories.

The academic trend of oral history often focuses on research methodology. These include standards for participant selection, consistency of approaches and subject matter, organization of questions, systems of transcription, and archiving. The focus on the primary source aspect of the oral history interview makes it dependent on rigorous attention to the details of the interview experience. This puts much less emphasis on the publication issues for the interviews. Contemporary new media organizations like the Museu da Pessoa/Museum of the Person or Storycorps take a broader view of the process, recognizing that new media provides a bridge between primary oral recordings and appreciation by audiences by working to make the source documents, and the excerpted stories, immediately accessible to a public.

Mobile and Transmedia Storytelling

The state of the art in Digital Storytelling, in both the commercial entertainment, but increasingly at the non-commercial and community level, is the use of mobile devices in the storytelling process, and their link to other platforms of media that will engage audiences in different ways with the same or related content. The mainstream media has focused these efforts in new ways to integrate social media and smartphone lifestyles with the marketing of their media projects, but many artists are exploring ways to use transmedia as a vehicle for social engagement. Designer and producer Lance Weiler (www.lanceweiler.com) has developed several projects that have a film component to be consumed in theaters or online; an interactive, web-narrative, a game component, a mobile/place-based component and even analog arts activities. In his Pandemic 1.0, participants enter a "control center" and find themselves engaged in helping the fictional characters respond to an epidemic by a mobile-based game that takes people out into the local community.

We can imagine a project about local food can have a grassroots documentary process with images, video, voiceover, and editing on a smartphone or tablet, that links to an app that has a game using parts the content in a mobile GPS treasure hunt, that links to a website that engages audiences in sharing their food stories, that links to the Netflix version of the documentary on Michael Pollan's *Botany of Desire*. At the end of the day, the participants watch their film from a mobile projector hooked to the smartphone and projected on a sheet strung between two fruit trees at the community garden. Our image of the story having one vehicle, much less how each vehicle complements the other, and advances a narrative process, is now in reach of many project designers. We will see many extraordinary projects of this type in the coming years.

Interlude 2
Wynne's Story

I was supposed to be an observer.

When I first came to the Kalasha Valleys in Northern Pakistan to conduct PhD dissertation research on Kalasha women's culture, I was stunned by the din and buzz of daily life in this small, pastoral place. I taped it on my state-of-the-art cassette recorder, thinking no one would believe me otherwise. But when I came home two years later, and played it to astonish my friends and colleagues, I didn't hear chaotic noise any more – I heard the very particular words and voices of individual men, women and children who had become real to me.

Even though I was especially interested in observing their *bashali*, the communal menstrual house where women went when they were menstruating and to give birth, I'd never actually held a newborn before.

I waited anxiously for the birth of Taleem Khana Nana's child. When the time came, together with the midwife, we walked the half mile up-valley to the *bashali* in the middle of night, our way lit by little torches of resin soaked wood. The birth was quick. The baby boy was big and healthy. The midwife cut the cord, swaddled him up, and then made a special sweet cream of wheat porridge for Taleem Khana Nana. All night, we *bashali* women, even me, took turns holding the baby around the fire while his mother slept. Taleem Khana Nana said I was his aunt, and said I should have a baby girl, and then we would marry our children and we'd be *"khaltabar."*

I documented the many rituals and visitations that happen in babies' first weeks of life, as they are blessed and welcomed into the community.

Then, about a week after mother and child came home, he got sick. With the help of my by now worn copy of *Where There is No Doctor* I decided that he had pneumonia. A penicillin shot would likely cure him, the book said. Boys from the neighborhood raced to find the only young man in the valley with keys to the dispensary. But he had gone to the high pastures and was several hours away. The other women from Chet Guru took turns walking around with the baby. But sometimes I was the one holding him … and in between his heaving breaths, he was so still … so blue.

"Look," I said, "let's take him to Chitral! There's a jeep in the baazar. Let's go." But Taleem Khana Nana said she wanted to wait for her husband to come home, surely he would be home soon and then he would come with me to take the baby. I said we should go now. I said I would pay for the jeep and the hospital. She said, "Surely he'll come. Let's wait."

I was 26, just married, didn't have kids, didn't even know how to bake a cake … but I realized that I could have taken that baby, with or without his mother, and gone to Chitral. She would have let me.

They all would have let me.

But I didn't.

Instead I sat outside, on the ground, and held the baby, as the other women, one by one, went home to tend to their own children.

One last huge gasp for breath ended in stillness.

I don't remember what happened exactly after that, but someone took the dead baby from me and sent me home.

I didn't write about this, or the funeral that followed, or even the birth, in any of my work. I finished my dissertation, published a book, but after my daughters were born, I never went back to the field.

Participant-Observation
—Wynne Maggi, 2011
This digital story can be viewed at
http://www.youtube.com/watch?v=zo8xrY0XxT4&feature=plcp

Thoughts by Daniel Weinshenker

When Wynne walked into the old hog barn that we use for our workshops in Lyons, CO at Stonebridge Farm, I don't think she had any idea. I surely didn't. But, as always, I'm open to it.

We went around the story circle, and when it came to Wynne, she said that she used to be an anthropologist and was going to tell the story of a woman she observed in her research in a rural village in Pakistan … talk about her customs relating to menstruation, bathing houses, and post-partum traditions between mothers and babies.

This was part of a training of facilitators, so we had a discussion during a break. We all agreed that Wynne's process was going to be interesting, since it seemed that she had come to tell someone else's story. Similar to her research as an anthropologist, she was an observer, not a participant.

When we joined back again for the story circle and a facilitator asked who wanted to go first, Wynne volunteered because, as she said, she was going to make it "easy" on us, because she was just going to tell someone else's story. I maybe saw a couple facilitators roll their eyes. I maybe rolled mine.

Wynne proceeded to talk about this rural Pakistani woman and her traditions and actions and life. It was research. Pure research … and looking around the room, I could tell that few people were listening deeply. I knew I wasn't either. She continued on for five minutes or so and came to a stop.

This is a hard place to be in this work. Probably for everyone involved. We teach something. Someone comes to do something other than what we're teaching. Sometimes they know it, sometimes they don't. Sometimes there's a nudging or a pulling or a direct discussion about it.

But the facilitators-in-training were new. So nobody said anything. And I usually jump in, but I had an overwhelming sense that all that was necessary was the space. The space (and the silence and the witnessing as part of that space).

It was a group of twenty people sitting around the old wood tables in the hog barn. In the silence we could hear the sound of the irrigation canal outside the back door, the ticking of the timer for the water pump, a tractor, and the horns and the commerce of the Cemex plant across the road – the train cars lugging the heavy around.

Ten seconds. Twenty seconds. Half a minute maybe.

And then Wynne broke into tears. Not just tears, but full weeping.

And after catching her breath, said:

"Or there's this story …, " which became the script you read above.

Sometimes, or maybe even all the time, all we need to do is observe, sometimes all that's needed is to be listened to, to be known, to witnesses someone telling a story and letting them hear the echo and then letting them become a participant in it for the very first time.

At the end she leaned back on her rickety old chair on the strangely even floor and said: "I've never told anyone that story before."

Now she had.

And it became real to her. It became real to us.

5

Seven Steps Of Digital Storytelling

During the first few years of our workshops, we would discuss with participants what made a story a digital story, and what made a digital story a good digital story. We came up with an initial lecture, the Seven Elements, that outlined the fundamentals of digital storytelling. We discovered that presenting them at the beginning of workshops greatly improved the process and the stories told.

Our emphasis in this introductory process started with a simple idea. Show an example, and briefly discuss the relative merit of the piece using one or more of the elements. The main goal of this section of the workshop was to creatively inspire the storytellers.

As our organization developed a national and international audience, the Seven Elements were often used by countless facilitators, and cited frequently in references to the CDS model. Internally, many of our own teachers began to adapt and amend the lecture in ways that suggested we needed to revise and rethink our approach.

For the last two years, we have given this lecture as the Seven Steps. This edition represents our current thinking about these components of storymaking. They were never meant as a prescribed "catechism" of storytelling, more simply a framework for the discussion of the aesthetic quality of this particular form.

During our group process called the story circle, which is discussed at length later in the book, these steps are often called upon to form clarifying questions to aid the storyteller in their process. What meaning and insight comes from the story? How does talking about it make them feel? Is there a scene, a moment, which acts as an axis point, to illustrate change?

Increasingly, we are moving our participants into a mindset where they can more fully visualize their story, and imagine how it sounds, before they even begin to write their script. So what images do the storytellers see, and what music or ambient sound do they hear? And finally how might the elements interweave in the edit, and where might the story end up in the world, and how could this change the story when the process is complete? After the story circle is completed, and the storyteller has had some time alone with his or her thoughts, they can then let all of these considerations inform them as they sit down to write.

We want stories. We love stories. Stories keep us alive. Stories that come from a place of deep insight and with a knowing wink to their audience, and stories that tease us into examining our own feelings and beliefs, and stories that guide us on our own path. But most importantly, stories told as stories, that honor the simple idea that we want to relive what the author experienced in time and place.

Step 1: Owning Your Insights

At seven, I learned about race.

Johnny Ramirez always got into trouble.

One morning, on a dare, we convinced Johnny to cut up an old bull snake and throw the pieces of it into the pickle barrel in front of Johnson's store.

We just ran away.

…

I spent my first six years on the west side of San Antonio, in a Mexican neighborhood. Then we moved to Vickery, an odd small town, surrounded by North Dallas. There were not many Latinos.

…

I remember later that day looking out the window of Mrs. Morgan's class and seeing Johnny's mom taking him home from school, latched on to his ear like a lobster. Johnny was crying, "Ay, Mama, let go, let go!"

Several of us giggled and snickered under our breaths. "Quiet class!" Mrs. Morgan apparently failed to see the humor.

Later that day we went to his house, and his mom came out to meet us, and spoke in Spanish, telling us to scram. As we left, my other Anglo friends started making fun of his mom, in loud voices, mocking her in their own version of a Spanglish. They burst out laughing. I just stood there.

I didn't think it was funny.

Johnny's family was never really welcome in Vickery. Later that year, they moved out of the neighborhood. Johnny wasn't missed.

But I never forgot.

For each and every storyteller, we are focused on creating a story that feels unique and powerful. Unique in that we hear the author describe the events and issues of the story in a way that is only theirs to provide, that the perspective feels like it emerged from honest self-reflection. Powerful in that we want the stories to give an intimate glance at the struggle the author faced in reacting to events, how the events changed them. Put another way, we want to help storytellers move through a process of self-discovery about the why of their story.

After asking "What's the story you want to tell?", our next question is "What do you think your story means?" We want to hear not just what the story is about in the obvious sense: "It's about my mom, my vacation, my first real job …" But what it's really about is the storyteller, as the person who lived through the story, takes some particular lesson from the experience, a lesson that serves them in some way in negotiating their lives in the world.

In this example, the story process could have started as an essay about growing up in this one neighborhood in Dallas. The resulting draft might have been a series of broadly told memories of my childhood inspired by a group of old photos. But suppose I was asked, "why are these experiences coming up for you?" And I realized I have been thinking a great deal about how different my own children's experience of life was from my own – in particular, the relative tolerance of the San Francisco Bay area compared to 1960s Texas. So the story evolves to a specific experience where I was taught about race. With this new clarity of purpose, I was able to take my 1,000-word essay, with many stories about many characters, to a 200-word story about Johnny told in three scenes. Purpose provides that path.

We realize finding and clarifying your story's insight is not easy. There may not be a light bulb flashing above your head at the start of the process. How can you best find your way toward a deeper insight?

One way is to consider what jumps out for you in the story right now. All stories told, if they come from deep inside us, can be said to be about this moment. The shadow of your current life shapes the story. I might tell the Johnny Ramirez story fifteen ways over my lifetime, but the small changes, the ways the story shifts in emphasis and tone, express something different about me as the author.

The writing process, as a form of self-reflection, can move you from an awareness of "I am" to a deeper awareness of "I have been ... I am becoming ... I am ... and I will be ..." As life proceeds and is reflected upon, how you have been shaped by experience can be better understood. The stories have the chance to ripen. Stories that may have confused a storyteller for years, that have held dormant insights, might now bear the fruit of new knowledge.

My story might have also changed because someone just before me in a story circle talked about facing their own issues around discrimination. A group process invites us to see how our stories are connected. As you process out loud with others, the heart of the story may come to light, elucidating new layers of meaning. Which is why the story circle is often critical for a storyteller's writing process.

Insight is related to many other questions that can arise for the storyteller. Even if you address the core insight and unique voice for the story, you may still feel you need to shape the story for a specific audience, or a specific purpose. You may also feel the story may need more context to be understood.

In our experience, if you burden the beginning of your process with the external expectations, you can easily interrupt or edit the little voice inside your head that is working through why the story has great personal meaning for you. You may stop short of mining the depths, because you are concerned about your own safety, privacy, and confidentiality. We argue, as we address in Step Seven, about sharing your story, that the beginning of the process, while holding the awareness of purpose in terms of themes you may want to address, should not be driven by the external outcome, or the need for context. The story should be told as you would to a dear friend, a loved one, with a minimum of context, and a maximum of directness about the events as they happened. Then, as you complete a strong draft, you can consider those issues more fully, in how the shared story needs to be re-framed for the audience.

Telling an Organizational Story

But what if the story you're trying to tell isn't really yours? What if it's not about "my" anything: my job, my mom, or my vacation." And instead, it's about "ours?" "Our life together, our divorce?" Or what if it's about "theirs?" "Their community center, their after-school program?" What then?

Here's Esperanza's journey of how she found and clarified the story she wanted and needed to tell:

Esperanza has decided to make a story about her non-profit, Familias Unidas, a community organization assisting low-income Latino families with negotiating the social service systems.

From the organizational brochure, and from all the grant proposals she has written, she has a great deal of information about why her organization exists and why it deserves continued community support. She also has ten years of photographs from her work with community members, special events, staff members, and the several times the organization has been recognized with awards.

But as she thinks about the purpose of her story, she realizes that the organization's mission statement fails to capture the emotional essence of what they truly do, or why she's even a part of it. If the digital story is going to be presented to their supporters at the Christmas fundraiser, and then be placed on the website, it needs to move people and not just present a list of activities, goals, and objectives.

Esperanza decides to create a portrait of the Sanchez family, one of the families Familias Unidas has worked with. When she goes to meet with them, they express interest, but as they talk about the role of Familias Unidas in their lives, Esperanza realizes their story only touches on one or two of the six programs the organization offers. She realizes that she needs several families to capture a broad enough view about the organization in order to connect with the different stakeholders in her communities of support. "This is so much work," she thinks, "and this will never get done."

She is the director of the program, and as it is, she barely has time to work on the project. That night, she speaks with her partner, Carolina, who laughs about how Esperanza is always getting overwhelmed. "This is just like how you started the whole thing, fresh out of college," Carolina says. "You were just full of ideals. You started helping a few of your cousin's friends get some paperwork turned in for the local clinic, and the next thing I know, you were helping everyone in the barrio. You hardly slept then."

Esperanza remembered these times, how passionate she felt, and how her passion inspired others to take up this work and to give donations to support it. "Maybe that's the story," she says aloud, "not just what we do, but why we do it, why I do it, and how caring starts with just one person."

She calls her cousin and asks if he would be willing to tell the story of those first projects. He says he would be honored. She starts writing, and the words flow. From this beginning story, she connects the Sanchez family's experience to show how the program became legitimized, and she finishes with a reflection on her own growth and the gifts that this work has given her.

At midnight, she closes her laptop. Esperanza sees the movie playing in her head. "I know just the images to use."

Whether the story starts as deeply personal, or like Esperanza, evolves to have a strong personal connection, as facilitators, we are working to hold the space for your movement toward deeper and clearer insight. This work is never easy. It can be humbling for the facilitator. But it can also be enriching, enlivening and inspiring in every way.

Step 2: Owning Your Emotions

Sue was the third person to present an idea in the story circle. She was proud of the fact that she had prepared a draft of a script. She opened her laptop, and started to read, but all of the sudden it was if a ghost had taken her voice. She tried to say the words, but her voice cracked, nothing came out. She sat back, tears welling in her eyes. "I did not think I was that emotional about this story, but I just can't say these words ... I just can't."

This is common experience for story facilitators. Even with scripts that have taken what appeared to be a neutral attitude on a personal subject, the emotional power underneath the words can ooze out of us. Our most important stories tap into the profound, and sometimes our bodies know this better than our conscious mind.

As a first step, we help storytellers find and clarify the meaning contained within their stories, but even as they work through the subject and theme, we want to help them become aware of how the story feels – the emotional resonance of their story. In this way, meaning and emotion are intertwined.

Just as the process of landing on the story's principal insight unveils itself over your writing process, so does the depth of emotion that of the story. Big emotions may surface at the beginning of your process, that you may feel are inappropriate for the story you imagine sharing. But only by listening to those emotions, owning they exist and are part of the reason you are drawn to this particular version of the story, can you effectively tackle a process of refinement of your tone and a deeper perspective on what you are asking the story to achieve.

To help storytellers identify the emotions in their story, we ask a series of questions regarding their process: "As you shared your story, or story idea, what emotions did you experience? Can you identify at what points in sharing your story you felt certain emotions? If you experienced more than one emotion, were they contrasting?"

As the storyteller gains awareness of their emotional connection to the story, they can begin to think about how others might connect on an emotional level. To help storytellers decide how to convey emotional content, we ask a second set of questions: "Which emotions will best help the audience understand the journey contained within your story? Is there an overall tone that captures a central theme? Can you convey your emotions without directly using "feeling" words or relying on clichés to describe them? For example, how can you imply the idea of happiness without saying, 'I felt happy?'"

When we reflect on the emotions within in our stories, we realize that they can be complex, and with this realization we oftentimes discover deeper layers of a story's meaning. For example, stories of wedding celebrations can also be about overcoming loneliness and facing new struggles in forging lasting partnerships. Joyous births can also be about working through the fear of shouldering new responsibility. Restful vacations can also be about recognizing the stress that shapes our daily lives. Grieving the loss of a loved one can also be about appreciating the wisdom that they have imparted. Thus having an awareness of the contrasting and complex nature of a story's emotional content will not only help get us in touch with the core of the story's meaning, but also determine which emotions to include, and in what sequence to present them to help the audience understand the story.

Taking ownership of the emotions contained within a story will also help the audience connect on a deeper level. But the inclusion of emotions doesn't mean that your audience will meaningfully connect to it, so emotion alone is not the goal. When we, as an audience, hear a story that has an exaggerated tug to emotion, we read it as dishonesty. Conversely, if it seems devoid of emotion, without a hint of struggle or conflict, then we don't believe it either.

So when a storyteller wants the audience to pause long enough to listen, to listen deeply and trust them as a storyteller, they have to convey a sense of awareness and ownership of the emotions contained with their story. We want to help the storytellers be as aware of their emotions as they can be, and demonstrate to the audience that they believe in what they are saying, and are "in" their story. Unless the storyteller trusts that the audience will connect with the underlying issues of their story, they may not be fully honest with themselves or the audience.

Most audiences know that if the storyteller chooses to leave out information and describes details through inference instead of evidence, then there must be a good reason. But they can also tell the difference between being reticent and indirect, and being purposely superficial. The storyteller may or may not want to disclose intimate details, but it is beneficial for them to demonstrate a respect for their audience.

In story work, as a storyteller reflects on their sense of what the story is about and becomes aware of its emotional content, they must also choose the just-so voice that suits it. And rather than using language constructed for a society that can be judgmental and threatening, the storyteller instead peels back the protective layers and finds the voice that conveys their emotional honesty, as if speaking to a trusted friend.

Within every community, and within every shared experience, there are many different ideas of what it means to disclose information. Therefore, knowing your intended audience can shape the emotional content of your story. The degree of emotional content is also culturally specific, as storytellers are familiar with the codes and clues within their own communities. When a storyteller trusts that they are listening deeply to their own heart and imagines the thoughtful appreciation of a specific audience, they will share what is appropriate to share.

People are rarely presented with opportunities for deep, connected listening, and if they are presented with them, they often don't take the opportunity to listen with a depth that matches that of the speaker's. Therefore, our practice is predicated on providing a safe space for telling and listening to emotionally honest stories. Stories that emerge in this sacred space of deep listening can source our emotional core, and can surprise both the teller and the listener. Storytellers in our workshops often choose to address difficult issues – to wink at, stare, and sometimes engage, the demons inside. When you visit the www.storycenter.org website and view the digital stories we have chosen to share, you will see that they are diverse in theme but consistent in their emotional honesty. To paraphrase Boston-based storyteller, the late Brother Blue, the stories feel like they are traveling the shortest distance from the heart of the storyteller to the viewer's own heart.

Step 3: Finding The Moment

> A story isn't about a moment in time, a story is about the moment in time.
> W. D. Wetherell

We borrow a truism from John Gardner that the plots of all stories can be boiled down to one of two types: 1) "A stranger came to town..." or 2) "We went on a vacation."

In other words, at some moment in your life, change came to you or you went towards change. As you become clear about the meaning of your story, you can bring your story to life, by taking us into that moment of change.

But out of the sequence of events in your narrative, which event best shows how you came to new insight, what forced you into a new perspective about the subject. I have a writing prompt, start a sentence with "The phone rang ..." and talk about a time when the phone rang and you heard news that changed you forever. Almost all of us have moments with the stranger, as a bringer of good news or bad news, that arrive with a phone call.

To help storytellers find this moment, we ask a series of questions: "Was there a moment when things changed? Were you aware of it at the time? If not, what was the moment you became aware that things had changed? Is there more than one possible moment to choose from? If so, do they convey different meanings? Which most accurately conveys the meaning in your story? Can you describe the moment in detail?" Once this moment of change is identified, we help storytellers determine how it will be used to shape the story.

Because our lives comprise an infinite number of moments of small shifts in perspective, of evolving, rather than distinct or dramatic shifts, we often find it hard to point to a moment. In the decisive moment writing prompt (see Chapter 7), we force the issue, and people will tend to write about a dramatic event. Ironically, while the "phone rang" might seem like the best moment to land the story in a specific event, it might be a month or a year later, when you are making toast, or driving to work, or any number of otherwise mundane moments of quiet reflection, when the full weight of what happened finally comes to clarity. Particularly with traumatic events, shock and working through the stages of grief means you may not be self-aware about the importance or meaning of the change for months or years.

Whether the storyteller became aware of it at the time or in reflection, we want to help them find the moment of change that best represents the insight that they wish to convey. In the Johnny Ramirez story, I present three moments: Johnny being dared to throw the snake in the barrel, Johnny being taken home from school by his mother, and being at his house and having other kids make fun of his family's Spanish. The moments build upon each other; at the beginning of the story I was part of group that set Johnny up, and later I laughed at him as he was being dragged home by his mother. The turning point was when I chose not to laugh at my friends making fun of Johnny's family speaking Spanish. Landing in that moment shows how I changed, shows my response in a situation. In hindsight, I could see that by not joining my peers taunting, I was choosing to be different. I took a vacation from the social norm.

Compelling stories reproduce the events in an immersive way. They prompt the audience to ask questions about their own experiences and look for larger truths. Compelling storytellers construct scenes to show how change happened, how they dealt with it, what they were like before the change, and what they are like after. A storyteller sharing their insight within a story says to the audience, "This is what has happened and this is what I have learned." By building a scene around the moment of change, the storyteller is "showing," rather than "telling."

"Showing" through scene is part of the pleasure for the audience as they are drawn into the moment of change and actively construct their own interpretations. If you can paint the audience a portrait of both you, and your experience of the moment of change, then you are creating a scene. As you recall the moment of change, ask yourself these questions: What do you see? What do you hear? What's being said? What are your thoughts? What are your feelings? What is the context behind your feelings? Have you been in this situation before or since? Have you been in these surroundings, or had these thoughts or feelings before or since? When? Is that part of this story?

How much of a scene you build around the moment of change, how you integrate that scene into the story, and the total number of scenes depends on how much information the audience needs to know in order to understand. What happened before that moment, what happened after? Does the audience need more or less information? What are the key details that will help the audience appreciate the moment of change? Over the course of a three- to five-minute piece, a digital story can consist of a single scene, or it can consist of several. Because the format is relatively short, it's important to select your scenes with care and establish them concretely to ensure that they are contributing to the overall piece.

As the audience, we uncover meaning in the way the storyteller has shaped their story. The events of the story lead us to conclusions but don't constrict our own discovery, and the moment of change and the scenes built around it lead the audience to a river of understanding. However, they are the ones who have to jump in. And in this way they become participants in the narrative; to make that jump, to fill that void.

Step 4: Seeing Your Story

Finding the moment of change in your story and describing it within a scene is the starting point to telling the story as a story. However, because we help storytellers share their stories in the form of a digital story, we also want to look at how the use of visuals and sound bring things to life for the audience. There are many choices that come along with designing how the audience will "see" and "hear" the digital story. Let's begin with visuals. We discuss visual choices early in the story conception process so that storytellers consider how the use of images will shape their story. In order to "see" their story, we help storytellers describe the images that come to mind, understand what those images convey, find or create those images, and then determine how best to use them to convey their intended meaning.

As part of this process of creating a visual narrative, we ask storytellers: "What images come to mind when recalling the moment of change in the story? What images come to mind for other parts of the story?" At this point in the process, we want storytellers to simply call these images to mind, whatever they are, without being concerned about whether or not they exist as actual photos. Next, we want storytellers to explore the meaning that these images convey, and so we ask them: "Why this image? What is it conveying to you? Is the meaning explicit or implicit? Does it have more than one meaning? If so, can you describe the multiple meanings?" Once the storyteller is clear about the meaning they want to convey with their visuals, we help them decide how they will find or create these images, and how they will use them. We ask: "Do you already have these images or will you need to find or create them? How could you use the images that you already have to convey your meaning?"

In her first digital storytelling workshop, designer and filmmaker Lina Hoshino decided to tell her mother's story about the evolution of her name into Chinese and Japanese as a result of the Japanese Occupation and then the Chinese Civil War in Taiwan. At one point in her digital story, Lina shows the Nationalist Party leader, Chiang Kai-shek, in a series of images as she discusses the history. But rather than simply showing the entire formal portrait that she found in the public domain (as part of the F.D. Roosevelt Library), she chose to present the image as a series of crops and a pan.

The original image that she found (Figure 5.1) shows the stately dictator seated with a sword in one hand and a prominently placed medal on his uniform. Lina dissects the full portrait into three cropped details that feature the medal (Figure 5.2), the resting fist (Figure 5.3), and the other hand holding the decorated hilt of the sword (Figure 5.4). After these three images, she then shows the portrait at shoulder height (Figure 5.5) and then slowly pans in and slightly to the left ending on the final frame (Figure 5.6).

Compositionally, the shots move from the medal in the left third, to the fist in the center, to the hilt/hand in the right third. The next shot, the cropped portrait of Chiang, remains in the right third of the frame. Dynamic motion across the frame is created with these detailed stills. In contrast, the slow pan returns our eyes towards the left side of the frame as we are carried along the gaze of the subject. Chiang's Kuomintang army came to Lina's mother's home island of Taiwan with imperial intent. Lina amplifies this through her cropping of the image to the focus on the visual representations of power – details of the medal, gloved fist, martial hilt, and gaze of the leader.

When thinking about creating a digital story, many storytellers who are new to the form will simply envision an image that mirrors each of the different points throughout their entire narrative. These types of literal or direct images that are

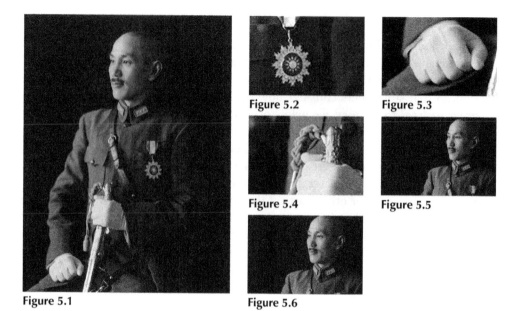

Figure 5.1

Figure 5.2

Figure 5.3

Figure 5.4

Figure 5.5

Figure 5.6

used to illustrate a story are called explicit imagery. Explicit imagery is useful for conveying the necessary details of your story or helping to set the scene for your audience. For example, when a storyteller says, "This is the house where I grew up" and shows a photo of a house, the audience understands that this is literally "the house." By intentionally choosing to show the house, the storyteller is also letting us know that it is important for us to see this house in order to understand the details of their story. When considering which images to use and how to use them, we want to help storytellers be clear about the important details that would not be understood or appreciated without the use of explicit imagery. To do this, we ask: "Would the audience be able to understand the story's meaning without this image?"

However, not all aspects of a story's meaning are best conveyed through the use of explicit imagery. When considering an image, a storyteller can ask: "Is this image conveying another layer of meaning?" If so, then the image has an implicit use. Implicit imagery is useful for implying or representing another meaning beyond an image's explicit or literal meaning. Two common techniques for a storyteller to convey their meaning through the use of implicit imagery are visual metaphor and juxtaposition.

When calling images to mind from the moment of change in their story, a storyteller may select an aspect of the scene that stands out for them, but is not an explicit illustration of the event. For example, when sharing a story about losing a childhood home and describing the moment of change, a storyteller may find that a nearby tree, rather than the house itself, is the dominant image they call to mind. As they consider the significance of the tree in their story, they may discover that it represents the idea of stability in their life. The use of an image of a tree to convey stability in their story is a visual metaphor.

The images you choose and the way you combine them will work to create additional layers of meaning. The placement of one image followed by another to create a new layer of meaning is called juxtaposition. An image of a house followed by an image of cardboard boxes, for example, conveys moving. However, until we know more of the story, we may not know if the message is really about loss, freedom, or maybe both. If the next image is an open road, this could represent freedom. Audiences "read" the juxtaposition of visual images as having implicit meaning that goes beyond what one of the other images explicitly means on its own.

A limitation of material can spark creativity. A storyteller may not possess photos from the major scenes in his or her life. Most people have pictures of their weddings, but who has pictures of their divorce proceedings? Storytellers in our workshops may have only a few photos to work with, or none at all. But paying attention to the images that come to mind when initially sharing the story will help lead the way in creating a visual narrative. And although production time of new material is limited in our workshops, if storytellers are clear about what they want to create, then taking pictures, shooting short segments of video footage, or drawing and scanning images are all good options.

The length of our workshops is typically limited to about three to five days. This constraint on time can help the creative process, but it can also lead to choices about images that are less often considered than the words they accompany. For example, composing a visual narrative with images grabbed from an Internet search can be a quick solution, but oftentimes these images can take away from the integrity of the story. But more importantly, if storytellers have not allowed time early on to see how their images can do some of the heavy lifting of storytelling, they may find they would have altered their script to work with the images they ultimately use.

Well-chosen images act as mediators between the narrative and the audience. As stated in earlier discussions, audiences enjoy stories that lead them to a metaphorical river of meaning and require them to "jump in" in order to make their own connections. Images can grab the hands of the audience and show them the river's immensity. And images have the power to reveal something to the audience that words just can't say.

Step 5: Hearing Your Story

We've just looked at how visuals help bring a story to life. Now, let's look at sound. The recorded voice of the storyteller telling their story is what makes what we call a "digital story" a digital story – not a music video or narrated slideshow. By this point in the process, the emotional tone of the story has been identified, and sound is one of the best ways to convey that tone – through the way the voice-over is performed, the words that are spoken, and the ambient sound and music that work with the narrative. When considering the use of sound, we help storytellers by asking: "Beyond the recorded voiceover, would the story and the scenes within it be enhanced by the use of additional layers of sound? Would the use of ambient sound or music highlight the turning point in your story?"

In digital stories, voice not only tells a vital narrative but it also captures the essence of the narrator, their unique character, and their connection to the lived experience. One's voice is a truly great gift as it is a testament to one's fragility and strength. But why does voice matter so much? In a speech, for example, we are listening for an applause line. In a lecture, we are listening for the major points, or an outline of information. But in a story, we are listening for the shape of an organic, rhythmic quality that allows us to drift into reverie. Here we have a complex interaction between following the story and allowing the associative memories the story conjures up to flow around us. If an image acts as the hand that leads us into the river, the voice is the riverbed below our feet.

When writing a voice-over, it is important to remember that the piece, in its final form, will move from being words on the page to being spoken aloud. And unlike a speech or spoken-word performance, this spoken narration will exist within a digital story complete with accompanying images and possibly other layers of sound. Because of this film-like format, storytellers want to pay special attention to their choice of words and phrasing and the impact they will have. Less is often more, both in descriptive detail, and in the formality of language. This form is served well by the storyteller mimicking how they speak when they tell a story to a friend, unscripted and unrehearsed, for the first time after having just experienced it.

They use incomplete or broken sentences, interrupted thoughts, and a haunting precision of choice words that make the details come alive for both the teller and listener. The more the spoken voice is inserted into the written script, the more the qualities of a person will come across and pull the audience into the story.

Digital stories that have the recorded voice as the only audio track can be tremendously powerful at conveying tone and meaning. When considering whether or not to add layers of sound, we help storytellers approach the process by starting with as little additional sound as possible and then ask: "Is this enhancing the story, or taking away from it?" If it is enhancing the story, then add a little more and ask the question again. One way to add some sound is to think about the ambient sounds that come up when recalling the moment of change in the story. When we listen to the scenes in our stories, they may include sounds that exist in the background of everyday life – traffic, birds, airplanes, voices, for example. These types of sounds help create a sense of place for the audience. There is no question that ambient sound can add complexity to a story. They help to set the scene and feeling, and its addition helps the audience better understand the significance of a scene, especially if there is a dominant sound that best captures its essence. When creating these ambient sounds, it may be simplest to record them from the available sounds nearby rather than search for pre-existing recordings. Also, the use of your recorded voice or that of another person to create additional layers of ambient sound can be very powerful, yet very simple.

As with ambient sound, storytellers can consider how the minimal use of music can enhance a story by giving it rhythm and character. From an early age we become aware that music can alter our perception of visual information. We see how music in a film stirs up an emotional response very different from what the visual information inherently suggests. By trying out different pieces of music you can change not only the story's tone, but also its meaning and direction. The use of instrumental music, whatever the genre, can enhance the style and meaning of the story's text and visual narratives without competing with the voiceover. While popular lyrical music may work, mistakes are sometimes made in mixing the story of the song and the voiceover in a way that gives an unintended conflict of meaning. However, by intentionally juxtaposing the messages, you may create another layer of meaning that adds depth and complexity to your story.

In our experience, storytellers have an intuitive sense of the music that is appropriate for a digital story. People walk around with songs playing in their heads which can set the mood of one's day, change the way we perceive spaces and places, and establish a rhythm for our steps.

A Note on Copyright

Your writing, recorded voice, and personal images belong to you. When you consider using others' music, you cross into the territory of deciding what should be the appropriate fair use of the copyrighted material. Put simply, whatever the music choice, honor it by providing a credit at the end of the piece. If you are going to make money directly or indirectly by the presentation or distribution of the piece you have created, then you should have the artist's permission to use the music. Fortunately there are a growing number of legal online music collections that provide free and affordable media, as well as software to assist you in designing a soundtrack that is wholly yours.

Step 6: Assembling Your Story

At this point in the process you have found and clarified what your story is about and how it sits with you today. You have also established the overall tone you want to convey. You've identified a moment of change and begun making choices about how to use visuals and sound to bring the story and scenes to life for your audience. Now you are ready to assemble your story by spreading out your notes and images and composing your script and storyboard. This requires answering two questions: How are you structuring the story? And, within that structure, how are the layers of visual and audio narratives working together? But those aren't simple questions. Where do you start? Let's look at the question of structure. You've identified the moment of change, but at what point in the story will it appear? Is it at the beginning, middle, end, or is it divided up at different points throughout the story? Or is it the entire story? What other details or scenes are necessary to provide context for the moment of change? And in what order will the information be sequenced?

When we tell stories for the first time after we have just experienced an event, we may want to launch right in, but if we see a confused or disinterested look on our listener's face then we should know to stop and say, "Wait, let me back up. In order to appreciate what I'm telling you, you have to know this ..." In essence, we understand that the listener is lacking some important information in order to "get it," and so we choose to provide our audience with a back story, or exposition. In going back to fill in details for our audience, depending how well they know us and know our life's ongoing narrative, we may find ourselves believing that we need to tell them everything, but quickly realize that this is impossible. A complete telling of every bit of detail is never really "complete," and in the process we begin editing, choosing which details we feel are the most necessary to include in order to construct meaning. In this real-time editing process, we are absorbing our listener's experience and making many choices about where their interest is peaked, where they seem lost, and where they are with us on the journey.

This process of telling stories and reading the audience's reaction is critical to understanding story structure. It helps answer the questions: What are the necessary parts of my story? How will telling this part shape the story differently or take it in a different direction? Knowing which pieces of information are necessary to include allows us to then determine the best way to order those pieces and keep our audience engaged. As the storyteller, we know where the treasure (insight) is hidden, and we are giving our audience clues to find it.

The joy of storytelling comes in determining how much to tell them and at what point. As our narrative literacy progresses from the comprehension of nursery rhymes towards a more intricate understanding of complex narratives, we desire more subtlety in a story's form. As the audience, we are less likely to look for intended morals and spelled-out meanings, and will instead draw from it what we find important. But presenting the conflicts, problems, or unanswered questions with subtlety requires not only identifying the right conflict but the right amount of conflict.

Daniel Weinshenker describes building tension in a story's structure by using a cat analogy: When you are playing with a cat and holding a string for it to chase, if you make it too simple, it will get offended, or bored, and likely walk away. If you make it too difficult and never let it catch the string, then it will give up. But the joy in the game is finding the balance between making it just hard enough to challenge the cat, keeping him engaged in trying to catch the string, and letting him savor it when he does.

In other words, don't give away too much information all at once. Allow your audience to enjoy the challenge. And rather than establishing a chronological telling of events with the moment of change positioned as the story's climax, you might instead try moving the moment of change to the beginning with little or no context, which may leave the moment hanging to pique the interest of the audience, and then go back and fill in more and more details and scenes and allow the audience to piece together the meaning and resolution. However, to do this you need to pay special attention to your audience's experience. For example, if you begin the story with something provocative and don't reveal the piece that explains it until the end, you may need to remind the audience about the question in the first place so they can savor the ending.

Once the basic structure of the story is outlined, the next step is scripting and storyboarding, or in other words, laying out how the visual and audio narratives will complement each other over the duration of the piece to best tell the story. The most common approach that storytellers take to planning their story in our workshops is to write notes in the margins of their script in order to reference where certain images or sounds will occur. In the Chapter 8 we discuss storyboarding in detail, and provide a sample template that includes a series of tracks that you can fill in with notes about the visuals and their effects, voice-over and sound. As you determine how your visual and audio narratives are working together within each of these layers, ask yourself: Do I want them to be redundant, complementary, juxtaposing, or disjunctive?

Considering the above question will not only help you determine how the various layers contribute to the story, but it will also help you economize each in relationship to one another. You can ask yourself: If I have an image that conveys my meaning better than words can, how can I use my words to tell another aspect of the scene? In digital stories, the way we combine the layers to convey meaning allows us to economize the presentation of information and lets our audience make the connections. For example, if we hear a phone ring and the storyteller says, "I held my breath as I got the news ..." and we see a photo of a loved one fade to black, we may understand that the storyteller is conveying a sense of loss. This process of the audience understanding bits and pieces of information as a single idea is called "closure." And as we edit down our scripts and choose each of our images, we need to think about how we set up opportunities for the audience to provide closure with each layer of the story independently, as well as in relation to each other. Oftentimes, this means your script requires fewer words. In an effort to help our storytellers, we provide formal constraints in the production of their digital stories: A word count of 250–375, and fewer than twenty images or video segments. This type of creative limitation helps the storyteller figure out what's most important in his or her story, while also helping to organize their time in the production process.

Digital stories contain multiple visual and audio layers.
    The visual layers are:

- The composition of a single image
- The combination of multiple images within a single frame, either through collage or fading over time
- The juxtaposition of a series of images over time
- Movement applied to a single image, either by panning or zooming or the juxtaposition of a series of cropped details from the whole image
- The use of text on screen in relation to visuals, spoken narration, or sound.

The audio layers are:

- Recorded voice-over
- Recorded voice-over in relation to sound, either music or ambient sound
- Music alone or in contrast to another piece of music.

After your story edits are assembled, pacing is one of the final considerations in creating a digital story because it requires an assessment of how all the layers of information are working over the entire length of the piece. When pacing your story, ask yourself: How does the pacing contribute to the story's meaning? How would pace, or rhythm, bring emphasis to the moment of change?

A story's rhythm conveys an added layer of meaning. A fast pace with quick edits and upbeat music can convey urgency. A slow pace with gradual transitions and extended shots may convey calmness. A mechanically paced story may work nicely for a piece about the monotony of an assembly line job, but for an adventure story it will flatten the experience of the joys and hardships that the audience is expecting to savor. Adjusting the pace of your story provides an opportunity for the audience to listen more clearly. Stories can move along at an even pace, stop to take a deep breath, and then proceed. Creating space for silence, for example, provides the audience with time for all layers of the story to be absorbed. Even if you think your story is paced too slowly, chances are your audience will appreciate more time than you think to allow their minds to explore the thoughts and emotions that are being stirred within them.

The assemblage of your story takes time, and isn't easy. However, our best advice is to keep it simple.

Step 7: Sharing Your Story

At this point in the process, the layers of the story have been assembled. Finding and clarifying the insight, and creating the digital story have taken the storyteller on a journey of self-understanding. The story and the insight it conveys may have evolved throughout the process. Therefore, it is important to take time now to revisit the context in which the story was initially described in order to determine the relevant information to include when the story is being shared. To help storytellers do this, we ask: "Who is your audience? What was your purpose in creating the story? Has the purpose shifted during the process of creating the piece? In what presentation will your digital story be viewed? And what life will the story have after it's completed?"

Before the final version is exported, consider the audience once more, but this time in terms of how you will present the digital story. You may be planning to show it to one individual, one time, for a specific reason. Or you may be planning to share it online with as many people as possible. But for most storytellers their plans fall somewhere in between, or they may not yet know the full extent that they will eventually share their story. But in any event, it's important to consider the contextualizing information you want to convey to your audience, both as part of the digital story and alongside it.

During our workshops we ask if storytellers want to say anything before their story is screened. Some say, "No, I'll let the story speak for itself," and others tell a bit more in order to set it up. When we share stories on our own website we provide a short description of the story and the storyteller's responses to a few questions: Tell us a little about yourself. Why did you choose this story to tell? How have you changed as a result of telling this story?

Knowing more about the story, the storyteller, or both, can reveal a new depth of appreciation by the audience. For example, the First Interlude of this book features Monte Hallis' *Tanya*, a story about how Monte discovers the meaning of friendship through knowing Tanya during her fight with AIDS. The back story she provided in person before her story was screened at the workshop was that Tanya had passed away. The story around a piece changes and expands over time.

Considering your audience at this point in the production process may alter how you complete the final edits. If you know who the audience will be for your piece and what they know about you, then it will help determine how much context you decide to provide about the story. Contextualizing information can be either within or outside of the story's script. If your intended audience already knows certain details about you and your story, then it will help determine which details you include in your script, and which details can instead be revealed through outside contextualizing information. You may choose to contextualize the story outside of the script, but still within the actual piece, by providing a title screen at the beginning and text screens at either the beginning or end that display additional information. This is a common technique used in films in order to set up a story, or communicate what happened to a character or situation thereafter.

Being clear about your purpose in creating the story and how it may have shifted during the process of creating the piece will help you determine how you present and share your story. In our programmatic custom workshops, sometimes the storytellers are recruited with the understanding that their stories will address a certain topic and be presented in a specific context. For example, in a project with foster youth, their host organization may ask if they would like to participate in a workshop in which they tell a personal story about their idea of the "permanency" of family, and have their story be included in a training program for social workers. The storytellers are informed about the expectation before agreeing to attend the workshop. And within the workshop, they are invited to share their larger life story during the first of two story circles. Then during a second story circle they focus their story in a way that is meaningful and timely to them, and also addresses the specific purpose with which the stories are to be shared. Knowing that their story will have this additional audience and purpose will help them appropriately frame their story. In the interview that follows in this book, Amy Hill discusses the issue of presenting stories within their intended context.

If you know the presentation setting in which your audience will view your digital story, then it will help you determine what kind of contextualizing materials should accompany the piece, and will also provide more time during the digital story to focus on other content in the story. For example, if a storyteller makes a story about the successes of their after-school program with the intention of presenting it on their organization's website, they know that the audience will be able to learn more by exploring the information online, and therefore won't need be concerned with including it in the digital story.

Whether your piece will be integrated into a live or published presentation, or is but one in a series of related digital stories that you create, or one that acts as a prompt to elicit others' stories, it is wise to prepare in advance by thinking through all of the possibilities as your story goes forth to live its life.

Finally

The storytelling process is a journey. And in our workshops, we approach this journey as a facilitated group process. We believe that the connections made between people in the story circle help to focus and inspire each individual throughout the process. For many of the storytellers we help, the digital story they create in our workshops may be the only digital story they ever make, in part because overcoming the challenge of finding and clarifying the insights and emotions in their story is not easily done alone. Therefore, we recommend that digital storytellers connect with others to share ideas and work through these steps together.

6

The Story Circle

Facilitating the Digital Storytelling Workshop

At the end of every workshop I teach, I express gratitude for being allowed to help people make their stories. The process continues to feel as rich and varied as every individual that comes through the door. People tell us at CDS that we have a great job, and we cannot argue, it is a privilege to listen and work with people through story. From the beginning of our work, people were interested in how they could become facilitators in our methods. We ran many formal training of trainers between 1993 and 2003, developed many facilitative guides, including this textbook. But it was not until 2004 we began to sharpen our perspective about the process, and develop much more formal materials for the training.

In the early years of our organization we averaged some two to three dozen workshops per year. We now facilitate as many as 90 workshops every year. That sheer volume has meant we had to have a team of experienced professionals who could find themselves in virtually any context, with any grouping of people, and deliver a transformational experience. This breadth of our experience, within numerous sectors, deepens our understanding of what this work has to offer to the larger field of facilitation. This chapter explores the form of the workshop, and the approach of the facilitation to each part of the experience.

The Symphony of Sharing Lives – A Story

The workshop started as many do. With shy introductions, the sorting out of housekeeping issues, and welcoming statements. We presented the overview and steps, but in the most abbreviated way. It was an evening workshop, and we did not want to wear people out with a lecture. Our community-based co-facilitators introduced the guidelines for the story circle, people listened, they were already well processed in group dynamics. As survivors, connected to public health environments, sharing in circles was a familiar, albeit uncomfortable experience, for most of the youth involved.

We started at the head of a long table. I remember the shy young man, hair hanging down, who spoke first, talking about an abusive father. His tone was upbeat, and he attempted to pull forgiveness out of the narrative, but it was raw. The rawness hung in the room. I remember thinking, "that will make it tough for the next person." I was responding to this feeling of hanging tension. Many times in the past, I had seen people in line after a "heavy" story, draw back into themselves. They were protecting themselves from the pain that a powerful story evoked in their own memories, but they also wanted to hold the power of the story in the room. They wanted to honor what had been heard … as something sacred … as something worthy of our ongoing consideration. I didn't want others in the room to be burdened by this feeling, so I called out to the storyteller in recognition and thanks. I also might have said something to release the tension, "Wow, that was intense." I did not want to take anything away from the solemnity or pain that the initial story had presented, but I wanted to make us all realize we were being held in the trance, and we needed to make space for the next story.

The next story was about losing a friend to violence, the next story about the abuse of an uncle and the rupture of immigration, the next story was about being homeless with a mother addicted to drugs, it went on and on. We reached a story about a girl and her sister. They had already lost their mother before either had reached six years. But this story was about another loss. It provided a detail-by-detail account of the day the storyteller was with her little sister, together at a camp, swimming. The little sister suddenly comes to her screaming in pain, her head was exploding, she slumped over in the storytellers' arms. A few hours later, the younger sister was dead. A cerebral embolism. The telling had a quality of such immediacy, that each of us left ourselves, left our bodies and arrived like witnessing ghosts at that pool, at that moment, holding a loved one in confusion and anguish. To see a teen perform this was stunning. How could one suffer … how could one suffer such a loss?

At this point, as I am sure anyone that has done counseling work with survivors, there is a natural impulse to check out of the story, to turn on a neutral set of ears, in order not to feel what the feelings are in their full intensity. This time, I did not feel like this was a choice. There was a prolonged silence.

No comments. No discussion. A recognition put in the simple phrase, "Thank you, your story honors us as listeners."

The community facilitators reminded us all to go home and do something to honor ourselves, hold a dear one, take a hot bath, write down thoughts, sit in quiet recognition.

We left for the night.

I later described to my colleagues at CDS the feeling that I had witnessed a symphony of suffering, the themes intersecting and building upon each other, moving towards transcendence.

I have had many amazing experiences in the story circles I have facilitated. Surprising revelations, synchronistic connections, fascinating patterns of care and support, kindness and compassion, and unbelievable creative breakthroughs. This one workshop remains outside my normal frame of reference, compared to many others that I have led working with similar groups of people, with similar life experience. It was a teaching moment for my life, and I am sure it will stay with me forever.

Approaches to Facilitation

When you enter into the role of leading a group, no matter your experience, through a creative process, you always feel inadequate to the task. At least I believe you should, because humans are so complex, and their potential for interactions so vast, that if you think you are in control, you are deeply deluded.

I have used the metaphor of midwifery, not because I know that art, but as a parent of two children born at home, with the support of an expert midwife, with my full participation in holding my wife through the entire birthing process, I have this metaphor fixed in my mind. Stories emerge in their own good time, and the success of their emergence has factors not dissimilar to those of the birthing child, patterns of healthy support need to be present at all times, but the centering of the work is on the parent to the story. This is critical. It is their story, not your own, and their mysteries in how they know when it is just time to deliver, are theirs. All one can do is create the space, the context, the encouragement and the support with a firm resolve that you believe the person is capable of the miracle of writing and producing a transformative story.

The metaphor can be extended to the idea of appropriate intervention. When one knows that something is not quite right, and one gains that ability to decipher another person's process, your training and knowledge should provide a basis for engaging folks in dialogue about their process. Self-knowledge, maturity and a strong sense of ethical precaution, are your main assets at all times. Reading the difference between relative shyness and strong-willed self-reliance is not easy. But the cues are usually there, in all the minute interactions you have witnessed from the moment someone arrives, in their body language, and in knowing your own sense of shyness and self-assertion.

In traditional processes of group therapy, there are several perspectives about what constitutes a safe and supportive environment. They begin with a sense of the shared nature of human suffering, the universal character of our primary relationships and how they inform and impair our lives, the moments of learning and discovery, as well as the losses and traumas that occur in our lives. The experience of working in a group process is inherently democratic and altruistic, everyone understands that they have something to give in support, even as they have something to take as experience, knowledge and hopefully, an improved story. We also understand the creative environment to be essentially hopeful, that whatever we bring into the story process, the work is to make beauty and insight out of it. The process is also very much about supporting interaction and a sense of group cohesion. As much as anything, it is a chance to work through interaction on one's own awareness of others' process of growth and resiliency, and through them to take a long look at your own process (Yalom and Leszcz 2005).

There are particularities to working in group creative process that have been explored extensively in the therapeutic expressive arts in visual/plastic arts, music, dance-movement, and drama. Because they stand upon the general consensus of ethical approaches of group therapeutic models, they avoid judgment, or aesthetic review. Part of the defining character of expressive arts is that the product is celebrated for any and all inherent value. Interpretation and reflection by individuals on their own work, by the group, and by the facilitator, is oriented to insight. The degree to which those insights assist with one's own self-understanding, and improved wellbeing is paramount. Success is defined by the whole experience of the process, not the end-point artifact.

While our model endeavors to hold the artistically judgment-free process perspective of expressive arts facilitation, we are also trying to integrate the arts-based aesthetic valuation of a formal arts class. In our minds, striving for technique and comparative success of one's film can be self-assessed, the work can stand as a statement of an attempt at a new level of quality for an individual. The issues of one's vulnerability to critique can be moderated by having no inherent judgment or valuation by the instructors or fellow storytellers. In our workshops, there are no grades for projects, and we resist being part of projects that include any competitive or exclusive outcomes for some storytellers over others. Our feeling is that storytellers can be coached around a number of aesthetic choices – from their thinking through the way their stories are structured, the wordsmithing of their language, what choices they make around visuals, the approach of integration of elements and pacing. The extent of the coaching is based on formal or informal assessments of the individual goals, or the goals of the project for which the stories are intended, balanced precisely with the perceived willingness of the storyteller to accept, receive and integrate feedback.

The art of facilitation is in listening for the storyteller's conscious and unconscious vulnerabilities – to delicately probe the borders of the extent their ego can withstand critique. Over time, erring on the side of caution yields a safer and consistently more successful process, while pushing a storyteller at precisely the right moment with the right suggestion can yield a transformative breakthrough for the story, and the storyteller. Some qualified risk versus reward is part of our intention. We want our storytellers to go deeper, farther, be more complexly nuanced than they may have before in their creative process. And our storytellers usually appreciate the coaching. The appropriate metaphor for this engagement is the skillful chiropractic adjustment rather than a surgical excision. The right snap of a lightly suggested idea, allows the storyteller to realign themselves to a healthy outcome. By contrast, if the storyteller feels the surgeon's knife, or the facilitators overpowering sense of certainty in an opinion about the story, while this may mean the story is received as more successful, the patient may suffer the cure.

We consider the shared practice of refining one's facilitative method as it itself a knowledge base filled with stories to illustrate nuanced decisions in context. Communities of practice in our methods exist around the world, and becoming part of these conversations, as well as seeking continued training through our center, is the only way to improve and master your technique.

A Small Miracle

Sam couldn't quite believe it. His movie had just been played. Everyone was applauding. His eyes were squishy with tears. He felt like the leaden jacket he had been carrying on his shoulders about his father had just been hung on the coat rack. At least for this moment, he felt he had a way to let go.

But 24 hours ago, finishing his story, much less finishing the workshop, seemed a ridiculous ambition.

...

Sam heard the footsteps of the facilitator as they approached.

"How's it going?"

Telling them to f**k off seemed inappropriate, but that was his first thought. "Why did I take this stupid workshop?" He thought to himself. "I can't tell this story, I barely made it through the recording session without breaking down, and now I have no clue what images to use. I brought all these photos of my dad and I when I was a kid, but now they have nothing to do with what I wrote. I wrote about a conversation I had with him just before he died. How do you make find images for that. I'm screwed. Just screwed."

"Good, yeh, I think I'm good." Sam didn't feel like looking up at the facilitator. "Maybe if I look busy they'll go to the next person," he thought to himself.

"Mind if I sit and take a look" she asked him. Sam decided his lunch was beginning to disagree with him.

"Sure" he said aloud but inside he thought "Might as well face the music. If I can admit I still love my dad after all he did to my family, I guess I can face this process like a grown man"

...

The applause was lifted and the facilitator smiled at him and patted his shoulder. "Great job. I knew you could do it, " she whispered.

Sam would spend the next month trying to understand how he got out of that workshop with a story. It felt like magic.

The Workshop Process Unpacked

This workshop process does feel like magic to me. How we get folks from the first digging around in their hearts a bit to these little hunks of golden narrative, has me look for elves and guardian angels over my shoulder. The methods honed over the last two decades, and the skills developed by my colleagues in the field in the process, are not too difficult describe, and hopefully understand. To start with, as suggested above, is a value system of facilitation borrowed from therapeutic engagement and community organizing. But one also needs to dissect the specific model, and how it works as an enclosed system.

Let's take a broad overview to the core steps in the classic digital storytelling workshop process. We have developed a basic timeline and tasklist that helps organize the process.

The typical digital storytelling workshop is three full days, or 21 hours of instruction. The scope of the work is determined as much by the film duration as any other component. We propose a 250–375 word count, and a limit of fifteen images or small video snippets. This generates a two- to four-minute digital story. In some cases when we know, for one reason or another, that the technical side of the workshop will be complicated, or the amount of time for preparation is limited, we suggest a 150 word count and a one- to two-minute duration as a good target for a story.

Day One

Workshop Timeline

Introductions
Seven Steps Lecture
Story circle
Individualized support on script, image selection, storyboard
Possible voiceover recording

Day Two

Complete Scripts
Voiceover recording
Software tutorial
Complete image selection and import
Complete rough edit

Day Three

Individual support in final design and production
Screening of films

Introductions

The hosting and process of introductions starts the process. We are aware that the success of the workshop begins with how people enter the room, how they are recognized and welcomed, and how they are made to feel comfortable. Once settled, we focus on learning the basics of each person, name, where they are from, work as it relates to this process, and we request a one sentence introduction of the story idea, even if it is, "I have no idea."

Having lengthy introductions of a large group can exhaust the participants right at the start, and folks may commit to ideas in the introduction process if allowed to expand upon them before the formal process of the story circle. Our hope is to move quickly past introductions to the initial lecture, and allow people to settle over an initial hour or so. We feel that people enter into processes slowly, and leave their contexts, the places and issues they left at home or work, only after some warming up to this focused process. By waiting for them to expand on their ideas until after the lecture, and within the story circle, it allows them to drop into their emotions, and reshape their workshop goals and story ideas with a fresh, and centered perspective. People usually have some idea for their story, may even have prepared a script, but we count on the initiation of the Seven Steps lecture , and each part of the story circle process, to re-orient them.

The Seven Steps Lecture

The initial lecture that occurs in a workshop serves four purposes:

1   As suggested, it is a time for the participants to "arrive" in the new venue, to step away from their thoughts and concerns outside the workshop, and step into the special workshop time and space.
2   It acts as an introduction to the aesthetic framework for the workshop process. the stories shown and dissected through the Seven Step process direct the participants to a goal of depth, design, and duration.
3   It demonstrates the credibility and authority of the facilitator, assuring the participants that the leadership for the workshop is grounded in a process of understanding that is clear and precise. While people want room to explore, and to project an inclusive perspective of artistic latitude, the setting of solid expectations to be supported by the facilitator tends to assure people that they are in good hands.
4   The lecture is meant to inspire. The facilitator's own enthusiasm, emotional connection, sense of wonder and excitement about helping people make stories, can bring people into the story circle infused with that shared energy. I often refer to my version of this lecture as a sermon, because I want to bring a joyful awareness of story-as-salvation to the process. This is not a time for intellectual dissertation, it is a time to pick up the tools and make things happen, and if I can project a sense that the process promises transformation, people will step out of themselves in the story circle in surprising ways.

At each workshop, we assess the efficacy of our lessons and adjust accordingly. The Seven Steps can become the three steps if we feel the audience is completely new to aesthetic discussions, and will quickly bore at a lecture. While we generally do not make the lecture discursive, we allow for questions and responses; if we have a smaller group, or the additional time, we might show a film, give a brief overview to a step, and invite a discussion of the issues.

Again, I argue the role of this lecture is to put space between arrival and initiation. We recognize people are still trying to stop worrying about the email back at the office, or – for those whom these kind of artsy/creative discussions are anathema – trying to relax and let the facilitator talk and joke about ideas, bringing them new perspectives and insights about story.

While we certainly believe that the seminar-style learning environment is positive, we caution against thinking that people who walk in the door as strangers are equally ready to engage in a discussion about how to make a digital story. Naturally a rapidly started group dynamic encourages people to join in from their normal level of assertion. That could mean folks may say little, or it could mean they have an opinion about the topics. Ranking of expertise in these dynamics becomes an invitation to passivity for some. It is better to start a mutual and equitable dialogue with the shared stories in the story circle, where they lead with the authority of their own lives.

At times, particularly when we are blessed with additional time, we will also explore icebreakers, writing to prompts and/or creative exercises, as a prelude to the story circle. These can complement the lecture in specific ways, expanding the storyteller's perspective about how their story might be shaped.

The Story Circle

At the heart of the entire process is our work in the story circle. When successful, the thinking of each and every participant shifts dramatically from their initial conception of their purpose and goals in the workshop, to the perspective they take out of the circle process and forward into the rest of the workshop.

We always limit the story circle to the facilitator(s) and a group of storytellers. We do not find it useful to have non-participants also engaged in the feedback. The process works to move toward depth because of the quality of safety. That safety includes that everyone is in this together, they have an oar in the water, and the resourcefulness and courage of one storyteller inspires the resourcefulness and courage of the next.

This is the first time the storyteller has to more fully present an idea, or ideas, to the group about what they want to consider as their story for the workshop. There is usually a time limitation for the circle. Storytellers may have anywhere from 10–30 minutes to work through the idea and receive feedback. While some people bring drafts of scripts, and are encouraged to share them, the pre-workshop preparatory materials do not encourage over working an idea prior to attendance. Coming with only a small concept, as in what the subject might be, and why they might be interested in the subject, is enough to start the discussion. As suggested, often by the end of the lecture, the idea has shifted. What was considered a superficial or distanced approach to a subject, now shift to a subject that feels closer to the immediate needs of the storyteller's emotional and intellectual concern. The process has seven distinct considerations for the facilitator to assure the depth and effectiveness of the process:

1 *Clarity of Ground Rules* – As facilitators, we have taken to heart that the articulation of distinct rules of process and engagement are critical to group success. They set an appropriate tone of mutual respect, and an idea of what authority the facilitator, and the group, has in managing input directed at the storyteller, and the direction of all aspects of the conversation. In general the ground rules we use are familiar to anyone in group process: confidentiality, do not interrupt each other, keep feedback positive and constructive, stay on topic, couch feedback in the conditional not the declarative, or use questions rather than statements, and be aware of one's tendency to dominate or conversely shy from group dialogue.

2 *Protecting the Storyteller* – As facilitators in a creative process, we emphasize that the storyteller should always feel like they control the amount and substance of the feedback. If the storyteller wants to use the entire allotted time to talk out their idea, that is their preference. After the initial presentation of an idea, the starting point should always be what questions does the storyteller want us to address.

The storyteller is encouraged to direct where they feel the concept needs refining, and the facilitator strives to keep the discussion in those areas. As facilitators, we observe the comfort by which they present their ideas, and the sense of their readiness for considered feedback. We manage the discussion around the storyteller's vulnerability. We will check with the storyteller, making sure they want to continue on a line of discussion. As much as possible, the storyteller should run their own feedback session. The facilitator is simply there to assure that the storyteller gets what they need.

In the event that the storyteller, or even another participant, becomes overwhelmed and unable to pull themselves out of emotional crisis, the process is immediately stopped. The person is allowed to step out of the circle and recover, or perhaps to step out of the workshop and reconsider participation. In our workshops where storytellers will address emotionally difficult material, we have professional psychiatric or counseling staff available.

3   *Focusing Discussion of the Story* – The feedback time belongs to the storyteller, and the facilitator needs to contain the discussion on how the storyteller will complete a successful digital story within the constraints of the workshop environment. Invariably stories always beget stories, and expressions of shared experience, as a form of solidarity, can be useful. But allowing respondents to use the time of the storyteller to explore their own story can become a distraction. The facilitator should remind the group that we are not trying to fix the person, just their story.

4   *Time Management* – As suggested above, we maintain an equitable distribution of time for all participants. Naturally, as one moves through the story circle process, people will become fatigued. Our experience suggests that it is best to complete the circle in one sitting. Each story generates new depth, concentration and compassion. The stories build upon each other. We have found that breaking the spell of the story circle process disservices the storytellers who come later, the group never listens as deeply as it does on this first sitting. Keeping the process on schedule means some people may feel their process is not fully explored, but the facilitator can assure them that there will be time for continued one-on-one feedback.

5   *Shaping Process of Feedback* – Facilitators do not need to feel that they are the ultimate authority in giving feedback. Rather, we should feel we can defer to the group genius to assure full participation. As facilitators, we want to listen to the entire group process, with our focus on supporting the storyteller. This may mean we do not have the mental space for suggestions for shaping the story. By being attentive to the range of feedback, we can also bring our consideration of the various viewpoints expressed in the discussion to our work with the individual storyteller.

The facilitator is equally responsible to the general maintenance of order – reminding people about ground rules, making sure respondents are recognized in order, and the transitions from one storyteller to another goes smoothly.

6   *Identification of Broadly Applicable Lessons* – Of course, the advantage of being an experienced facilitator, is you may have many useful suggestions to shape an individual story. Ideally, your choice to share feedback should refer to both

the individual story, and to broadly applicable lessons for the other storytellers. Learning moments are many in the story circle process. Whether referencing the original Seven Steps lecture, or bringing new ideas to the discussion, the facilitator has a responsibility to abstract from a singular example, a more general rule.

7   *Closing Summation and Encouragement* – The exit from the story circle experience is as critical as the entry. Recognizing that the process may have brought up unexplored emotions, and may require support in various ways from the staff or peers, it is important to state that those resources are also part of the process. It is important to thank everyone for their participation. And it is also important to remind everyone that the process continues with individual support for each storyteller.

Script Review and Initial Image Work

We exit the story circle with the work of keeping the storytellers to task on creating an initial draft of writing. This initial draft is encouraged to be longer, from 500– 1,000 words, and allows us to consider the larger idea of the writer, and then focus our efforts on restructuring the arc of the narrative.

We each bring with us an approach to editing language, but our core precept is that we never change the way the person would say the words, and ideally we never add words, but merely restructure and subtract language with the writer for them to compare versions that trim the edit to the script maximum. Some people will take feedback on focus and approaches to the expression of concepts, and return to their own writing approach to attempt an edit. Other people prefer one-on-one collaboration that demonstrates potential edits that the author can accept or reject. The process is always iterative.

As part of the discussion about the edit is the beginning of image consideration, as images may inform the editing process. Certain images may allow implicit relationships to be explored that the written text has suggested, but can be left out, knowing the narration will use the images to provide additional meaning and clarification. We will discuss the storyboard process as part of the design discussion, but short of a thorough storyboard discussion, you can suggest scripts begin to indicate potential image choices to inform the final bits of editorial work on the narration.

Voice Recording

Standing or sitting a front of a microphone can be nerve-wracking for many people. The voiceover is a performance, and the performance requires the storyteller to feel the words they are saying. At the very least, they need not sound rushed or disengaged from the text. We encourage the storyteller to breath as they speak, and take deliberate time with each comma, each period, and certainly with the end of paragraphs. We ask them to imagine an audience listening to what is being said, where emphasis belongs, and how important concepts, or shifts in emphasis require pauses to allow the ideas to be held by the audience. We find a little bit of coaching, makes a world of difference. For some people, privacy serves the purpose of a relaxed read, but an equal number will find it difficult to progress through the reading without coaching and support, a listener to their story present in the room.

Many facilitating practitioners in the form have experienced wooden, stuttering, or awkward reading of scripts by storytellers who are challenged with reading a text comfortably. There are many ways to encourage low literacy level readers to succeed as well. It is possible to have a call and response approach with the storyteller, where instead of reading the text, they record the words that they have constructed, as they hear them spoken by the facilitator. Working through one sentence at a time, the facilitator says the words with an appropriate inflection, and the teller repeats with their own version of the inflection, until the script is completed. While this may sound unusual, the result can create a comfortable, and authentic sounding voiceover.

A Word About Technology

Since 1993, we have used a myriad of video-editing software applications and evolving versions of each. We also use different versions of audio-recording, image manipulation, video compression, word processor, browsers, email programs, etc. And of course we do this on each version of operating systems for Apple, Windows, and Linux computers. This textbook could not hope to provide an active list of what would be good for your specific needs in the classroom, community center or home. We will attempt to maintain some of this information on our companion website at www.routledge.com/cw/lambert.

What you should consider best for Digital Storytelling projects may not be intuitive. While this world has many low cost and free software programs for editing video – iMovie and Windows Movie Maker, for example – these softwares are not always the best for beginners. While issues of cost may determine the use of freeware, we have a history of trying to identify relatively low cost software that is robust enough to expand the creative palette of participants.

Every workshop has storytellers with a range of experience in computing and media production. If the software is too simple, the advanced users lose interest, but if it is too complicated, some storytellers are too daunted. Professional-level software is also generally more stable than free products, and that stability is vital to creating a positive experience for participants. Teaching a complex software at a simple level is always easier than trying to make a simple, but unstable, software behave appropriately in an intensive workshop.

We also realize that much of the artful finesse of highly experienced facilitators is precisely in their ability to troubleshoot hardware and software issues while never losing sight of the time limitations, production demands and very specific resiliency/ stress of the storyteller they are assisting. The lessons of our work are won through many, many cases of mistakes made by each of us, and the endless process of keeping our skills up to date with the shifting requirements of hardware/software configurations and versions.

Software Tutorial and Production

Digital Storytelling workshops are also about technology, and technology becomes the focus of the process as we enter the second day, with the voiceover completed and images selected.

As a critical mass of storytellers complete their voiceover recording, we want them to quickly move into editing. While some storytellers may have organized their materials "on paper" using script and storyboard, many, if not most, find it difficult to visualize their stories, until they begin editing. We want the tutorial to arrive just in time for this process to have immediate impact on the storytellers efforts.

Most of our tutorials are hands on. We have designed the tutorial materials with exactly the form of our workshops in mind, in both content, and in considering what features or tools need to be introduced, and how to build up competence by the repetition of these basic procedures. In teaching the tutorial, we are also trying to make the experience as gentle as possible. If you are not experienced in instructional technology teaching, you quickly realize that people find it quite difficult to follow a set of instructions between something demonstrated on a projected screen, and something on their own screen. One-on-one training is still by far the most effective way to learn, and we are generally expecting that acquisition of most procedures will only occur as the storyteller works through the process during the entire workshop. So we keep the tutorial simple but lively, expending no more than one hour to one and a half hours in this experience.

We also use the tutorial to get our first active assessment of technological literacy. Participants are invariably either slightly over-confident or more usually entirely self-effacing about their ability to use a computer and tackle the basics of software. The tutorial allows us to examine how much support will be needed to assist the individual during the production phase. Our first triage of facilitative support can come out of tutorial to assure that those in most need, will get the most assistance, and conversely, those that we assess are quite competent, are encouraged to explore the software themselves (even if they would love to get help in doing more sophisticated process than the workshop period allows.)

As the story above suggests, this point is a critical juncture for individual support because whatever creative blocks people may have, this provides an enormous playground for displacing time, instead of attending to a procedural focus with our suggested priorities of completing a rough edit, the storytellers will find themselves heading into dark holes of obsession with certain images, and certain design tools. We support individualized learning and creative approaches, but we attempt to distinguish what feels like a productive exploration, and what feels like a stalling action because the material is emotionally difficult, and the creative act – committing to one way of doing something for this one story – is daunting for nearly everyone.

With the tutorial accomplished, the individual production support also turns into the first general assessment of progress. We use workshop progress charts to monitor the writing and voiceover recording, but the chart becomes more and more handy as production begins. Typically we find the storyteller may have an idea of what the storyboard might be, and have a handful of images that they think relate to the story, but staring at the editing software for the first time, as in the story at the beginning of the chapter, the person may discover what looked to be easy, plopping a hand full of photographs into their story, suddenly turns out to be quite complicated.

We have found that if we provide only basic suggestions, or keep the stories on a strict template, we may in fact make our job easier, but in turn stifle many participants' initiative and inspiration. We want their introduction to new media and storytelling to have a magical, transformative feeling. Furthermore, we also want to provide a broad range of tools that participants with the usual range of experience (novices to professionals) have an appropriate amount of toys with which to play. So during the one-on-one support, particularly after the rough edit is complete, we will demonstrate possible approaches within the skill set of each of us as experienced editors and designers

In the production process, the true art of digital storytelling facilitation is seen when facilitators address each individual and each of his/her unique concerns. Each participant brings a different skill set to the table, and it is up to the facilitator to work with what is available. However, there isn't always enough facilitators to go around, so we encourage participants to assist other participants if their skill level permits.

Producing A Movie

To produce a digital movie, the production process involves four distinct steps:

1. Importing material to the computer – This involve scanning and digitizing audio and video either prior to or during the workshop. Recording the voiceover is a critical part of this process, and we usually insist on this being done in our lab in order to sustain quality.
2. Preparing media – In our situation, this typically consists of editing images in Photoshop. In a professional environment this might include pre-producing the audio and video work to enhance the quality of the original tape.
3. The initial video edit or rough edit – We encourage participants to first complete a rough cut of the movie that doesn't include transitions or special effects. The reason for this is that it allows the participant to have a general understanding of his or her piece. Furthermore, it helps identify the areas where images or video are insufficient for the edit.
4. Special effects, creating titles, audio mixing – The final changes that are made in a digital story look to enhance the piece by using filters, transitions, motion graphics, compositing, audio layers, and text generation available in digital video-editing software. Using these effects can be the most fun part of the project, but it is also where novice digital storytellers can become overwhelmed or lost in the possibilities. In order to prevent this from happening, we like to emphasize a specific set of tools that helps participants start simply at first, and then expand their creativity over time.

In the midst of these artistic processes, the maintenance and supervision of the computers, those unruly beasts that they are, is extremely important. We can assure all those who have tried to create a Digital Storytelling computer lab that the experience for the computers reaches a battlefield hospital proportion of symptoms, cures, work-arounds, and retirements. In fact, the battlefield hospital is an apt metaphor for the whole procedure. If you are well, we let you heal at your own pace, if you are critically challenged we step in with immediate procedure.

But, of course, and regrettably, on rare occasions we also have participants for whom no amount of intervention will result in a completed project on the deadline. When this final situation is the case, we work with them to ensure that their perspective on the process is as positive as possible. We play their voiceover and invite people to close their eyes and imagine the film, for example. At this point, a student might be feeling dismayed about the accomplishments, and it is our job to help them work with what they have so they cannot walk away empty-handed.

The Final Premiere

The final showing of storyteller's piece is the most critical and successful part of our workshop process. Before showing the films, we ask each storyteller to give comments about their efforts, and as we approach the appointed hour, the participants get to shed their anxieties.

As we bring the workshop to a close, we stop to recognize all that has been achieved. We also assure the participants that everyone would like additional time to complete their projects, and that each and everyone has a prerequisite disclaimer about the projects, regardless of their individual outcomes.

Many, many tears have been shed at these showings. The catharsis, the pride, the sense of awe at what others in the room have accomplished, and the resulting camaraderie, are all wonderfully satisfying outcomes of a successful workshop.

The circle is closed.

A Sacred Trust

As we said, at the Center for Digital Storytelling, we do not pretend to have license to function as therapeutic facilitators. The material that explains and markets our work does not suggest that this environment should be formally approached as a healing process. But it would be inconceivable, incomprehensible, and irresponsible if we did not recognize the emotional and spiritual consequence of this work.

The forbearers of story circle traditions are indeed ancient, and they can be found in all cultures. They of course remain vital in the root cultures that survive to this day, and most certainly in the living traditions of our native peoples and their ceremonies. Today, what we know is that when you gather people in a room, and listen, deeply listen, to what they are saying, and also, by example, encourage others to listen, magic happens.

The magic is simple. And we do not have many safe places to be heard.

Sharing personal and reflective storytelling in a group is a privilege, and for many of us, a sacred trust. Those of us who live fully in the modern world do not go easily into quietude and listening. We mainly talk at each other, not to each other. The result is the stressful sickness of modern living.

But however you help others to facilitate a story, respect the process and the participant's efforts. In the end, a well managed process guarantees the best digital stories will come to life ... and perhaps, live forever.

Interlude 3
Elizabeth's Story

My father and his brother arrived at Ellis Island in 1922, the only survivors of a pogrom in their Russian village. My mother moved to Harlem from rural French Canada. My parents' desire to see a better world led them to join the American Communist party and become union organizers.

In the 1950s, during the McCarthy era, my father was charged with conspiracy to overthrow the U.S. Government. For ten years, as the case dragged on, he was rarely able to work. When he did, he was confronted by men jeering, "Two red-hot Rosenbergs on the grill, one more to go." My mother's life was tense and frantic with fear.

It is against this backdrop that my story begins.

I didn't remember what happened when I was six years old until I was thirteen. Up until that time, I had been a quiet kid. After I remembered, I couldn't stop talking. I chattered about everything, anything – I just never told anyone exactly what happened. They knew from the police and my dad, but no one asked me. All I wanted was to be listened to and cared for. It isn't that my family didn't want to help me; there hadn't been any safety for them, and they didn't know how to give me something they never had.

(But they gave me a vision of global justice and a commitment to deep systemic change. These were the priorities, during this turbulent era. Individual stories were not valued. In the end, the charges against my father were dropped, and we moved to California.)

Over the years I dealt with what happened to me through psychotherapy, art, political organizing. Members of my family began to tell me their own silent stories – the rape and murder of my father's mother in a pogrom; the rape of my mother by her cousin, a priest … and eventually, my sister told me of her assault by the same man who had kidnapped, raped, sodomized, and threatened to kill me. With each story placed on my shoulders, I listened, comforted, and wept. But still there was no place and no one to whom to tell my story.

When I was 34, my mother told me that she wanted to go to counseling together, to deal with what happened to me. I said, "I'm all right, we don't need to go." She said, "I need to go, because I need to know what happened, and to talk about what it was like to not be able to protect you, and nearly lose you." We sat there in the gathering dusk, at her small, quiet house, holding hands, crying. Finally there it was: a place for me to tell my story.

But we never got to counseling. The following day my mother was raped and murdered by a young man in the neighborhood. Over the next months and years, I lived in a world of vast grief. My world fractured into other stories and images, and it was a very long time before I did indeed tell my story.

It wasn't until the second spring after her death that I started to find myself here, with the living, again. What sustained me and kept me from bitterness towards life? My art, my passion for justice, my hands in the garden soil, loved ones … and those loving words from my mother, on our last night.

—Elizabeth Ross, 2005
Project sponsored by Generation FIVE
The story can be viewed at www.silencespeaks.org/case-studies/40.html.

Thoughts from Amy Hill

With the creation of a narrative, a fragmented present tense becomes a coherent past tense. To narrate one's life is to have agency. To know and feel this agency is important for everyone, especially for those who have been victimized.

(Michelle Citron, 1999)

We sit side by side in the cramped office, staring at words on a page, reading about the unthinkable. Elizabeth's breathing seems shallow, and as I take in what she has written, I understand why. She's part of a workshop that I'm teaching in partnership with Generation FIVE, a nonprofit group that seeks to end childhood sexual abuse.

In that office, Elizabeth and I grapple with how to convey the essence of her personal wounding while also acknowledging the social and political structures within which the story unfolded. Like her, I feel torn. And as the workshop progresses, with participants finalizing their scripts, collecting images, and recording voiceover narration, we have to decide what approach to take to her story.

Elizabeth is concerned that bringing in the back story of her family's response to her molestation will make her piece too long. She has very little computer experience, and she is visibly drained. She worries that adding to the script will make it difficult for her to complete her story. I listen carefully, I pay attention to what her energy is telling me, in addition to what she's saying.

And in that moment, I make the decision to encourage her to move forward with her script just the way it is. The sparseness of her language, and her plan to use a combination of family photos and digital versions of her own artwork to illustrate the story feels very complete. We sit together in silence, for a while, and then I help her record narration.

But it doesn't take long for me to question my decision. After the workshop, as the months pass, I became aware that GenerationFIVE wasn't showing Elizabeth's story publicly. She explained that they felt uncomfortable with what they saw as its lack of attention to the interconnections between sexual abuse and politics.

While Elizabeth felt hurt by this and remarked upon the irony of her exclusion, given that much of her story focuses on the ways in which for so long, she was not listened to, she also shared that *she* was very happy with her piece. And that for her, this outweighed the disappointment of being "excluded" from the group.

And ultimately the "problem" was solved, when we began to develop a compilation DVD of the GenerationFIVE stories. Elizabeth drafted some written text providing background to her story, and we successfully integrated it into the piece. Everyone was happy, more or less … I went on to do several more workshops with GenerationFIVE, and Elizabeth became a dear friend.

7

Approaches to The Scripting Process

Prompts and Processes

After all these years of people bringing their stories to CDS, I would like to think the scripting process gets easier. But it doesn't. Writing for many is a painful process, and moving from the big idea of the story to the little script of a narrative is even more excruciating. To take some of the pain away, we want to treat the process of getting the words down on the page as a completely different subject.

In the preceding chapters we discussed the insights and structure for your story, how to work through a group process to hone in on a story idea, as well as the considerations for working with multiple forms of media. In this chapter we will discuss how to find your best creative voice for self-expression in writing, about how writing happens, and about what makes the way you write unique and powerful.

As with our approach to digital storytelling in general, we find that our practice is ideally suited to group settings. And while you can use these ideas to get started on your own, success happens just as often by comparing your work to others, and by hearing a variety of examples. So find a few friends, declare yourself a writer's group, gather once a week for a month, and share your writing. Your digital story will thank you for your efforts.

Our Friend, the 4 × 6 Index Card

Of all the suggestions that we have made in helping people to prepare their writing, the use of 4 × 6 index cards has garnered the most praise.

The idea is simple: novice and experienced writers alike inevitably suffer from a malady aptly called "blank page syndrome." The weight of filling a blank page, or more than likely, many pages, can easily crush our creative initiative, and as a result, cause us some difficulty in getting started. In our workshops, when we have found a person blankly staring at their monitors with a deer-in-the-headlights look in their eye, we like to hand them a 4 × 6 index card and say, "You have six minutes and only the space on the front and back of this card to create a draft of your story. Write whatever comes out and don't stop until either the time or the card runs out." We might also give them a prompt: "This is a postcard. Choose a person that you think this story is for and write them a postcard about the story. Start with, 'Dear.'"

The card is small, and it is finite. It seems possible, and perhaps even easy to fill. So for the novice, we are saying, "Just get this much down, and we'll work from there." And for writers confident in their ability to write countless pages of prose, this exercise is a creative challenge. To them, we say, "We know you could write a novel, now just try and say it in only this much space."

One of my favorite Mark Twain quotes is from a letter that he wrote to a friend: "Forgive me, this is a long letter. I would have written you a short letter, but I didn't have the time."

Shorter isn't always easier for the mature writer. The 4 × 6 card also helps condense the narrative by breaking the story down to its most basic elements and forcing a writer to ask, "What are my choices in the beginning? How quickly must I get into the action of the narrative?" Usually, this approach means sacrificing the long exposition that accompanies the first draft of a story. But in the end, if the writing is no longer than the front and back of a 4 × 6 card, or one double-spaced, typewritten page, it ensures that the writing will lead to a two-to-three minute story complete with narration.

Writing Exercises

In a group process, we are proponents of writing exercises. While we are fully aware of the potential and beauty of free writing, it's important to have a class spend ten to twenty minutes writing down whatever comes to their mind. I have found that the shared themes and ideas of a prompted idea can connect people to each other in wonderful ways.

This is my favorite prompt:

> In our lives there are moments, decisive moments, when the direction of our lives was pointed in a given direction, and because of the events of this moment, we are going in another direction. Poet Robert Frost shared this concept simply as "The Road Not Taken." The date of a major achievement, the time there was a particularly bad setback, the experiences of meeting a special person, the birth of a child, the end of a relationship, or the death of a loved one are all examples of these fork-in-the-road experiences. Right now, at this second, write about a decisive moment in your life. You have eight minutes.

The writing that comes from this prompt, when it comes unannounced at the beginning of a workshop, often goes straight to the emotional core of the author's life. The act of sharing of these kinds of stories can be instantly bonding for a group.

If the goal of the exercise is to prompt distant memories, we have not found a better approach than writing instructor Bill Roorbach's idea of having participants in the workshop first draw a map of the neighborhood where they grew up. Reaching back in one's memory to locate the layout of the streets, where friends lived, the names of friendly or strange neighbors, the way to the store, or the secret paths to school, inevitably opens up an infinite number of possible stories. The physicalization of a memory, trying to remember a time by remembering the places of that time, the places you traveled through on a daily basis, a neighborhood, a house, or a room, usually leads quickly to events that are rich with the kinds of meaningful inspections that make good stories.

There are innumerable prompts that might work for various situations. Sometimes these may have nothing to do with the subject initially being explored. Simply jumping into writing on some subject, can unlock the mind. Even if the writing is not further explored, the process may lead people back to their chosen story with new perspective.

Here is a short list of some themes for which prompts could also be built for powerful stories. Books about writing are filled with these exercises, so don't forget to pick up a few when it's time to delve deeper into your interest in writing beyond the digital storytelling experience:

- Write to a mentor or hero in your life to say thank you.
- Tell the story of a time when "it just didn't work" – a point, at your job or at some other event or activity, when you would've been typically competent or successful, and how that all changed when everything fell apart before your eyes.
- Describe a time when you felt really scared.
- Tell the story of a "first" – first kiss, first day on a job, first time trying something really difficult, the first time your heard a favorite song, etc.
- Tell something about the stuff in your life and what it reveals about you, a favorite appliance, a toy as a child, a keepsake, clothing or furniture.
- Tell a story about the body; a scar or injury, a family trait, your grandma's hands?
- Make a list of things you absolutely cannot stand, and things you feel you cannot live without, choose one from each column and make a story that connects them
- And of course, the old standby: Tell me a time when you were embarrassed?

These Stories from These Pictures

Digital stories often start with the pictures. Our easiest direction to anyone thinking about making a digital story is to look around his or her house and find images that provoke memories and stories that are meaningful. Then, see if there are other images around the house that are part of that story. And in the end, you will try to connect the memories that link all of these images together.

As we talk about storyboarding and structure, the notion of illustrating the script, or accentuating the writing with images, is emphasized as an outgrowth of a successful draft of the narrative. However, some people that come to the workshop have taken the absolutely opposite approach to the process. They will pull out the photos for their story, arrange them on a table, and sort them out in order from beginning to end. Then, with the story visually organized, they start writing. Is this approach effective? Of course it can be – great stories have emerged through this process.

As we discussed in the last chapter, this approach is not meant to hold back your writing, do not start with the concern over having or not having images. If you find that you would like to see an image in your story that you don't have available, you can look to an illustration, or appropriately implicit or metaphorical images you can find or create to capture the sense of the writing that suit the purposes of your story.

Getting into the Scene

We spoke about "finding the moment" in the Chapter 5, but it is worth re-visiting this idea in more detail here, as we think this is a key component to successful storytelling. When authors come to our Digital Storytelling workshops, we have them share first drafts and talk about their ideas for their stories. Oftentimes, I find myself discussing the notion of scene with the authors. As an example, I can take one approach to my own story about my father's death:

> Well first of all, let me just say, I was seventeen at the time and I had finished high school that summer. My dad had smoked three-packs-a-day, and had been trying to quit smoking for a couple of months. He was sixty-one, and had a difficult life as a union organizer working in Texas and throughout the South. But we had gone on a vacation the month before and he seemed like he was doing okay.
>
> He came down from his bedroom saying that he had a terrible pain.
>
> We called the doctor. The doctor said that it was probably an ulcer attack. He had had several of those. We waited. He got much worse. We decided to rush him to the hospital. It was a heart attack. He died within a half-hour. My mom was hysterical.
>
> It was a night I will always remember.

What we have is a fairly typical set of expository contexts, and a sequence of events that most people use to casually recall a major catastrophe in their lives. This approach is a fairly direct and distanced recitation of the facts, and it usually finishes with a statement that is conclusive. In this example, the recalled memory is understated and obvious to the extreme. If this were a dramatic dialogue, a speech by an actor pretending to be natural, it might work, but it does not convey the experience with clarity and depth.

But here is a description of the same memory that I shared at my mother's memorial in 2001, twenty-seven years after my father died:

> I will never forget the sound of my mom's voice when the doctor said, "George is dead."
>
> "God No! No! No!"
>
> A scream. A release. An explosion.
>
> The sound of her wail bounced off all the walls of the emergency room at Presbyterian Hospital in Dallas, bounced down the streets and through the trees, bounced out into the night sky, all the way across the universe of my young mind.
>
> In a single moment, a single pronouncement, everything changed for my mom. It divided her life in two, and it taught me that love can reach down into the cellular essence of awareness, and with its rupture, tear a human being in half.

What differentiates these two texts for me is the fact that in the second text, I am asking my audience to immediately journey in time with me to the exact instant when it all really happened. No context, other than the assumption that "George" must be someone really important, and the feelings, best as I remembered them, that accompanied the defining moment of the experience; my mom's reaction to the doctor's words. And finally, with over twenty-five years of perspective, what that means to me now.

In the above example, I tried to take the audience into the scene at the hospital. I could have described the way it looked and smelled, where we were standing moments before the doctor came up, and what happened afterwards, but all of that was assumed when I said it was the moment that my father was pronounced dead. Instead, it serviced the quality of the writing to strip away all of the descriptive material. We have found that audiences really can build an elaborate understanding of the story if they can get a sense of the context of an event. Furthermore, we know that much of what seems like important background, or exposition, is in fact superfluous to what really happened and what it really felt like to be there.

Taking the audience to the moment of an important scene, one that either initiates or concludes your tale, and putting them in your shoes, is why we listen to the story. We want to know how characters react. We want to imagine ourselves there as participants or witnesses, and we want to know what someone else takes away from the experience and uses to lead their own lives forward.

This idea of scene is related but separate from the terms of the specific disciplines of literature, theater and film. Dramatic scenes all have complex sets of conventions that allow us to observe the action of characters within a continuous time of the narrative. In our thinking about scene, we want to encourage people to share at least one portion of their narrative as a scene – to write as if they were there, inside the events as they unfolded, experiencing the shock, surprise, or amusement, for example, for the first time. For many stories, this strips away the superficial consideration of the events, and gets to the heart of the matter.

Character Studies and Personal Story

We know that most parents are multi-faceted, complex humans. In one story, it may serve to have the parent in the classic role of the ideal mentor, thereby filling one stereotype of parenthood. In another story, the parent may be a beast, or display beastly behavior, but if we are mature enough, and we are given one small nugget of context, for example: "When they got drunk, they would be mean," it is sufficient for us to imagine that they had good days as well. We are probably aware that the story is a cautionary tale about human behavior, not the evidence to indict the guilty party.

Lajos Egri, author of the bible for my training in dramatic theory, *The Art of Dramatic Writing*, reduced all great storytelling and theater to the author's understanding of the true nature of the characters he invents in the world of his narrative. Like most people, when I watch a film or a play, I know when character development has been rendered ineffective when I am able to say to myself, "You know, that character would have never said those words, or behaved in that way." In any story, the characters strengths and flaws drive the series of events forward, leading logically to the climactic clash or coming together that delivers the conclusion of the story.

When we write in the first person about real events and real people, we make the same choices as the fictional author, that is, describe those details of the character that are pertinent to the story. It is nothing short of egomaniacal to imagine that our characters are faithful portraits of actual people. In our digital stories, they are not even sketches, but rather, more like cartoons or contour drawings – brief and subtle outlines that highlight their most compelling, and relevant qualities.

Some of the writers that have participated in our workshops are fixated on elaborating their characters. They fear providing too simplistic a picture of the people they are describing, or their behavior in a given context, so they expand the narrative with a multiplicity of facets in order to feel more "fair." Personal storytellers are not judges or juries, they are faulty witnesses. And as faulty witnesses, we seek truth inside and around the simple lines of the sketch of their memories. We, the audience, are only capable of judging the approach they take to establishing the narrative, and whether or not their attitude and tone reflect balanced judgment or unreasonable accusation.

By letting the story dictate the degree to which we know the background of the character, we avoid cluttering some of the prose with assessments that cancel each other out. We can communicate which characteristic, for the purpose of the story, we can fill in with the broad brush of a stereotype sufficient enough for our small tale so the audience can fill in the character with the complexities of their own experiences.

Interviewing

What if writing is not an option? From the beginning, CDS found itself in environments or work with specific individuals where for reasons of literacy, language difference between instructors and participants, expedition of process, and the simplification of engagement with the storyteller, we work to the script through an interview process. In attempting to stay true to our ethical precepts, we still work to make the storyteller responsible for the edit, and we have developed a number of techniques to manage the process so our storytellers feel like their words are shaped by themselves, even if writing is never involved.

These techniques include recording the interview and then editing it side-by-side with the storytellers, as well transcribing the story in interview format, reviewing the edit with the storyteller, and then re-feeding the original lines to the storyteller for their recording sentence by sentence. If done well, we can not distinguish between these efforts and written pieces as texts (other than these pieces many times sound more natural).

At the same time we do refer to traditions of media journalism and documentary to inform our process, particularly how we might shape the interviews and the interview process.

Interviewing Techniques

Guidelines for the Interviewer

1 Study the questions so that you are not reading from the page, and feel free to ad lib. Being able to sustain eye contact assists the interviewee in relaxing and responding in a natural way.

2 Allow the interviewee to complete his or her thoughts. Unlike a radio or TV interviewer that is concerned with "dead air" in the conversation, give the interviewee all the time desired to think through and restate something that is a bit difficult to articulate. Interruptions can cause people to lose their train of thought or become self-aware and steer away from important, but perhaps emotionally difficult information. Let the interviewee tell you when he or she has finished a question before moving on to the next.

3 When appropriate, use your own intuition when asking questions to get more detailed responses. Often, a person's initial thoughts about a question only retrieves a broad outline of a memory. Feel free to request specifics or details that would clarify or expand upon a general response.

4 If the story is about information that is specifically painful or traumatic in the person's life, carefully assess how far you will allow the respondent to delve into these memories. In many situations where the interviewer is not a spouse or a loved one, you may cross into territory that is much better approached in a therapeutic environment with experienced guides or professionally trained advisors. We have come perilously close in interviews to taking people into an emotional state from which they cannot return at the session. This is embarrassing for the respondent, and an emotionally inconsiderate act on the part of the interviewer, as the interviewee may not have the therapeutic support to cope with these issues in the hours and days after the interview. Don't feel you need to hunt for emotionally charged material to make the interview effective. If it comes naturally and comfortably, so be it.

5 Finally, along with ensuring privacy in the interview, make sure everyone is comfortable: comfortable chairs, water at hand, and the microphone positioned so as not to disrupt ease of movement (a lavalier, or pin-on microphone, is the best).

Fragments of Understanding

When you are stuck, really stuck, as a storyteller working on a script, often as not it means you are still in the story. The story cannot write itself because what it represents for you in the moment, insight is emerging, but perspective is still months or years away. In our workshops, we suggest to certain writers, forget all the advice about "insight", "moments" and the circle of storytelling, and just write a poem. Fragments. Thoughts. Juxtaposed.

Perhaps the distinction between the reflective writing style emerging from our workshop environments and poetry is overstated. The purposed and immersive quality of story, as we understand it, is often derailed by people's relationship to the subject. The stories are inherently fractured, inconclusive, and confusing. So perhaps the writing, in an attempt at authenticity, should be the same.

Or put another way:

Never kneel to one
Notion of narrative
The needs of the narrator
Exceed those of the form

Excellent examples
Of enduring expression
Exist in abundance
And create their own norm.

Finally, A Few Words on Style

During my high school and early college days as a young journalist, I carried around a copy of *Elements of Style*, the William Strunk and E.B. White companion for all writers. I have to be frank, except for their call for economy, economy, economy, not much stuck in my sense of the rules of good style. In other words, I am the last person to teach anyone about formal issues of style. Having said that, Strunk and White might have been apoplectic at much of what I love in the styles of the writing of our students. What works, particularly as the words leave the page and are spoken by the authors, is not a case study in language usage according to conventions of grammar and syntax defended by the gatekeepers of the English – or any other – language.

What works is truth. By this, I mean that an author's truth about how he or she conceives of a personal way of storytelling is their style. How does truth happen in storytelling? Here is where the metaphor of journey, or quest, serves me best. Good writing has a destination and seeks the shortest path to the destination, but no shorter. The destination is usually the punch line, the pay-off, or the point of the story. Detours should never be accidental, unconscious, or indulgent. Each word and each apparent digression is critical to the final resolution of the characters' action.

I am a traditionalist in this idea, having never fallen for what feels to me to be a experimental conceit of an "anything goes" approach to narrative.

But that is my truth. I have had the pleasure of hearing thousands of people share their stories, and each with their own style of telling. In that sense, I accept that when it works, it works.

The good news about those of us living at the beginning of the twenty-first century is that we have an awareness regarding how we tell our stories, and how telling has much less impact than how we are heard. Stories do a number of things to people, but only a small part of what they do has to do with story content and our stylistic intentions. When people hear a story, what is occurring in their lives at that moment that either focuses or distracts their attention? What is the context in which the story is being heard? What is the ambience of the environment? And who else is in the audience? Context changes everything about the impact of a story on the listener.

So trust your own voice – the way it feels right to you to put things, and your own approach to these stories. And make sure that when it comes time to share your story, you are certain that the context best suited to your story is being appreciated to its fullest.

The Author's Reflections on First-Person Narrative

Critics of our work suggest that our emphasis on first-person perspective cannot allow for hybrid forms of narrative that include combining storytelling with persuasion, argumentation, analysis, and dispassionate reflection. We readily concede that our work is a reaction to the swing of the communication pendulum over the last two centuries from sentiment to objectivity.

The Industrial Revolution established a model for breaking information down to little nuggets of data. That dissolution process, like many industrial processes, provides the constituent elements, but leaves out the soul of things: a tomato can be made in a lab, but who wants to eat it when offered a homegrown garden tomato instead. This process can be extended to writing in that we often analyze with dispassionate authority, but we miss the essence. Our heads become too separated from our hearts.

In the social and natural sciences, objective observation and neutral communication have proven impossible – we change the thing observed by observing it. We carry the ideological and subconscious fetish of objectivity in all our thinking. A researcher or journalist can certainly synthesize, but the participant in the experience retains a privileged vantage point, and as audience, we want their narratives as unfiltered as possible, so that we can work through assessments from multiple perspectives.

From the very beginning we have believed in framing all narratives in the first person. This was simply more honest. Our unique perspective on experience is all we have, but it is just that. Our stories are not a doorway to truth, but they are one portal where light can fall through. And the more light, the better.

8

Storyboarding

A storyboard is a place to plan out a visual story in two dimensions. The first dimension is time: what happens first, next, and last. The second is interaction: how the audio – the voiceover narrative of your story and the music – interacts with the images or video. In addition, a storyboard is also a notation of where and how visual effects such as transitions, animations, or compositional organization of the screen will be used.

Storyboarding in the film world is a high art, bringing to life a vision of a scene. This composition includes imagining the many choices available to a director regarding camera placement, focal point, shot duration, possible edits, and camera-based effects such as panning and zooming. Storyboard artists combine illustration skills and a sense of stage business (where actors, props and sets are placed before the window of the camera), with cinematography and cinematic theory to write the roadmap for the director and film crew to organize every part of a film production.

The art of film storyboarding has taught anyone working on a story (from mega-movies to digital stories) one important lesson: planning on paper will save the enormous expense of time, energy, and money when it comes time to produce your work. Taking the time to organize your script in the context of a storyboard tells you what visual materials you require. If this exists, from the selection of images you have in your archive, then it just tells you the order of things and makes your edit go quickly. But much more importantly, especially for novice storytellers, storyboards clarify what you do not need, and saves you from scanning, photographing, shooting, designing, or recording things that don't fit into a particular story.

Recipe for Disaster

Our cautionary tale concerns Rick, just an average guy, getting ready to make his first digital story:

> "What a great morning," thought Rick, stepping out his back door and going to the little studio he had cleared out of a corner in his garage. "Today, I become a filmmaker. I am going to make my first digital story this weekend. Today, I'll assemble all the material I need. Tomorrow, I'll edit it all together."

Rick's story was a tribute to his parents. Their fortieth wedding anniversary was in a week, and he had a great idea about a retrospective on their lives. He had taken two large boxes of photos and a few old 8mm films from his parent's home earlier in the week. He was confident that if he could just sort through the stuff, the story would write itself. "I know that's how Ken Burns does it, just gather all the sources and piece it together like a puzzle."

He had his computer fired up. He had a scanner and digital camera handy, and the video camera set up on a tripod next to the old 8mm projector. He was going to project the film against a sheet he had hung on the wall and then record it. "Ingenious," he thought to himself.

The day began smoothly. Rick organized the photos into piles representing five decades of his parent's life together. "These are great," he thought. "I'll scan these eight from the 1950s, and these twelve from the 1960s, but the ones from the 1970s, when I was born, there are at least thirty of these I have got to use." And on it went. The piles grew, but no scanning yet. He broke for lunch.

Then came the film. "Old 8mm film is really beautiful, isn't it?" he thought. "My parents are going to love this part when I had my first little swimming pool. Wow. I'll just transfer it all, and then make my selections tomorrow during the edit." Despite a few glitches in the camera, he eventually got it right, and by 4 pm, the video was recorded. He thought about taking notes about which sections were on his two-hour tape, but since he was having so much fun reminiscing he never got around to it.

"I have to find the right music – old show tunes and stuff. And I need a few archival images, and I bet I can find that stuff on the Internet." After dinner he got online, and around 11 pm his eyes grew tired and his hand had gone numb. But he had everything he needed – just all in one big folder on the computer.

Rick woke up in the middle of the night and opened his eyes. "... The part where they are looking out over the Grand Canyon ... I can cut to a shot of me digging myself into the sandbox when I was three. That will be so cool. I can't wait to start."

The next day, he scanned his images, played with Photoshop, and he captured so much video on his computer that he ran out of hard drive space. He played with his morphing software. He did everything but start on the story. Sunday evening came and it was still a big mess. The workweek was a nightmare, so he only had a few hours to actually edit.

When the event approached on Saturday, the best thing he came up with was an extended music video, fourteen minutes long, with whole sections of images, film and titles bumping, flipping, and gyrating for reasons unknown. Several of his parents' friends fell asleep during the showing, and at the end there was a spattering of applause. Rick attributed the reaction to the heaviness of the gravy on the chicken stroganoff that was served at the dinner.

His mother, of course, cried through the whole thing.

His father, always supportive, thanked him, and said, "Rick, that was, well, really ... interesting."

Digital stories have an advantage over film production – you are often using available material at the core of your project as opposed to creating all-new footage. But as our story shows, the material itself can be profoundly compelling for the storyteller, particularly if it is a first visit in a long time. But without a script, and an idea of how the story is told, composing a digital story can overwhelm the best of us.

Rick's tale is the worst-case scenario for the digital storyteller: So much wonderful content and so many cool tools to play with, but so few ideas for how things will actually come together. We have met many people that have had symptoms of these obsessions, and in our workshops, we work to try and gently bring them back down to earth. We affirm that the material might seem irresistible, but we encourage students to write a first draft and complete a bit of storyboard work prior to diving into their family's photo archive.

Professional filmmakers use the storyboard as a critical production management tool, saving countless hours of experimentation by avoiding non-essential material. We want to encourage our participants to reach for their highest level of organization to maximize the precious time they have to create their stories. For many of our workshop participants, life may give them only a few such opportunities to really mine the archive for the critical stories of their lives. But we want to honor all different kinds of creative processes. For some, time is not so extravagant a luxury. If you can afford to excavate your archive completely, to fully examine the creative palette of multimedia tools, and to work through a series of drafts of your project to make a highly polished piece, the rewards are worth the effort.

Making a Storyboard

Our reference here is from a tutorial developed by the Center for Digital Storytelling in 1999 called MomnotMom, and is based on a reflection by staff member Thenmozhi Soundararajan.

The specific section that we refer to below consists of a title, six photographs, and a short video clip. The soundtrack is a nice piece of guitar music. We've laid out the storyboard on the next page.

Notice how few words of the voice-over are under each picture. Each line takes about six to ten seconds to speak. In general, three to four seconds is about the ideal length for any still image to appear on the screen. If it's too short, then it's hard for the viewer to recognize what's being shown; too long, and boredom sets in. If you're laying out your storyboard and find lines and lines of text under any one picture, rethink your script or your images.

Can the script be cut down, and can the image be left to fill-in for the missing words? If the text remains long, can more than one image illustrate the essential words? You may also want to use some effects to extend the viewer's interest in a single still image. But for now, try to use the best effect of all: letting images speak for themselves, and using words to say the rest.

Images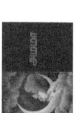

Effects Fade In   Image Pan   Image Pan   Image Pan   Image Pan

Transitions   Cross Dissolve

Voiceover There is a picture of my mother that I always keep with me.   It is a curious photo, because in most photos I always imagine that people pose for the future, but in this moment, this photograph, I feel like she is searching for her past.

Soundtrack Fade in
guitar chord progression

Images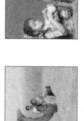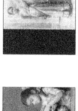

Effects Alpha Channel Motion

Transitions   Cross Dissolve   Cross Dissolve   Cross Dissolve   Cross Dissolve

Voiceover Across oceans and between cultures, a young woman, a doctor, a wife,
I think back to who she was as a girl,

Soundtrack guitar chord progression

Some Ways to Make Your Storyboard

1. Get a piece of posterboard, preferably large (22″ × 17″), and a packet of Post-it notes. Sort out the image material you plan to use and label each of the Post-it notes with the name and, if needed, a phrase describing the image.

2. Create five or six horizontal rows across your posterboard, leaving room for writing text below each Post-it. Fill in the text of your script in pencil, and place the appropriate images above the appropriate words. The Post-its will allow you to move things around or take them out as need be and you can erase the text if you want to move it around.

3. Instead of labeling Post-its with the name of each image, you could go to a copy place and photocopy your photos. Tape or glue your copied images to the Post-its, and lay out your storyboard. The advantage here is that, just as on the computer, you can easily move things around.

4. If you'd like to work on a smaller page, photocopy the blank storyboard template on the next page or visit www.storycenter.org/books and download the .pdf file.

5. If you are familiar with desktop publishing software like Quark XPress or Adobe's InDesign, or you know how to layout tables in Microsoft Word, and you know how to scan images, you can make your storyboard right on the computer.

6. Any of these methods will work. Do whatever is convenient and easy for you. A storyboard will speed up your work in many ways. It can show you where your voice-over should be cut before you record, and it may help you to determine if you have too many or too few images chosen before you begin scanning. Storyboarding is a valuable tool, and it can also be fun. Get others to join you in your storyboarding process and make it a collaborative project.

Images

Effects

Transitions

Voiceover

Soundtrack

Images

Effects

Transitions

Voiceover

Soundtrack

Interlude 4
Ray's Story

The place where I worked is no longer there.

I started working in this building when I was 14. It was a shell, we put a floor in, walls, shelves for a gift shop named "Chan & Chee" (for Chandler and Conchita). She was born in the same building. Two years later the steel ball struck the building. Now it's a county-owned garage.

Where the cars are parked, that used to be houses, the homes of my friends and extended family. That was the first place I recall them taking away peoples homes.

The row house down the street is no longer there. It was my grandparents' house, then it passed to my mom. We played basketball at the Stanton Freedman Bureau School just up the alley. My mom graduated from that school. That was my recreational place.

Gone is my Psychedelic Shack behind the house. It was "Ray's Place." Sheepskin rug, African prints, Indian bedspread, TV, record player. I'd go there after school and spend my weekends there… It was my escape, my Walden, my sanctuary.

We stayed here three more years after the store went, then we moved away. Shortly after, they tore the down the whole block, except for the school. To replace it with the Maryland Dept of Business and Management. 45 Calvert St.

Gone in an instant are the mortar and bricks that inhabited the souls that shaped, defined and shaded my young life.

I moved to West Baltimore in 1975. The brick row homes and the mortar that connected the community atmosphere was similar to what was I lost. Folks trying to hold on to what they have. Later I purchased a store-fronted building. I started working on it, improving it, while I was seeing the decline of other buildings. Just right next door to me they tore a building down. The wrecking ball has come again and the old feelings have begun to resurface.

But unlike Chan & Chee's gift shop, my Psychedelic Shack and our home, I'm putting earnest effort in to reclaiming community space. In the wrecking I still see renewal.

Wrecking and Renewal
– Ray Baylor

Thoughts by Stefani Sese

Ray is very active in the revitalization of his West Baltimore community. He came with his grant-writing hat on and couldn't break free of speaking in broad sweeping terms about the destruction urban renewal had wrought on once thriving black neighborhoods. He wrote several drafts but he just couldn't get away from the third person or the terminology to find the personal part of his story.

As we were looking at his photographs he began to describe his old neighborhood in Annapolis, MD. He showed me the old house; the place where he and his friends had played in the alley behind the all-black Freedman Bureau school; the store that he remembered working in. As he spoke, I typed what he was saying and asked questions. He had a treasure trove of rich detail and stories in the two photos of his old neighborhood, a place that no longer exists. He talked about his sanctuary behind the house, and I asked him to describe it. Best of all, he still had a photo of himself from that time! After a while, as he spoke and I typed, we had a text for Ray to edit. A personal story.

It's often very hard to write in a personal voice. Sometimes being passionate about what you are addressing in your story makes it even harder. It was a joy to take the journey with Ray and uncover the memories hidden in those old images.

The story circle is a key part of the CDS process, but the one-on-one work that happens between the facilitator and the storyteller is also where a lot of the final story-mining takes place. It's a matter of listening hard to what the photos are saying, to what's in between what the storyteller is telling you, in order to find the questions that will help someone discover their insight and their voice.

As I watch my old neighborhood shift subtly and then drastically in the wake of increased development and gentrification, I remember Ray's story.

He reminds us of the centrality of place. Laying down roots and creating memories contributes to building a thriving community. Ray's story is a reminder of how easily this can be destroyed if we are not mindful of how development occurs, who it benefits, and who it uproots.

9

Designing in Digital

Working with Digital Imaging, Audio, and Video

What makes good design in a digital story? This is a loaded question. If you went to a design school, you would be handed a set of principles and conventions for good design. The principles would cover color theory, composition, perspective, typography, photography, cinematic theory, as well as conventions in animation and motion graphics, and a touch of voiceover performance methods, music composition, and audio design to boot.

For the digital storyteller, unless you are moving toward a professional career, you can save yourself a year of fundamentals classes by using the oldest principle in design: mimic what you like.

In our workshops, we show specific pieces in which the storytellers made choices that we felt worked with the overall impact of their story. Some issues of design including pacing, images, and soundtrack, are obviously integral to the seven steps discussed in Chapter 5. In this chapter, we look more closely at some design issues to expand the discussion. We will discuss two movies, with illustrations, to examine a number of choices that are fairly typical in the early stages of digital media design.

We will not be addressing how the pieces were created. We felt that offering tutorials in this book would make it out-of-date almost as soon as the book was printed, so we have list of software tutorial resources available on our companion website at www.routledge.com/cw/lambert.

Thinking Like a Designer

> Design is the method of putting form and content together. Design, just as art, has multiple definitions; there is no single definition. Design can be art. Design can be aesthetics. Design is so simple, that's why it is so complicated.
>
> (Paul Rand, 2001)

My starting assumption is that you do not call yourself a designer. But maybe you do. For those of us who came into the arts outside the visual arts, design has an aura of mystery about it. I quote Paul Rand, the guy who brought us the IBM and ABC logos, as well as the Enron-crooked E, because I always thought the essence of our work was what Rand called "the defamiliarizing of the ordinary." How do we take something that is so simple, three letters in a logo, and make those letters seem iconically extraordinary. How do we take a urinal, as did Duchamp, put it on a pedestal, and call it Fountain, and declare it art – and nearly one hundred years later, most college-educated folks would know the piece as art.

Where design professionals like Rand are concerned with breaking through the noise mass market expectations to succeed in the highly competitive world world of advertising or contemporary art, our ambitions are small, but they can still lead to profoundly powerful communication.

The original impulse of our workshops was to have people tell stories into their family albums and home movies. What could be more ordinary? Most of our participants arrived with a story that relates to a collection of existing images.

As we discussed in the "seeing your story" step in Chapter 5, the first impulse is to stick an image from that collection everywhere there is a noun that suits the image, "when I was child", picture of me as a child … "me and dog" picture me and dog … "we played in the woods", picture of woods. To be explicit. To be direct. And as we said that can work.

But…

People with a chip on their shoulder about their sense of smarts call those choices, cliché. A great and nasty word. Most people who use it do not even know its origin, something French, they think. A cliché was a "ready-made phrase" cast into lead on the old printing press. Because people would say things like "In my humble opinion" a great deal, the printers who were setting type found it easier just to make one piece rather than set the separate words again and again. Stereotype comes from the same printing reference. "We knew that already. So when there is not a more vivid, exciting, surprising way of communicating the same meaning," we call it cliché.

Of course, what is cliché to some is still news to others. Originality is all about shared culture and context, what I might find trite and sentimental, you might find engrossingly powerful. And as listener, readers, in the age of magazines, billboards, television, and websites, we are all able to attune ourselves to expectations of a genre/ trope, and judge originality and surprise against the neverending flow of shifting expectations. Fashion, as we understand it, is nothing but attempts to reframe our expectations – to make the ordinary, what we thought we understood in what we were seeing/feeling, seem somehow new and unfamiliar.

As digital storytellers, you do not have to suffer endless an design process to surprise us. You simply need to think about how in the choices you are making, you are challenging yourself to not go with what is blindingly obvious. Allow for happy accidents, where an image that was meant for one part of the story, ends up as illustrating something completely different. Allow yourself, once in awhile, to think outside the enchilada.

Robert Kershaw's "Camaro Boy"

For the last several years, our teaching of visual design in the digital storytelling workshop has been advancing, in part because of the ways photographers and designers on our teaching staff have informed the process. Photographer and designer Rob Kershaw joined our staff in 2007, but his introduction to our work was in 2004, when he completed the workshop with a story about wandering and finding one's place, called "Camaro Boy" (www.youtube.com/watch?v=W_BBUYhV_M8&feature=plcp). There are many things we like about this piece, but one of the easiest ways to describe the success of this work, as a digital story, is that it is the story of two pictures.

Rob succeeds precisely because he takes exceedingly ordinary photos and makes us see them in new ways. His design choices force us to consider more than how Rob's life journey has evolved, but how seeing our lives through a progression of photos, becomes emblematic of success or failure to live out the expectations of our youth.

Rob's Script

1981. There's a photo of me with my brand-new used car – a 1976 Camaro, 350 – 4 barrel. Tough enough but not quite the muscle car it would appear especially not with its white vinyl upholstery, automatic transmission and tinny am/fm radio.

So there I am leaning on this car. Tough enough but not quite …

The photo's a bit of joke with my family. Who's that guy? Nice hair! And those shades! Mom's written on the back of the picture – "Rob's macho period" – as if I needed reminding.

The car was bought with the money I saved from the first job offered me out of college as a roughneck in a diamond drilling camp in northern Saskatchewan. Ask me what I thought I would be doing when I was 23, all green from the city, sweating it out in a noisy drill shack in the middle of nowhere or at least nowhere I had imagined this wouldn't have been it. But for some reason actually for the lack of any reason in particular I took the job.

So this "macho period," it was a weird time. It wasn't pretty.

Then there's this picture from my first hike in Banff National Park to Johnston Canyon. I'm a year older. I'd quit my job and escaped west in that Camaro. Couldn't face a summer hanging out in my hometown, playing baseball and drinking beer.

I like the macho shot. Ten years ago I was embarrassed. Now I'm okay with it. But I think I like the hiking picture better. I got rid of the Camaro, never moved back home, found a new job, went back to university got married, got un-married, moved on, stayed awhile and moved on again.

My grandfather liked this picture too. It hung by his bed in his one-room seniors' apartment – the only photo he had out before he died. Mom said it was his favorite photo, a reminder to him of the trips he wanted to take but never did. He wanted to be a sheep rancher in New Zealand but stayed in England, a shopkeeper all his life. Seems there were things he wanted to escape from, too.

I learned that later.

Robert Kershaw, "Camaro Boy, 2003"

In designing the piece, Rob made many choices that are great illustrations of a design process common to digital storytelling workshops. They are simple choices, but seen as a system of thinking, they can change even the simplest set of images, into a provocative visual narrative that completes the written narrative.

One Picture Becomes Many Pictures

The first fifty-five seconds of Rob's story is created out of one photograph. The essential photo of this story. Rob is standing by his Camaro, circa 1981, looking "macho" as he explains in the script. His writing addresses what we are seeing directly, so Rob could have had us stare at the image for the entire minute. Rob knew the static nature of the shot would have bored his audience, and detracted from the story's impact. His choices were either to find additional images, or to find a way to make the single image graphically more complicated to have us conceive of the image in more than one way.

He chose to create a series of vertical and horizontal slices of the video for us to consider as fragments of a whole, the use of the "reveal" through the slow assembling of the puzzle of the image. This fragmentary approach relies on Rob's own sense of what might generate a "graphic" interest for an audience, but at a deeper level, he was forcing us as audience to work, and engage, in the visual process.

His approach suggests your choices of cropping an image could be relatively abstract. Rob begins the initial four shots excluding the figure of him leaning against the car. We know by the script the idea of the image, but by allowing us to consider it from other angles, we are thinking more about the car, than about the person. Then at an appropriate moment in the script, when he discusses his haircut and sunglasses, the image crops to a medium close up of him, and the dialogue becomes more interior, less about the car, and more about the person being introduced.

Many single images have the potential for being considered as two, three, four or more separate cropped images that work as graphics for the story. Thinking about an image as having a graphic power in different ways it is sliced, frees you up from hunting for more images. And it also allows us to piece together visuals just as we are piecing together what meaning to pull out of the narrative.

Working Within the Frame

Another important design concept that Rob's story immediately engages is the concept of the frame – the horizontal rectangle of a video screen. The expectation of many digital stories is that they mimic the slideshow effect, a progression of images that fill the screen, and have us focus on the content of the image, rather than the frame within which they are being presented. We are all familiar with split screen films, but the photographic emphasis of Digital Storytelling suggests we can use the negative or blank space around an image for effect.

By challenging the way we see the artificial box of the screen, we are also calling attention to the graphic nature of the rectangle of the background canvas. The screen space is by default a black background, composition within the area of the canvas suggests priority, emphasis, and the focal point for our view. We can make each slide appear however we want within the canvas – images can be juxtaposed side by side, move through the screen space to draw our attention in a particular way, or layered on top of each other in a collage.

As the story progresses, Rob uses the screen space again when he presents the second image around which the story revolves. He tilts the image in the space, making us think of a photo left on a table. The presence of the image suddenly has a meaning in line with the narrative, as not just an image, but as an artifact to be picked up and examined.

Visual Pacing

In the seven steps, we talk about pacing as both a component of the writing, recording, and music, and how a story is assembled with visuals such that each layer emphasizes complementary or contrasting meanings and feelings. Here we want to explore visual pacing in more detail.

"Camaro Boy" succeeds to a great extent because of the visual pacing Rob employs as he advances the story. Each image is perfectly complemented to the approach of the narration and the use of music. In the initial section, the Camaro image advances at a five second per image pace until the first mention of him leaning against the car, where it lingers, until, in time with the voiceover, he switches to the closeup.

As he exits this image into darkness, he creates a visual pause that sets up the launching into the back story. Each of the next two images, appear static, holding our attention not so much to what we are seeing, but to what is being described in the words. A decisive moment, of taking a job as a diamond driller in Saskatchewan, for as he says… "the lack of any reason in particular" and he fades again.

The second section starts with the introduction of the image of the hiker by a creek. To start with, the image is off kilter, and it still has the tape on it. Here he lingers again, but uses a rotation, and a bit of zoom, to hold our attention, and draw us into a more serious consideration of this image. The image then fades out again to black to prepare us for the next shift, during which time in reintroduces the Camaro image. Repetition is part of pacing as well, for as viewers we can re-consider the image in a new way, based on what we have learned so far in the story.

Up to now, nearly two minutes into the film, four images have been used. But as he enters the next section, where he will cover some twenty years of living, the slow pacing shifts to a rapid fire series of nine images in ten seconds. This shift is jarring, but we barely make note of it, because it seems so appropriate for the way the script touches on big changes in such a reductive way. Life went on, like a flashing of scenes before our eyes, is suggested by the urgency of the pace.

As the story moves to closure, the last two images in the formal story, a return to the hiking photo, and a long pan on the grandfather, each image has the effect of circling the story back to a beginning, of how the Camaro Boy made it out to the west of Canada to discover himself as an adult, and how the little boy, foregrounded in the image of the grandfather, somehow escaped the fate of a man with unmet ambitions, unmet dreams. As the voiceover ends, we find Rob as man sitting graveside, the image provokes an unsettled, somewhat uncomfortable feeling, appropriate to Rob's script ending with, "I learned about those later…"

The pacing is carried with the credits, and pays off one last time with a "surprise" coda of Rob as a boy with a soap box style car. A nod as a visual allusion to the title, and to the idea that we are fated at a young age to our calling.

Implicit Use of Images

Finally, it is worth returning to the concept dealt with in depth in the "seeing your story" discussion of the seven steps. Rob uses two images to tell a story. Those images could have been the story. Several other images refer more or less directly to what is being described, images of Rob up a cliff side, an old VW, along a trail, and his grandfather watching the grandkids. But out of sixteen images used, nine are not related directly to what is being said. They are snaps out his album as a smaller child, the kind of images we all have, as if we disappear from memory at age twelve or so. What works with these images is that they themselves, as familiar representations of the family album, make us consider expectation of the child.

These four issues of "Camaro Boy" suit the vast majority of Digital Stories that have come through the Center. People start with existing photos, and as this story so well exemplifies, build the story around the images, presenting them in ways that surprise and engage in new ways.

Panning and Zooming

No tool is more associated with our style of work than the ability for a computer editing program to easily pan and zoom across an image. Panning refers to moving across the horizontal plane of a film shot, and zooming is moving in or out from a point on the image. Like any effect, panning should be practiced with restraint. Many first-time users find it irresistible, and pan and zoom on every image. In "Camaro Boy," Rob uses the generated pan three times, on the first of the parade of children images, on the camping image the first time, and finally to great effect on the closing image, of the grandfather and two children on the croquet lawn. The choice of reframing the shot in the pan to the grandfather and Rob as a little boy focuses us on the relationship…. both the distance, and the connection.

Barcelona Marathon – Design as Improvisation

As this edition was being composed, I found myself experimenting with a series of workshops using the iPhone/iPad as the focus of production and editing. We are leaving an era of keyboard and mouse based computing, the world will soon be screens small, medium, and large that we touch to design and communicate. In organizing the workshops I wanted to leave the stuffy rooms of our computer labs, and bring the process of reflection into story out to the streets. The photo and video camera, audio recorder, editor and distribution mechanism that is the smart phone, has ushered in a new era of improvised film making and design.

The second of my walking workshops took me to Barcelona, Spain. There a group of several storytellers from Europe, the United States and Africa, were led through the Ramblas and Passeig de Gràcia, Barceloneta and other parts of the city capturing images and discovering the stories they had to tell. Roberto Gerli, an architect turned design and communications specialist, decided to tell a story as a postcard home to his two children (https://vimeo.com/39278236).

Roberto's Script (from the original in Italian)

Ciao Angelica, Ciao Lorenzo, Ciao Amore

Let me introduce you my teacher, Joe "The Coach". He arrived from Berkeley.

To follow him was a Marathon. Three days and few hours left to sleep. It's simple for him going from one point to another.

But the point are thousands. It's easy to get lost. Where to start from?

As far as I remember, I have never been lost. On our travels, my father encouraged me to look " around the corner." Saying "don't be scared …. Wonderful things are just round the corner waiting for you, that are worth being … discovered … lived … savoured."

Travelling is an adventure.

Here 30 years ago there wasn't a seaside beach, there were industrial factories. It's beautiful to see that things can change.

Neus from Spain, Henning from Norway, Zoe from Greece, Aisha from Virginia, Dora from New York, and Simon from Switzerland. All together we followed Joe through a journey of emotions and digital bytes, connecting the dots.

An adventure for creating something new.

Life is a journey where you never get lost if there is love.

Thanks to you, I'm living through an incredible adventure

with Love ….and mucho gusto!

Papà (Dad)

Roberto Gerli, 2012

Roberto describes a workshop experience in Barcelona. The story subject is the story creation process. One level of the story is about what he did over a March weekend away from home. Another level are the issues of finding meaning in travel, and passing the value of adventure on to his children.

The travel memoir approach provided an ideal way to let his writing, and his thinking about the story, be driven by the visual material available at hand. The starting point for designing these improvised mobile digital stories is to find an appropriate angle into a subject – an angle that allows you to reflect on important ideas, such as encouraging your kids to be open to new experience. A traveler's postcard home allows for intimacy with the audience, and a way to take the direct experience in the moment as the basis for the story.

The story uses the metaphor of the marathon to suggest both the actual Barcelona Marathon (which we found blocking our way during our meander around the city) but also the effort-filled journey of his life. This is a good starting point of the improvised design process. As you explore an environment, what singular image, or in this case event/action, links best to your story idea? The unconscious lure of a visual subject is often an appropriate visual "hook" to some story lurking in the corners of your mind. That image becomes the metaphor to inform your writing process.

The Visual Treatment

The story starts with Roberto's portrait. He uses portraits as a form of visual repetition in the story. Most of the images are diverse, some with only a hint at implicit relationship. But his use of the portraits of the workshop participants allows him two things; to introduce the individuals in the group as supporting characters in his story, and to create a frame which we see repeated later in the story.

Roberto begins and ends his story with his own portrait, giving visual symmetry to the story. Many people feel that their visual treatment should avoid repetition, but as an audience, we are pleased to see a visual idea, or certain phrases, or a melody in music, reappear in the story.

Roberto's story also uses four instances of moving image, again shot on the fly as part of our exploration. The first shot is the video of the Marathon. He chose to capture it from low angle, focused on the running bodies, more than the expressions of the runners, or the general context of the street.

In the second use of video, he swings around in a self-portrait at the Olympic beach, playing with perspective, before giving us a shot of people strolling down the street. Finally, the marathon returns, but this time, we see faces and expression of the runners, and the audience and city streets. While confident that Roberto was not overly conceptualizing his shot selection in production, nor in the edit of the story, we can see that in each circumstance the effect of the video was to contrast movement to the static image. His choices to use video were where the movement represented a shift in perspective, the change in his point of view, or a new insight. The clips are quite short, but they enliven the way we see the narrative.

The other visual theme that is explored is points, or dots – points or dots on a map, points as multicolored berries and fruit and cups of juice, or point references in graphics filled with dots. The connecting the dots idea emerged in a discussion about travel and meaning during the story circle, it was clear that the connection between his father's joy of traveling, and Roberto's own, was something he wanted to link to his children as well.

The remainder of the images show his talent at capturing different parts of a landscape; a homeless character sleeping in a corner, narrow streets peeking out to the shore, a four-paneled beach scene, the tourist cart, a pile of peppers and the smile of a clerk at the market. These fill out the story, but they also compel the audience to read the juxtapositions of image and text in new ways. Part of the lesson of Roberto's story is that some visual play is pleasurable for an audience. We do not mind that the implicit relationships are stretched, we just enjoy the journey, as a journey.

Final Note

We have seen a great deal of creative brilliance in the face of the unwavering deadline of our workshops. This is one of the advantages of compressing this work into a few days. Like the 4 × 6 cards or folded piece of paper, it forces us to strip away non-essential elements. We have found in our process, as well as in considering the processes of other artists, that often what is finished, polished, and refined becomes over-polished and over-refined and lacks the directness and spontaneity of the initial drafts.

Intuition is the largest part of experimentation. If most of our students stopped right after they completed their script, and meditated on the message of their work – the story's interrelationship to their entire way of looking at the world – and then went for a walk with a camera or video camera, they could successfully create an effective film just from the elements that would appear before them.

Perhaps this way of looking at digital storytelling is a bit too Zen, but it corresponds with our experience.

10

Distribution, Ethics, and the Politics of Engagement

When we believe what we see bears witness to the way the world is, it can form the basis for our orientation to or action within the world.
Bill Nichols *Introduction to Documentary*, Indiana University Press
(November 15, 2001)

"Do no harm." The easiest of statements turns out to be the most complicated to realize. In virtually all practices of the "helping" professions, what starts as well-meaning intention becomes a minefield of unintended consequences. The offer of help, made with sincerity and compassion, becomes instead a relationship fraught with expectation, interdependence, power, and on all sides, vulnerability.

CDS was founded out of the legacy of anti-colonial, liberationist perspectives that carried a critique of power and the numerous ways rank is unconsciously expressed in engagements between classes, races, and gender. From the beginning, we saw the need to provide mechanisms of community engagement and self-determination for communities that self-identified as having need for support and solidarity. We worked with local Native American, Latino, African-American, LGBTQ, and women's communities in finding ways to develop programs that would serve those communities. We attempted to honor the wisdom of many, many activists from these communities about how best to approach storywork in a cross-cultural, cross-class, and at times cross-gender/sexual identity, context.

We realized that the lived experience of people or peoples who have faced systematic forms of discrimination and oppression must be honored as authoritative perspectives on their own lives. Individuals need to be supported in telling their own story; in their own way, to the audiences they choose. Telling someone else's story, besides being sketchy, as my son would say, does not address the process of that person's own liberation. And ironically, the act of appropriating someone else's voice diminishes the person who appropriated the story, in much the same way it diminishes the person's for whom the story belongs. No one wins.

In the struggle for cultural equity in the arts, we focused much discussion on the concept of First Voice. That in artistic collaborations with local communities, we should strive that people should speak for themselves, and as often as possible that gatherings of storytellers should be facilitated within the community, by community members, for the general benefit of the community (as opposed to an outside audience).

For some of us, we borrowed from approaches to popular literacy, to place great value on "conscientization" – the process of developing a critical awareness of one's social reality through reflection. Even as one addresses negative narratives told by a dominant culture about a community, one also has to look at the way power plays out within a community, and how the shadow of a larger oppression in society is cast on all of our individual interactions.

This thinking was a cornerstone in the development of our methods. I knew that leading a process, whether leading as a teacher-artist, of a facilitator-organizer, carried with it the baggage of my own ideology, history and culture, the baggage of all those that assist me, and of course the baggage of all those I hoped to assist. We drill down to individual stories to address how much the way we live is scripted, by history, by social and cultural norms, by our own unique journey through a contradictory, and at times hostile, world.

Self-aware politics could only take our work so far. In my years as an activist, rallying people around a shared perspective on issues, inviting them to take up organizing for their own and their communities benefit, you learn a great deal about the ways people are silenced by tradition, by language, by nuanced communication of privilege. But that does not prepare you to develop particular systems of professional ethical protocol. For that we needed to work more closely with progressive professionals in the human services communities, to give our work more substantive understanding of not only how to develop guidelines, but how best to make them work in practice.

Even so, professional ethics have grown out of story. No singular rule book for engagement can cover the countless cases in the real world practice of professionals. To deepen understanding, people discuss the fundamental issues of providing safety, dignity, equality, and positive support in terms of a given case. They tell a story. So the circle never ends. And CDS has much more to learn.

In the first couple of years of our work, we had a workshop in a small community where a participant went through the three-day process working on a very painful story. She had decided to speak out about the ongoing domestic abuse of a child she knew from the school where she taught. It was a poetic reflection, spoken in metaphor, it seemed dignified and respectful, an important way to address the powerlessness educators sometimes feel in assisting young people caught up in family violence.

In the hour before we were to complete the work she came up to me.

"I really need to make sure this story does not leave the room. Would you mind if I simply delete the project and all the contents?"

"Without a back-up?" I gulped. I was concerned she might regret not having some repository for exploring the story in the future.

"No. This process was for me. To deal with my feelings of helplessness about what happened, but it is not my story. I am happy to just delete it and move on."

"Sure, it's your story" I heard myself say, not quite believing someone would dispose of three days of work so casually.

She closed the folder. Dragged it to the trash on the desktop, and emptied the trash.

"Thank you for a wonderful workshop."

This story poses one end of the spectrum of the process versus product dynamic, but our approach to ethics always has to slide back and forth across that spectrum to deal with the needs of our storytellers, and the needs of projects that enable the storytellers to participate and sustain our work.

In this chapter, while we start with the lens of our particular viewpoint on the distribution of digital stories, we will also briefly address the larger issues of ethics in group process and the politics of social change engagement, as a whole.

The Genie Stays in the Bottle

From the beginning of our work, there was a tension between the private process of storywork and the public presentation of the artifact created as part of the workshop. Despite an assumption that the stories were likely to be shared by us or the collaborating organizations, we immediately sank into a pattern that continues to the present, as much as possible, the workshop process belonged to the storyteller, how they choose to use it was in their control, and that meant that any public presentation of the story, including sharing within the group, was left to the storyteller.

In addition to my training in community activism and cultural work, I came from a theater background deeply dedicated to freedom of expression. We were renowned for presenting many transgressive performance artists that the cultural conservatives of the day were actively working to de-fund and censor. So as we began this work, I felt it was important to establish that no subject was taboo for the workshop environment. In the first set of open workshops in 1994 people were sharing stories about incest, about issues of "deviant" sexuality, about criminal violations against them or their loved ones. In all of those cases, stories were shown within the workshop setting. This was San Francisco, after all, and people were generally used to diverse perspectives of what was considered socially acceptable discourse.

Even so, it was clear that it was perhaps not my role to encourage the publication of these stories. And if I was feeling like I had to choose one story over another, especially if I felt that choice was made because the content might offend someone, I had a dilemma. I would not censor someone. Better to just leave the stories with the storytellers, and if they decided to publish I could point to that publication.

Two things occurred as a result, we never built a formal publication process into the open workshops, and we turned that problem into a principle. I argued that our role as facilitators of free creative expression meant we should leave publication up to the participants. The ethos of self-determination was throughout. People would, at times, be asked to be part of compendium of stories to be used as examples for training, but generally we told people the stories were their own .

CDS also emerged as part of the independent new media community of the early to mid-1990s. We felt we were storming the ramparts of traditional media hegemony through the invention of many-to-many publication. The idea of do-it-yourself media publishing was everywhere, and our workshop was meant to give the tool of publication to the people. We imagined all of our participants going on to pursue their video editing and new media voice as artists, activists, prosumers.

In addition, we were distrustful of distorting influence that celebrity created. Several times we were asked about creating the equivalent of "America's Most Heartfelt Stories" as a broadcast mechanism, and we were simply disdainful. We saw from the Oprah Winfrey show, where Dana was once asked to prepare a story for the launch of iMovie, how the idea of our work as self-awareness could be turned into sentimental tripe. I knew we had a model for transformative process, and in my mind, the apparatus for sustaining the sacred nature of the process, with an intention for publication, if it could be done, was beyond the scope and resource of the model we had created.

The Explosion of Participatory Media Practices

The media arts field had twenty years of effort in developing various grassroots strategies for community engagement by the time we began our work in the 1990s. Providing ways for people to make media that would find its way onto the limited broadcast mechanisms, public television and cable access, had been the emphasis. But as a way to engage large numbers in learning or using the tools of media production and distribution, these projects were quite limited.

The digital moment changed everything. Suddenly prices for the toolset for video production dropped dramatically, and with the coming of the web, people have ever-expanding options for distribution. Independent and alternative digital media projects exploded around the world, with soup to nuts approaches for creating, distributing, and archiving stories in all shapes and sizes.

With the advent of blogging and social media, nearly every organization of any scale has developed a mechanism for sharing media, and consequently a need for having it produced. Traditional broadcast standard producers are being kept plenty busy by the demands for media. But the idea of sharing media coming from the field, either as snippets of video that take you to the scene of relevant events, short YouTube talking head reports, or as more considered documents made in some training or engagement process like Digital Storytelling, has become increasingly possible.

Those partaking in these processes may have little experience in media engagement, and little familiarity with approaches to ethics. With millions making media, the likelihood of abuse, confusion and even tragic consequence, is high. For those of us in organizations that self-identify as agents of positive social change, there may be a tendency to have faith that ethics will be considered in all engagements. In our experience, that faith is misplaced. Even if one never becomes a media facilitator or producer of community-based project, becoming reasonably well-versed in the ethics of engagement seems a critical part of professional project management.

Building An Ethics Framework from Documentary and Human Services Perspectives

On our journey we have learned a great deal more about approaches to ethics from two sets of practitioners that raised these issues as an active and ongoing challenge for participatory digital media.

The first were the media professionals, from documentary and journalistic backgrounds, that had been appropriately trained to concern themselves with accuracy of representation, neutrality or balance in opinion, thoroughness of research/competency in subject, consistency of production quality as regards representing a subject, but also the contract between interviewer and subject as it pertained to the extent and purpose of use of image, voice, and artifacts of the subject, and the general safety and appropriate confidentiality of the subjects. These concerns were implicitly tied to the power the documentarian had over the people they engaged in their projects. The ethical guidelines were based on a professional expectation that they would not abuse the power, or at least limit the negative impact of their engagement with their subjects.

Documentarians know precisely how easy it is to either put words in people's mouths that are not what was intended, or edit the words in a context that extracts contradictory meaning from what was originally intended. They know that an agenda for a project, from the funding source, to the perceived optimal outcome by a larger social, or even quite local, consensus, distorts people's honest and authentic perspectives. One might go on a project wanting to tell a story about climate change on a local community, but discover that the story the community wants to tell is about substance abuse and dysfunction, about family and resiliency. How the documentarian balances the resource expectations with the community's own interest is critical.

The second group, hybrid media educator/social workers, were people that had backgrounds in behavioral and mental health, counseling and psychological services, arts education or other health and wellbeing professions and had turned toward media as an engagement/education/advocacy tool. In our organization, Amy Hill, founder of the SilenceSpeaks project (see interview in Chapter 12), worked in public health for many years even as she acquired skills as a media professional in documentary. Amy, and countless other colleagues, brought with them professional standards of care that reflected a century of self-assessment within those professions, and several decades of critical re-assessment based on post-colonial perspectives on class, race, and gender. These professionals had much, much more to say about how one engages in processes that have an inherent psychological or social outcome for the individual storyteller. Among the many things the contemporary social service professional ethical framework provides are considerations about how people are affected by being either included as a subject by a media maker (as an interviewee), or as part of a storytelling or media engagement process. The issues of agency/consent, safety/risk, emotional/psychological support before, during and after, loom larger for these professionals than journalists and documentarians. In addition, the degree of expectation becomes a large issue, what should people expect from a process. People are aware that the fifteen minutes of fame and celebrity comes often through someone pointing a video camera at them, they are aware getting the news about their issues might change policy, they are hopeful that the story will improve some aspect of their lives from the outside; but coming from the service perspective, the emphasis of expectation becomes less about what the story will do as it reaches a broad audience, and more about what it will do for the storyteller, and the immediate community. Participatory media processes put a much larger focus on local conditions, and local benefit, than do traditional documentary processes.

From these and other sources we have taken general inspiration, and have begun to refine our own guidelines (See Addendum: Silence Speaks Ethical Guidelines). While many of these guidelines were developed where there exists a stark contrast between of the lives of the facilitators and the lives of the storytellers, the ideas inside of these

In a World of Do-It-Yourself, Why Do Ethics Still Matter?

As participatory media models expand, as huge number of protesters in the Middle East or the Midwest, figure out how to shoot a video, write a commentary, tell a story and post it onto YouTube or Facebook, why does it matter that we sustain the dialogue on ethics? People are speaking for themselves, communities have more and more forums for visibility, audiences can take or leave official channels of information and search out more authentic and reliable information about the things that concern and affect them.

Rookie reporters still make rookie mistakes. Sources of eyewitness evidence are faulty, what is projected as "what happened" if not verified from numerous sources, becomes propaganda, rumor, and slander. The wonderful part of the web is that it does its own fact checking, mistakes in projected perception often find an audience with countering view of the facts, other eyewitnesses, other perspectives on meaning. Almost because of the idea that you will be called on your errors, the conversation about what you are telling and why it matters that you try to be balanced and self-aware of your bias, still needs to be a core part of the training and support dialogue for participatory projects. There needs to be ways for consistent vetting and feedback about the way subjects were engaged and procedures followed inside a process. Grassroots media trainers and facilitators may not have the resource to follow up and sustain the quality of awareness necessary for ethical concerns to be a natural part of the conversation from first contact to the final process of presentation, but they can point the way, and short of in-depth professional training, can suggest that people revisit these issues consistently.

In addition, the context for presentation is often under the control of the facilitator, and this alone becomes an area rich with challenge, as with the example above about the needs of a funding resource, and the needs of the community.

Finally, in processes like Digital Storytelling, the authors are turning the camera on themselves, to make sense of their own lives. With self as subject, the most help you need is in your own thoughtfulness and self-awareness. Ethics growing out of mindfulness and/or spiritual perspectives start with the simple mantra of loving kindness; you want, and you want all others, to feel safe, healthy, happy and at peace. You deserve dignity. So does everyone else. If this thinking deeply informs how you represent yourself, and what you say about others, this can become an essential perspective to making wise ethical choices.

Interlude 5
Zahid's Story

Every year, I celebrate one Eid festival with my mother, and another one with Hosne Ara's mother.

She has no one except me.

My father had wanted me to study to be like my grandfather, a great Sufi of Bangladesh. But my passion for my life was different than my father's.

One rainy morning, against his wishes, I left my sweet home, the village where I was born. I reached the port city of Chittagong, where I began my studies of journalism.

I joined a local newspaper as university correspondent, then, the country's premier English daily – *The Bangladesh Observer*.

I loved working for repressed people. If I heard any cry from any corner, I ran towards them, listened their sufferings attentively, took pictures and wrote news story. It was my long awaited dream.

In school we were told to observe. To write. To stay detached.

But this is not my way.

I was assigned to investigate an acid-burnt housewife at the nearby hospital. Because her family couldn't afford the high dowry, her mother-in-law threw acid on her body…

I went there with the guise of being her cousin.

Hosne Ara's body was 80 percent burned, except her mouth, and two shiny eyes. What I saw was not a human being, but rather, an alive roast.

But she was fully conscious and able to talk. She tried to extend her hands towards me, but couldn't.

Urging me, Bhaia (brother), please write for me that those doctors would not help. I want justice, and please don't forget my mother…

Suddenly, a physician came to interrogate me and called his colleagues. Later, I learned he was the relative of Hosne Ara's mother-in-law, and didn't intend to disclose the information about the incident to the media.

They took my bag, discovering that I am a journalist.

In a separate room they beat me until I was senseless, tied my hands and left. They returned and broke my left hand and right leg with an iron rod. I floated in blood. Someone suggested hanging me from the ceiling fan. They tightened my neck with the bed cover and were attempting to tie it to the fan, when the police broke down the door.

The journalism community burst out in protest. Every newspaper, television channel and radio station published and broadcast news of the incident. My colleagues filed a case with the police.

But the doctors filed two cases against me. I was harassed.

After a long recovery, I returned to my newspaper office, only to be dismissed without concern. I learned later a bribe was involved.

Again, I was threatened, so I fled, leaving everything ... my computer, bed, books ... ... and my sweet dream.

I cried all the way to Dhaka.

My face was too familiar, and no newspaper would hire me.

Still, I couldn't forget Hosne Ara, the housewife who died for lack of a dowry, and with no medical care.

With some activist friends, we knocked door to door for her justice. I gave up my own case to fight hers. In late 2008, a judge finally gave the verdict.

But the soil of Bangladesh is still not safe for the housewife.

Or the journalist,

... Like me.

—Zahid Al Amin

Thoughts by Allison Myers

Zahid knew to take the last turn in the story circle. When he finished talking, no one said anything ... it felt like minutes passed.

When he handed me a script, it was almost 2,000 words. I remember taking a deep breath.

We were in Bangladesh working with storytellers representing various NGOs from south Asia. Every workshop has twists and challenges – quirky technology keeps you hopping, or stories that hold onto you for weeks afterwards, but *this* workshop was the ultimate opportunity for me to practice presence ... in chaos.

With seemingly endless tea breaks cutting into production time, incessantly honking horns that made clean audio recording tricky – even on the 15th floor, multiple power outages taking out unsaved edits, and a national strike that left us a day short, it was a miracle we finished with ten wonderful stories, or finished at all.

The intensity of Zahid's perseverance and desire to tell his story, walking again through this traumatic saga that he had never fully shared, was striking. A lot was at stake. Overcoming our language barrier, we talked through his story in a lengthy interview process. I typed while he talked. He told me his father wanted him to be a Sufi holy man, laughing when he said all he wanted was to be a journalist.

I wrote that down.

He asked me to edit the draft for him overnight. I felt the weight as a facilitator of walking the sacred line between helping someone through a difficult story, and having my fingers in it. Our handprints are inextricably on the stories, by the questions we ask, the way we respond, and the choices we help the storyteller make.

And we have to tread so lightly.

The best I had to offer Zahid, was my presence. It seemed my most important task was to support him in walking through to the other side of his story.

And here's a glimpse of the other side.

He had invited about thirty journalists and peers to the workshop screening of the stories.

But with the long script, the lost day, the language barriers, the challenges of finding a compelling way to illustrate the story, and the power outages, Zahid's story was nowhere near complete. The screening was in thirty minutes.

But we both knew that the talking and the writing had only taken him half way. He needed to come full circle. And there was an audience of his professional peers – the journalism community that had supported him, and also rejected him – waiting in the other room while we sweated it out, literally, at an ever-crashing computer.

His story was played last – with huge gaps in the visuals, the music too low.

But after the last note of Hari Prasad's haunting flute faded out on his audio, the room was silent for the second time that week.

This time I held my breath.

Then suddenly, the crowd leapt to their feet, exploding in applause. Zahid stood before his peers and openly wept.

And it dawned on me, that *this* was a *holy* moment, for Zahid the journalist, and also for me.

11

Applications of Digital Storytelling

Over the last fifteen years, Digital Storytelling has been applied to many different contexts, and has encountered an enormous range of possibilities. In the following chapters, we present conversations with a group of practitioners in the context of community engagement, violence prevention and public health, and education. As a preface, this chapter addresses the potential scope of this practice as it has been adapted to meet the needs of those in an ever-broadening range of fields.

Telling an Organization's Story

Whether you are working for a commercial enterprise or a civic group, trying to capture an organization's story is a common idea for a Digital Storytelling project. For some, the story is just another piece of marketing material, a step up from a PowerPoint presentation, but a step below spending $20,000 on a new promotional video. For others, the style of personal narrative in a piece that is produced with a minimal, but elegant design stands out as a new way of communicating meaning and values in relationship to the products or services the organization offers.

Our work in organizational storytelling has ranged from the smallest one-person consultations, to assisting marketing professionals working with large corporations. The thrust of organizational stories revolves around the question, what does the organization mean to you? And as the person whose work revolves around representing the organization, you need to have a good answer to this question. But no matter how good you are at making up reasons for your support, if your answer doesn't stir emotion or connect with an aspect of your life's calling, then in our book, you are not likely to be that effective in any of the materials you create.

Our approach is to start with a person's story that connects their own life experience to the organization's mission or brand. It may not be the story that makes it into your next speech, or the one that is showcased on your website, but until you share an experience with the audience, you won't be able to effectively represent other people's experiences and the resulting connection to the product.

Persuasion or as a Prompt to Action

We once had a student arrive at one of our open workshops in Berkeley who said that she was going to do a project about her boyfriend, and at the end of the movie, she wanted the final words to be a marriage proposal. It was our first marriage proposal digital story, and we thought it was one of the most compelling uses of a digital story as a prompt to action we had seen.

The story form invites the audience to consider issues, to have a deeper sense of why something is important, and that naturally orients people to consider the idea or approach to the experience. Motivational communication is all about storytelling, and the right story can inspire someone to get up and act, to change their position, to get others involved in a cause.

Reflective Practice

At our Center, mindfulness expert Jon Kabat-Zinn has become a major influence on several of our staff, myself included. If you are not familiar with his work, he can be summed up as a non-denominational meditation expert. His background is in healthcare, and he has brought meditation and mindfulness practices in the US medical community to a position of broad acceptance. As with most mindfulness instruction, the trick is to put yourself so completely in the present moment that all the thoughts you have become, as he so well put it, a waterfall that you can stand behind and observe.

Most creative work has a component of effort that is useful for deeper reflection. As you focus in on your piece of writing, or drop into your editing process, you can feel yourself stepping outside of the normal noise and chatter of your day to day. You become present, and step into a zone of awareness that is, if not heightened, then refreshingly free from distraction. The concentration required to edit video, especially in a workshop process, especially with yourself and something you deeply care about at the center of your process, can take you into this enchanted state.

I have come to believe that the process of writing and speaking your words, then editing with that mix of your own voice, and images that perhaps carry their own powerful meaning. Digital Storytelling is a form of reflective practice. This reanimation of the image artifact as part of the edit makes you feel as if you thinking about people, places, and objects in new ways. The plasticity of images, music, voice, the very playfulness of arranging and re-arranging meaning by visual sequence and juxtaposition, the entire process becomes regenerative for many people.

Health and Human Services

Everyday stories by local community members about pressing health and social problems have become a valued source of information and inspiration for providers, educators, and policymakers. In 1999 we launched our public health and violence prevention work with the Silence Speaks program (see the interview with Amy Hill in Chapter 12). While the broader health sector was at first slow to recognize the power of sharing stories digitally, the application of our methods has proliferated at a startling rate (see the interview with Pip Hardy and Tony Sumner in Chapter 14).

Digital storytelling today has been employed not only as a tool for professional reflection, but also as a method for capturing intimate stories by service consumers. In the tradition of narrative medicine, for example, these stories assist providers in understanding the nuances of how race, class, language, and culture inform people's understanding of their own health and wellness in ways that are different from Western medicine's views on illness.

At the community-based level, digital stories have played a critical role in social marketing campaigns for individual and community-wide behavioral change. For example, our work with the Partners for Fit Youth Network (PFY) in Santa Barbara, California, and a project on chronic disease prevention in Salinas, California, both have positioned local voices and images as the message bearers of critical health promotion information, as a way to prevent adolescent obesity and diabetes. From these two brief examples, it is clear that stories are being crafted and contextualized to point to the social determinants of ill health. Therefore, sharing this work on a larger scale enables public health advocates to call for health equity and highlight the ways in which inequities impact communities.

When compared to other service sectors the health sector has witnessed the greatest adoption of digital storytelling as a qualitative research methodology. Like PhotoVoice, for example, our process has been adapted as a form of community-based participatory research (CBPR) to examine the attitudes of young Latinas regarding pregnancy and mothering; barriers to breast cancer screening and treatment for rural women; and the role of traditional knowledge in health promotion among Alaska Native communities.

Whether the focus is on healing and reflection for providers and consumers, educating remote communities with relevant and meaningful story-based content, inspiring systemic change, or research/program evaluation, we know that the honest, first-person voices that arise from digital storytelling will continue to play a pivotal role in the health and human services sectors in the years to come.

Intergenerational Connection

When we began our work at the Digital Clubhouse in Silicon Valley in 1996, we quickly discovered that digital storytelling was an excellent tool for fostering connections across generations. Since its inception, the Clubhouse was organized around a principle of serving a diverse cross-section of the south San Francisco Bay community, with an emphasis on seniors and youth. Since that time, a large number of senior focused workshops have been organized, including over a half dozen World War II Memories projects. The seniors bring the stories, the youth assist with multimedia production, and the middle generation acts as the organizational glue.

Cross-generational storytelling provides a platform for our elders to share stories with a broader community, especially for the younger populations. Instead of experiencing new technology as just a digital playground, they see the potential impact it can have for all people involved. Digital Storytelling also affords young people the opportunity to confront frailty, aging, mortality, and disability associated with aging. Furthermore, Digital Storytelling is also an appropriate adjunct to community- or university-based oral history projects with elders.

Disability

It was also at the Digital Clubhouse where we began exploring the relevancy of Digital Storytelling practice for the many differently abled people in our communities. One of our first projects was, "My Life As A Movie." The project was predicated on the fact that many high-school-aged youth with disabilities face difficulties in finding appropriate part-time or full-time employment; we believe that providing these youth with a chance to create a digital reflection about their lives, their strengths, and their skills, could help them in their job search.

In the course of the workshop, we met many extraordinary youth, several of whom became an integral part of the Clubhouse youth program. We also were first familiarized with the advances in assistive technology that allow participants like Kevin Lichtenberg, who operated the computer using an infrared mouse/tracking device attached to his forehead, to design and create their own stories. Giving voice takes on new meaning when those with hearing disabilities can "see" their voice for the first time displayed as a waveform on a computer screen.

Since this time, we have had several opportunities to work with members of the disability community to develop digital stories. In particular, in our collaboration with Professor Sue Schweik at the University of California, Berkeley, and activist/artist Neil Marcus, we developed a Digital Storytelling component within a college course on Creative Writing and the Body. The class aimed to foster dialogue about disability and many of the larger cultural issues that are raised by our perceptions of selves and our bodies. This meant confronting issues about the notion of limitation, and talking about how our stories are shaped whether we are perceived to be visibly whole, visibly limited, or invisibly limited in countless ways.

The stories of struggle, the stories of resolve, and the stories of frustration and beauty were captured elegantly in the Digital Storytelling process. The larger canon of literary and creative accomplishment coming from differently abled communities continue to be served by various adaptations of Digital Storytelling processes.

Youth Programs

Three months after we started the San Francisco Digital Media Center in 1994, we found ourselves working with Ron Light, a local educational media expert, to develop D*LAB. D*LAB would remain a program of our center for almost four years, allowing us to sustain an active body of work with teens from San Francisco's many diverse communities. In our projects we explored digital video stories, as well as web-based stories and special workshops with specific schools. Additionally, we looked at the Title VI program of the San Francisco Unified School District, and also worked with Native American youth.

Daniel Weinshenker's many years of working with the Downtown Area Visual Arts program, leading youth through the process of developing high-quality stories, has also demonstrated how youth can meet the challenge of writing meaningful and powerful prose. The 826 Center movement, Streetside Stories, the National Writing Projects' local youth programs, Adobe Youth Voices, and many others, have made Digital Storytelling a critical part of youth media strategy.

These experiences affirmed our attitude that young people, despite feeling adept at multimedia tools, long for environments where freedom of expression is possible – where they can choose what story to tell and decide how it should be told. After-school environments are often where effective youth-based projects can best be developed. These efforts give youth a sense of real world consequence that is a critical component of a constructive educational philosophy. And for the most part, the students and instructors are not weighed down with the criteria of assessment and bureaucratic inertia that plagues many of our public school settings.

As has also been stated by a number of our colleagues working in the context of media literacy with youth, Digital Storytelling plays an ideal intermediary role between the observations and analysis of media (the classic media literacy curriculum), and full-on film and video production. We learn most about the way media affects us by manipulating media and making our own editing decisions.

Youth video, animation and film projects have for years demonstrated that the desire to speak in the language of film is virtually universal among young people. However, the expense in time and resources in organizing film production inhibits accessibility. Digital Storytelling puts the participant in the editing chair with a minimal amount of preparation, and without the lengthy process of shooting, reviewing, capturing, and working with video clips. Young people walk away from their first video-editing experience with a new set of eyes and ears, as they see how special effects and design decisions are constructed and work upon the minds of viewers.

With the commitment to educational technology use in classrooms and youth programs throughout the developed and developing worlds, digital storytelling and other forms of digital media publishing are becoming key parts of curricula and programming at many youth centers and after-school programs.

Identity and Diversity

Race, gender, class, and sexual orientation are natural subjects for storytelling, as stories provide ways to address these difficult, complicated issues by bridging and negotiating difference. Many of the discussions about "digital divides," "serving those at risk," and "cultural equity" are sophisticated euphemisms for discussions of racism, sexism, and homophobia in the public sphere.

Digital Storytelling has been seen as a useful tool for two of the more complex aspects of this discussion. First and foremost, a post-colonial perspective suggests people within every culture have the right to carry on conversations, form organizations, and amalgamate their own stories outside of the mainstream cultural discourse.

Integration into a dominant society that sustains aspects of the legacies of genocide, segregation, and racism in many of its institutional practices is not necessarily the end goal of cultural pluralism. We have encouraged the development of programs to assist people within African-American, Latino, Asian-Pacific Islander, Native American, and LGBTQ communities to capture their own stories, using approaches and methods that reflect both historical cultural practices and contemporary expressions and ideas within these communities. The conversation with Yvonne Pratt in Chapter 11 addresses these issues in more detail.

As an example, through our associates China Ching and Thenmozhi Soundararajan, we were involved in the Spring of 2001, in a workshop with a group of Native Californian activists who were part of the Circle of Voices project. On principle, the workshop did not allow visitors or observers to attend, and the artifacts photographed for inclusion in stories, many of which represented sacred items to the various communities, were not shared with those outside the circle of participants. As a final precaution, at the end of the project, none of the associated digitized materials were allowed to remain at our center, nor were the stories distributed or exhibited outside the community in any fashion.

Another aspect of a culturally democratic practice is to provide media-based mechanisms for people who have felt excluded from the channels of economic and political access to share their stories publicly. We have encouraged all of our participants to imagine their stories as having broad relevancy to a larger public, and where appropriate, work directly with our collaborative partners to seek broadcast (radio and television) and other avenues for distribution.

Inevitably, changing from an "I" point of view to a "we" becomes a more sensitive dialogue in these particular pieces that address racial and social justice. Giving witness as an individual coalesces with a sense of collective will, and with a view that suggests any document reporting on the conditions people face need also include a sense of collective responsibility.

Since our beginnings, we have sought to sustain a diversity of participation in our workshops held throughout the country. We have an ongoing scholarship and outreach effort to engage communities of color, and much of our specific work in public health, community development, and social services focuses on low-income and immigrant communities. When possible, we also provide pro bono technical and production support to the grassroots efforts of our colleagues working both locally and internationally.

Activism

While community-based discussions about root identity and diversity reflect a certain degree of activist perspective, the use of Digital Storytelling as part of the community organizer's tool kit has its own set of considerations.

When my father arrived in a small, east Texas town to begin a labor-organizing project at the local garment factory, his first project was the creation of an agitational newsletter. The newsletter captured stories about what was going on in the plant, which abuses were being perpetrated by which managers, what plans the company had to keep employees in line, and what funny incidents demonstrated flashes of spontaneous resistance. He told stories, as much as possible, in the words of the folks living the experience.

In my own activist experience, while I prided myself on being able to knock out an effective, rabble-rousing speech, I knew what made my arguments for change and resistance effective were the most direct examples of courage and leadership that I had observed. Capturing these stories was what breathed life into our ideology.

Of course, part of the problem with political people on both the left and the right is that they often make sure that the stories projected suit their ideologies and political programs. The "politically correct" stories are the only ones that surface in their campaigns. In a long-range view, common sense suggests that the activist would do well to leave the sifting of arguments within a range of stories to the audience, and instead focus on facilitating voice and educational empowerment as broadly as possible.

Your own political stance aside, imagining how Digital Storytelling can be easily integrated into strategies for change is not difficult. In our own programs, we have worked with countless activists to develop projects that address the issues they care about so deeply, and the media has been presented as part of community meetings, assemblies, policymaking venues, political rallies and in organizing packages distributed to their constituents.

In addition, using the Digital Storytelling workshop as a group cohesion exercise has been shown to be effective. If the resources are available, gathering a group of organizers together to share their own stories and learn the process and the tool set can orient and energize a campaign.

Immigrants and Refugees

The immigrant youth of the Mission District were some of the first participants in the CDS Digital Storytelling workshops. Their stories were often one of the first ways they were able to explore their voice in a creative context, and have their stories find audiences inside and outside their communities. From the beginning, immigrant and refugee voice was seen as a vital area of development for our work, because the family- and community-centered format was easily adapted to the ways in which immigrants process the rupture between their former and current lives. In addition, the tool set was easily adapted to bilingual and multi-lingual settings, allowing English as Second Language students to explore their writing and reading out loud, as well as with native language speakers to work with subtitles.

We have many excellent examples of projects in this sector. Among the more effective was our partnership in the Seattle Refugee Youth Project. Beginning in 2010, the Voice of Migration project connected youth from Burma, Bhutan, Eritrea, and Russia, between the ages of 14 and 19. The community celebration of stories attracted citywide attention, and brought new recognition to the issue facing these specific communities, and generated a greater sense of cohesion and inclusion for the participants and their families.

International Development

As our work spread from its initial base in California across oceans and continents, it began to find a place in the development sector, which for decades has explored and promoted the value of participatory communications strategies. With its emphasis on first-person narrative and meaningful involvement in the media production process, Digital Storytelling represents a user-friendly approach to participatory video, a method practiced widely in the context of international health and community development initiatives in Africa, south Asia, and Latin America.

Those involved in international projects face many challenges when implementing a storytelling process that is appropriate for resource-poor environments. For example, what adaptations are required for Digital Storytelling with individuals and communities that lack a written literacy or even a written version of their first language? And in terms of cultural sensitivity, how does one approach issues related to representation, privacy, story ownership, and program sustainability in the context of colonialism and media exploitation – two factors that are pervasive in development work?

Our approach has been to emphasize partnerships with local NGOs well versed in the needs and issues of their area, and to push for work that goes well beyond the mere documentation of stories to integrate personal narrative into existing health and human rights agendas. Flexibility has been key to the success of projects in Uganda and South Africa, where we have brought testimonial practices into the process of story development, and worked closely with skilled interpreters to capture and edit the narratives of workshop participants. While digital story creators have historically relied on personal archives of photos and video clips to develop visual treatments for their stories, work in the development sector has required the integration of photography and artful creation for participants who lack such image collections.

An emphasis on organizational capacity building and sustainability has also characterized much of our international work. In Brazil, we trained staff at the Museu da Pessoa (Museum of the Person) in Digital Storytelling methods and supported them in adapting the process for a large-scale youth voice initiative. In South Africa, our ongoing collaboration with the Sonke Gender Justice Network has also involved facilitator training and mentoring for staff, as well as additional partnerships to ensure a long-term presence to support the continued evolution of the work throughout the region.

K-12 and Higher Education Curricula

Educators from K-12 schools as well as colleges and universities have been an integral part of our practice from the start. The leading proponents of educational technology for project-based learning identified Digital Storytelling as one of the most obvious and effective methods within a broad cross-section of curricular areas. Writing and voice, reflections on civic processes, oral histories, and essays on major subject areas are just some of the ways the work has been integrated into curriculums across grade levels.

We imagine a much broader role for Digital Storytelling in an integrated constructivist learning setting that easily could address science and math as well. We agree with the philosophy that if children remember the stories of their own learning processes and can readily apply their unique sets of strengths and intelligences, they will develop their own strategies for learning. Because it goes well beyond the facts and formulas they are expected to regurgitate as evidence of their mastery of knowledge, Digital Storytelling will support not only the academic success of students but also their life success.

Building a portfolio of how students approached problems through digital storytelling could provide a vivid and enjoyable mechanism for charting the development of their learning over time. Just imagine a student capping her/his educational career with an interactive performance of stories showing work on projects from kindergarten through college, and projecting them at the graduation party.

For educators at either the K-12 or college levels, learning not only how to facilitate Digital Storytelling but also how to articulate judgments about the design of video with the same authority they have in relation to text can take years of training and practice. But today, the necessary tool sets and the training of educators to use them have found their way into classrooms across the U.S. and around the world.

Scenario Planning/Futures Thinking

In 1997, we began a multi-year collaboration with the Menlo Park-based Institute for the Future (IFTF) to look at the role of Digital Storytelling in scenario development. IFTF has always integrated a narrative approach into its reporting methodology by combining essays that examine major technological trends with fictional scenarios involving characters as consumers and managers a decade or more into the future. They were also involved in looking at the ways that new media technologies could be more thoroughly integrated into knowledge management and organizational communication practices. Because Digital Storytelling fits so well with their own methodologies and practices, in 1998 they commissioned us to create a white paper on our work (which served as the core of the first edition of this book).

Of particular interest to us were a pair of projects involving educators and high-school youth (in 2000), and then community members (in 2001), where IFTF and members of our staff collaborated on extended workshops to both educate participants about the implications of the trends being examined in IFTF research, and gather stories about their views of the future and the impact of technology on their lives.

In the work with educators and students, we were struck by the ability of each group to imagine the impact that technological progress would have on their personal and professional lives. With the community members who were also involved in a longer assessment of their then-current attitudes toward technology, we were impressed by the ease with which they imagined integrating the commitments and values they held most dear into a future, and with their ability to envision some of the enabling technologies on the horizon. In both cases, workshop participants recognized that technological progress had a Janus-like role in their lives, enabling and oppressing at the same time.

The stories themselves were surprisingly powerful, given that the style of speculative writing and the notion of illustrating the future in image was new to all participants. We found that the process assisted all of the participants in thinking more broadly about historical change in their communities. We hope to see the emergence of much more elaborate programs for capturing and developing stories about how individuals view their futures, as a process for initiating dialogue about large-scale community development and the impact of global climate change and other pressing issues.

Professional Evaluation

Myriad approaches to periodic review and assessment exist within various professions and sectors. Management consultants in both the commercial and civic arenas have developed numerous ways to give organizations and individuals the opportunity to take stock of their development and morale. Storytelling opportunities have been presented in group settings, or as one-on-one dialogues. And as with any reflective practice, the process is usually more important than the product. Unfortunately, written reports usually disappear into files and filing cabinets and never again see the light of day and have little in the way of reflective substance.

In the last five years, we have witnessed interest among a growing number of professionals to use Digital Storytelling as a way to give the product of their assessment processes new and more enduring meaning. Capturing one's professional process over the course of a year as a classroom teacher, for example, with the production of a multimedia story as the final assessment piece, provides a wide array of topics to explore. The professional can look at her/his relationship to students by recording the students at work, or at their own development of new styles of teaching and testing by documenting themselves as teachers. They can also explore themes and issues around their personal life or the larger context of their school or district as a way of setting the backdrop for a story.

With a grant from the Spencer Foundation, we worked with the National Writing Project (NWP) to collaborate with a group of rural educators from around the U.S. in a project to encourage this kind of assessment. The resulting stories have found their way into countless dialogues with other educators and have inspired numerous school districts to consider projects to capture the reflections of classroom teachers.

In another project with First Five of Alameda County, we were able to bring together representatives of some seven organizations supported by this early childhood and family project to tell their stories about the role of this program. The stories were integrated into a final report with formal evaluations of both quantitative and qualitative materials, and presented on the website connected to the report.

When stories are completed in an environment of shared reflection, they can inspire and lead to more in-depth reflections by the storytellers' peers. The portfolio of each of these projects offered a treasure trove of detail on programmatic impact, as well as valuable and inspirational material on learning and engagement in their respective fields. These multimedia stories provide an effective and entertaining way of presenting the arguments of administrators and managers about changes needed in organizational thinking.

Team Building

During the height of the dot com boom in the late 1990s, hardly a week went by without a national news story about how project management professionals were busy cooking up "experiences" that would enable the members of teams to bond more closely. The examples included fire walking, rope courses, sports camps, extreme hiking, and other outdoor adventures. Undoubtedly, people who are forced by circumstance to execute complex projects over periods of intense activity will operate more effectively if they are initiated through an ego-stripping test of endurance and nerve. The physical test as a communal rite of passage is an ancient ritual.

But it would seem that the extremity of some of these experiences is perhaps a bit overstated for the relatively mundane application of the average professional project, no matter how stressful such a project may become. They also seem much more suited to a traditional view of male-dominated cultures where physical prowess and leadership are considered interchangeable.

A number of our clients in both civic and commercial organizations have suggested that the strongest application of our work is in amplifying the process of the personal story exchange. While developing intimacies through personal stories is a common part of informal professional life, storytelling circles, and the more intense production madness of a digital storytelling workshop, gets to the heart of the matter much more directly.

We have witnessed the solidarity that typically develops among people in the context of workshops, and while, thus far, this outcome has been unintended, we are watching with interest to see where and when it will be taken up and examined more fully.

Journalism

With the advent of widely available high-speed internet access, journalism has emerged as a sector that is exploring many innovative uses for digital storytelling or multimedia reporting. While it would seem that the journalistic profession is built on story, ethical concerns have tended to divorce authors' personal experiences from their treatment of stories. But for many of us, emotional content is at the heart of effective journalism.

Our colleague, Jane Stevens, formerly with the *New York Times* and now working as an independent science journalist, has developed her own approach and theories about new multimedia authorship for journalists. In this context, she approached us to collaborate on a few workshops to train some of her peers on Digital Storytelling practice.

Back in the late 1990s, Jane was one of the first people to correctly point out that the traditional divisions of labor between print journalists, photographers, and video journalists were dissolving as more and more news was developed as entertainment. At the same time, online journalism and the number of freelance journalists were growing, and a much more complex relationship between journalists and audiences in the reporting of news resulted. Stevens continues to see journalists as both multimedia storytellers, often with recognizable personal styles, and news facilitators, working with sources that are helping to craft their own stories, and developing their own web-based platforms for sharing them.

Following the initial work with Jane, we were asked to train staff at the BBC on Digital Storytelling methods, and they subsequently launched a large-scale on-line broadcast initiative called Capture Wales (http://www.bbc.co.uk/digitalstorytelling), the first of many "citizen journalism" approaches to our methods to emerge.

Today, news outlets around the world offer incredibly sophisticated forms of multimedia-based online journalism, as Twitter, Facebook and YouTube collects and shares user-generated content that gains a wider and wider amount of our attention. In our work, we continue to emphasize the value of first-person narrative, participatory production, and group processes for shaping and sharing meaningful stories. When these values align with journalism and other media outlets, both storytellers and viewers benefit immensely.

Technology Training

Ironically, technology training, perhaps the most obvious application for the skill set we use in Digital Storytelling, is in some ways the least interesting to us organizationally. We realize that the digital divide is alive and well along both socio-economic and cultural lines, as well as along lines of age and gender – both in the U.S. and throughout the world. Getting access to digital media production tool sets is far from a closed issue, especially as these discussions expand globally, so providing access is a critically important part of our work.

At the same time, we are not overly concerned about the ways that innumerable communities seeking access will ultimately be able to put their hands on the tools. As costs decrease, creative community solutions such as community-based technology access centers can pool their resources and service a large number of people. We also recognize that digital video/multimedia production and training curricula has been developed and refined over the years by a plethora of non-profit media centers, as well as colleges and universities, for people who want in-depth knowledge of the tools. Opportunities such as these may represent a better option than our workshops, which emphasize narrative and story rather than the intricacies of software use.

Place and Planning

In the last decade, the popular use of geographic information systems (GIS) through tools like Google Earth and Google Maps, have become endlessly useful in communities putting meaning into place in new and powerful ways. Along with innovations in data visualization, and to lesser extent augmented reality, countless projects are mashing up stories with statistical and geocentric location. One of the most exciting uses of this material is related to community-based learning and urban planning. In our own work, beginning with our 1994–1998 collaboration with the

Ukiah Players Theater, located in Mendocino County, we have been examining place-based storytelling in these contexts. In Houston, Texas; New Orleans, Louisiana; and Tuscaloosa, Alabama, we worked on a prototype workshop process to engage community members in talking about their community, and linking the stories to the discussions of redevelopment and resource development for communities. This work was captured on the website, now archived at www.storymapping.org, which has also shared the stories of several other place-based projects from around the world.

Conservation, Local Wisdom, and Environmental Justice

The place work has a natural allegiance to environmental activism in all its forms. Stories of place become ways to discuss land resource management, indigenous land rights, climate, disproportionate public health impacts on the poor, and countless other issues becoming part of our national and international civic dialogues. CDS has had numerous projects taking the workshops to frontline communities in these debates.

In Canada, staff member Rob Kershaw has developed a perspective on our work in these areas called the Witness Tree initiative. The focus of his work has been in connecting to local communities to develop a sustainable story process for capturing stories as part of action-research methods. This work has included ongoing series of projects with First Nation communities. These communities include the Métis of Fishing Lake, Alberta (see Chapter 13 interview with Yvonne Pratt); First Nations and Métis, in High Level, Alberta; Inuit in Labrador and Sahtu Dene of Deline, Northwest Territories. The subjects addressed include job development and skills for youth, oral histories, and climate change.

The Future of ~~Digital~~ Storytelling

Every month brings a new application for Digital Storytelling somewhere in the world. We follow them every way we can, but in all the countries, in all the contexts, in all the languages and modalities of expression, we can only speculate about where this work has found new territory.

As we look five or ten years ahead, we recognize the word digital has less and less meaning. Human expression finds its way to digital in every context, and the distribution of material without a digital version, has become more of a political statement or stylistic preference, than a practical reality. If you want to share a story, why not make it digital and post it somewhere.

So if everything is digital, is Digital Storytelling a less-and-less useful idea? Does the brand have legs, as the marketing professionals might say.

We enjoy the nuance of this specific genre, and we believe this genre has much more growing to do. Millions of people are moving from Facebook posts with pictures, to composing small stories with images. Each step of the way, there will be a role for slightly more advanced early adapters to assist a novice in their steps into this process. But this work we do, and why we are appreciated for doing it, will be less and less showing people how to put a pan on an image, or to improve the quality of a recording. Even now we define ourselves first as storyworkers, as story coaches, as story enablers, mid-wives, collaborating artists, and narrative alchemists.

The future of our work is learning how to hold the state-of-the-art in popular use of digital media in one hand, while becoming ever more effective at supporting people in their storytelling. We are moving forward to ancient technologies. Technologies that are older and more difficult than print, electronic, and digital communication. They are the dynamics of listening. Listening beyond words, beyond conscious intention of a teller, to the shape of a feeling as it moves from emotion to language. We have much more to learn, and apply, in these arts and sciences. We invite you to join us in this journey.

12

Silence Speaks

Interview with Amy Hill

Amy Hill is a public health consultant and staff member of the Center for Digital Storytelling, where she directs the Silence Speaks initiative (www.silencespeaks.org). Originally a collaboration with an organization called Third World Majority, Silence Speaks has expanded its initial focus on violence prevention to include a variety of gender, health, and human rights issues. This interview was conducted in 2002 and updated in 2012.

Joe Lambert: How did you get involved in Digital Storytelling?

Amy Hill: I came to this work in 2000, when I had reached at a point of frustration with the limitations of the digital media approaches that I saw in the context of public health approaches to violence prevention. At that time, I had been working in public health, largely focused on women's health issues, for about 12 years. Back in the 1990s, the use of digital/multimedia tools and productions in these sectors, at least at the local level, centered largely on didactic classroom presentations and curricula that did not seem to me to speak to the actual experiences of violence survivors. When I found out about Digital Storytelling, I thought that it would be an effective way to incorporate visual media into community education and public awareness campaigns related to addressing and preventing violence against women. As I came to understand the therapeutic potential of Digital Storytelling, through the process of working with some of the most difficult and painful stories from my own life, I saw clearly that Digital Storytelling could also offer a potentially transformative experience for survivors and witnesses of violence and trauma.

Joe: When did you first make a digital story?

Amy: My first experience was with the Digital Clubhouse Network (DCN) in Mountain View, California, which I found through the research and consulting I was doing as coordinator of a 1998–99 technology training and capacity building project for domestic violence shelter agencies and prevention programs across the state. At that time, these agencies and programs were underutilizing emerging digital technology tools and the Internet, so I was looking for interesting ways to engage them, beyond dry, introductory training on basic software applications. I stumbled upon the DCN on the web, and I contacted them, and they invited me to a Digital Storytelling workshop that was specifically for representatives of non-profit agencies. The DCN methodology was a bit different from that typically employed by CDS. The DCN teamed storytellers up with young people who handled the computer production work. The workshop participants wrote and recorded scripts, brought photos and video clips, and provided direction to the youth, on the edits of their stories. I took away two key things from that experience. One was that in telling my *own* story about violence within my family, I realized that it would be incredibly valuable and much more nurturing to hold special workshops for groups of people dealing specifically with issues of trauma. It was difficult for me to feel safe and really open up, in a more general context where people were creating stories about a variety of experiences. The second take away point was an understanding of the importance of offering a much more participatory production process, to guide storytellers in editing their own stories rather than giving them a more passive role. My understanding of the strength of this approach grew as I began working directly with CDS to develop the Silence Speaks program.

Joe: In your own experience, why do you think Digital Storytelling is useful as a reflective practice?

Amy: From the perspective of working in the field of violence prevention, a fair amount of media is produced in the guise of health education, much of it involving fairly canned, unrealistic scenarios. Many people in the field do not find these kinds of videos helpful. In having gone through the Digital Storytelling process myself, in having told my own story, and in having coordinated numerous workshops with survivors and witnesses of trauma, there is a level of sincerity that comes through in digital stories that has a way of deeply moving viewers. The digital story is a different kind of representation than a dramatized approach – the fact that stories contain recordings and images of real people rather than actors enables them to really touch people.

Because I have a history of working with a number of domestic violence agencies, Silence Speaks has ended up working with many agency staff members. For these projects, there has been a great deal of discussion about where to draw the line between working directly with survivors and working with staff, in setting up workshops. Of course the line is actually quite blurry, because so many people who work in the field actually have some direct experience with violence – as either a survivor or a witness – in their own lives. Because staff members in these agencies understand that there is such a great need for their services, they tend to work many, many hours, for little money. As a result, we have found that across the field, they don't have much time to reflect back on how their own experiences affect the work that they do, in ways that allow some realization or catharsis or transformation in terms of their particular healing journeys. Nor do they often have time to step back and look at how events in their lives have shaped their relationships, their professions, and their politics. So participating in workshops has been enormously powerful for agency staff. Workshops have served as amazing team-building experiences, and where we have brought together representatives from multiple agencies, have also been effective in building support and collaboration across organizations and sectors.

People have told stories about a broad spectrum of issues related to violence; from human rights work in Colombia, to a young man who told a story about his past involvement in gangs and how it informs his current work as a youth counselor. This spectrum of story allows people to make connections regarding the ways that the same social, cultural, economic, and political structures influence forms of violence that are typically viewed quite independently.

Joe: What do you see is unique to your approach to Digital Storytelling? As you have moved toward a therapeutic practice, what sort of ethical and political questions have you had to address?

Amy: The Silence Speaks approach to Digital Storytelling is unique in a number of ways. While trauma may happen to individuals, it is widely recognized as a social and political phenomenon, deeply influenced by the power dynamics which shape human interaction. I define traumatic experience broadly, to encompass violence, oppression, stigma, and marginalization occurring in the context of families, communities, institutions, or armed conflicts. I also believe that while definitions can be useful for establishing a shared understanding among researchers, clinicians, and activists, rigid definitions of "trauma" can also limit inquiry and unfairly pathologize both individuals and groups. This has been particularly true in the context of the growing body of work that I've been doing overseas. I therefore use the term "trauma" with caution and choose to support workshop participants in identifying themselves and describing their experiences *as they see fit*.

For Silence Speaks, I approach each new partnership (and all of our work is done in partnership with community organizations) with great care, assessing the needs and capacities of collaborators and engaging them in a process of dialogue to outline goals and objectives, design workshop participant recruitment strategies, and orient staff to the role we require them to play in providing emotional support to storytellers – before, during, and after workshops. I take special care to ensure a safe container, during workshops, in which the participant can unravel her/his narrative and then piece it back together into a coherent story. I have studied various theories of trauma over the years, and I bring that knowledge, as well as my background as a certified sexual assault hotline counselor and meditation practitioner, into my work as a facilitator. Above all, I'm committed to remaining transparent and open, to the best of my abilities, during workshops, because I believe this is critical to being able to listen in a way that invites people to safely touch into their vulnerability. The exchange between teller and listener that happens in this space of presence is where much of the healing lies.

I also adjust the standard CDS curriculum in a number of ways. First, Silence Speaks workshops are almost always longer than three days (the length of a typical CDS workshop). This allows greater space and time for participants to explore their issues, bond with their peers, and receive the gentle support and guidance of facilitators. Second, I integrate gentle warm-up activities, particularly those that involve physical movement and awareness, into the workshop process, as a way of acknowledging and addressing the ways that histories of violence and trauma can be deeply held in the body. I owe my colleagues at Generation FIVE (www.generationfive.org) a debt of gratitude for introducing me to this somatics-based approach to working with trauma. And last, I take quite seriously the importance of workshop closure.

For some projects, this means tapping the expertise of partners to develop and carry out ceremonies or rituals that are done at the end of the process. For others, it means making sure that follow-up procedures are in place – such as telephone or in-person debriefing meetings, group get-togethers for participants, etc. – to give workshop participants a place to land, in the days and weeks after sharing their stories.

In terms of ethical issues, there are too many to name, here, but the one that stands out to me revolves around concepts of "consent." This includes both consent to participate in a workshop and consent to allow one's story to be shown publicly. When I started Silence Speaks, YouTube didn't exist, and most nonprofits lacked the technical capacity to readily put video up online. While I had a vision for how digital stories could support broad-based public information and advocacy campaigns, the nature and history of the work caused that vision to take a back seat to the evolution of the therapeutic aspects of the Digital Storytelling process. Today, in 2012, that landscape has changed dramatically; not only is video online ubiquitous, but many additional channels for distributing multimedia content have arisen – smart phones, Twitter, Facebook, and other social media forms are becoming woven into the fabric of everyday life. Whether or not this current social media frenzy will last is open to debate, but what is true is that it has greatly complicated and magnified the ethical challenges inherent to bringing highly sensitive personal narratives and images into public spheres. I have come to view consent as a process, rather than as a one-time activity involving forms and signatures. I believe it is incumbent upon facilitators and project sponsors to be transparent from the outset about their desires to share stories publicly, and to support workshop participants in making good decisions about what they feel comfortable saying and showing, in their stories – or in making the decision *not* to participate, particularly if there is any possibility that doing so might put participants at risk of harm.

Joe: What about the participant's sense of social agency, do you think this shapes their sense of contributing to struggles against violence?

Amy: Yes; in my experience, I have seen many participants undergo a radical shift in their ideas of what they are going to do with their story projects, from when they first hear about a workshop, to when they arrive and are oriented to the Digital Storytelling process, and again as they move through producing their pieces. As a testament to their commitment to having an impact on the world, we have found that many people are comfortable with Silence Speaks and our community partners sharing their stories in community settings, on websites or compilation DVDs, at conferences and trainings, at film festivals. They see these opportunities as a way to showcase their work, stimulate dialogue about the issues, and, ideally, prompt viewers to take action. About five years ago, an intern with us did her master of social work thesis as a qualitative study of Silence Speaks. Study participants reported that sharing their completed digital stories with others led them to feel a sense of social agency whereby they believed their digital stories impacted or had the potential to impact others. And I can say that whenever I have presented the work, or when I have received comments via email about the Silence Speaks website, the response has been hugely supportive both from individual survivors and grassroots groups or professionals dealing with violence.

Joe: Even in our public workshops, people are willing to take risks with emotional material, and ordinarily they are prepared for the emotional impact of this work, but sometime they are not. How do you address people's potential for going into crisis as part of the workshop experience?

Amy: This is an important piece of learning from our early work with Silence Speaks. While I've found that in general, people tend to self-select when they are ready to participate in something like Digital Storytelling, we make sure from the outset of outreach strategies that potential storytellers understand the workshop is not appropriate for someone currently in crisis or coming out of a crisis situation. To expect that someone suffering from a multitude of symptoms of post traumatic stress or from the daily challenges of trying to find food and shelter will be able to narrate a story and function well in a group process is not only unrealistic but potentially dangerous. We make this vividly clear to our project partners and in our materials and in any conversation we have with would-be storytellers. In addition, we have worked with a social worker who has considerable expertise in counseling and supporting trauma survivors to develop a self-assessment questionnaire for potential participants to think through before they decide whether they feel prepared to attend a workshop. The questions include: Have you told the story before? What was your experience when you told the story? How do you think it will be to tell the story in a group of other survivors? What kind of support do you think you might need, both in the context of the workshop and beyond? How do you feel about the idea of your completed story being shown publicly?

While none of us working on Silence Speaks are licensed therapists, we do, as teachers, have a great deal of experience in the field. We also require that our project partners make staff available on site for the duration of workshops, to provide any necessary additional emotional support to participants. I do want to stress that we have never had a "dangerous" situation and in fact I have found that storytellers in some of the Center's general workshops that I've taught had had a more difficult time addressing very sensitive material than Silence Speaks participants. I suspect this is due to the fact that with Silence Speaks, we always work in close collaboration with grassroots groups and organizations that are skilled in counseling, violence prevention education, and advocacy etc., and in reaching out to potential workshop participants, they lean towards people who they believe are ready to speak out. This ensures that the participants who they recruit to make stories have had some prior exposure to making their own stories known, in a group setting.

Joe: Do you have an intuitive assessment of how your experience in working in these therapeutic contexts might be relevant to other areas of the health professions?

Amy: Fortunately, we have led enough Silence Speaks workshops to have a body of work that I believe is adding an important contribution to the world of therapeutic interventions. The pioneering work of Silence Speaks has directly influenced the content and shape of many other CDS projects, particularly those which have focused on supporting young people currently or formerly involved in foster care, mental health, and/or juvenile justice systems. In describing the therapeutic benefit, for participants, of creating stories, I think the best way to express it is through a comment by one Silence Speaks participant, who said that the workshop experience allowed her for the first time to have complete control over the telling of a story about a situation over which she had no control. So the workshop process, for her, enabled her to reclaim her own experience and achieve autonomy and agency in how she portrayed the experience back to the rest of world. This is a generally shared feeling about the Digital Storytelling process: the sense that it can be intensely cathartic. It is one thing to sit with a therapist or in a group therapy session and just talk about one's experience, but it is something all together different to put recorded words to the experience, create a visual treatment of it, and incorporate music and all the multimedia elements ...

It's also true that Silence Speaks practices link directly to practices in narrative therapy and art therapy. Narrative therapy has addressed both the general power of rewriting the life story you carry with you, as well as the specific impact that the writing process has in prompting reflection and feedback in a therapeutic environment. In fact, studies in psychology show that a combination of descriptive writing (for example, what happened to me ...) *and* reflective writing (for example, how it affected me ...) can have the biggest positive impact on well being. This fits perfectly with our Digital Storytelling methods, which encourages work that blends these two approaches to narrating a story. And, as is true of art therapy practices, Silence Speaks workshops enable people to access multiple ways of conveying meaning in order to represent their experiences. While talking and writing go far, they do not tap into the visual and auditory modes of perception that come into play when we hear music or view still/moving images. For many workshop participants, looking at an old scrapbook, taking a photograph, or drawing a picture can be a profound starting point for crafting a story. If a traumatic experience rendered someone speechless in the past, a chance to not only describe what happened but also develop a visual portrait of the experience can be especially transformative. This is particularly true in the case of those who were very young and therefore pre-verbal when the trauma occurred.

But I shy away from convention and clichéd notions of "closure" and happy endings. When it comes to how violence is represented, I believe strongly that there is no linear path from "victim" to "survivor"; that we move in and out of these kinds of identities in a much more fluid way and learn ultimately how to cope with periodically resurfacing pain. One early Silence Speaks storyteller put it really well when she said, in her story, "You never really get over it; you just wake up one morning, and it's not the first thing you think about."

Joe: I had the experience early in the history of CDS that was particularly poignant to me of working with an incest survivor. I realized that for a survivor, going through the family album can be a painful journey into a territory of denial that is represented in the snapshots of "happy" family gatherings. In the specific piece, there was a photo of a parent, the father in this case, who was the abuser, and the image captured in the body language of the child, and even in the expression on her face, a sense of separation and distance. In working on her edit, she was able to deconstruct that image, to call attention to details, and take control of the meaning of the image in a new way. And as she talked about her experience, her voice added another layer of depth and complexity. It was enormously powerful.

Amy: Your story reminds me of a wonderful book that provided inspiration for me when I was starting Silence Speaks, *Home Movies and Other Necessary Fictions,* by Michelle Citron, a feminist filmmaker and theorist at the University of Chicago. She made a film that uses home movies from her family to explore power dynamics in her family. It was her way of taking ownership in a production sense, of experiences which when she was as a child had situated her on the other side of the camera. So she twists this around and takes on the role, in this case, of her father, who was the one with the camera when she was a child. She was quite well-versed in filmmaking and had the necessary production training to do this. As with your example, Silence Speaks creates a space where people who do not have these skills can access multimedia tools to explore a very similar process, to re-examine, explore, and reclaim events from their own lives. I think this is really groundbreaking. There is also a way in which some modes of creative arts or narrative therapy can be inappropriately clinical and over-professionalized and therefore not very accessible in a community context. The whole notion of talk therapy to begin with is a very Western, Anglo concept with really no parallel in many immigrant communities, indigenous communities, and various cultural communities around the world, particularly in the global South. So formal therapies can turn off many people, particularly people of color. As such, I am hesitant to align too closely with the therapeutic arena.

Joe: In that sense it relates more to the notions of co-counseling and peer counseling movements that have tried to position themselves not as oppositional to the professional medical priesthood, but as effective alternatives for a large number of people. Are there other adaptations in your practice?

Amy: In terms of adaptations, two early experiences informed my thinking for the work I've done more recently. First, in 2002, I taught a workshop with Navajo and Hopi women, sponsored by an organization in Arizona called Tuba City for Family Harmony. The participants really could not come for three days, with issues of jobs, childcare, and transportation, and such. So we rethought the workshop, and fortunately we had a small number of participants and were able to work one-on-one as counselors to assist them in making stories, each on her own timetable. They recorded their scripts, and did the editing, but we had to present software tutorials individually. This workshop also raised the potential for working with survivors who not only have experienced trauma in their own lives but also are carrying around a profound amount of historical grief due to the legacy of the American Indian genocide. This unfolding of trauma across generations at both the singular and societal level is something that I became eager to explore and indeed did go on to explore, at length, through a significant body of work in partnership with a South African NGO called Sonke Gender Justice Network. (To read about this project and view stories, visit www.genderjustice.org.za/digital-stories/tools/digital-stories.)

Later, in 2007, I taught a workshop in northern Uganda, with young people formerly involved with fighting forces in the country. This session served as a pilot for methods that I've subsequently used elsewhere in Uganda, as well as in Republic of Congo (Congo-Brazzaville), rural South Africa, and Nepal, to address extremely resource-poor settings and challenges of language and literacy. As with all Silence Speaks projects, the workshop was closely supported by a group of Ugandan counselors who had been working extensively with the young people to reintegrate them back into their home villages. I also engaged these counselors as interpreters/ translators; without them, the process of developing and recording scripts, and preparing subtitles (all of the stories are told in the participants' mother tongues), would have been impossible. I also adapted the concept of "participatory" that is such a cornerstone of the CDS method. It was not possible to access computers for each storyteller, so we supported them in taking photos on site and in drawing pictures, and then we did detailed storyboarding activities to enable the facilitators to edit the stories into finished videos. So the workshop was true to the core aspects of Digital Storytelling, as I see them: first person narrative; group process; and participatory production, even though the definition of "participatory" was modified to accommodate local circumstances.

Joe: There are a number of ethical considerations when you are working in resource-poor environments, and I think we have to be especially thoughtful about how the collaborators and the Digital Storytelling facilitators communicate with participants about expectations, follow-up, and the use of stories.

Amy: This has definitely been true of my extensive Silence Speaks work overseas, these past five or six years. Through the partnership with Sonke Gender Justice, I developed a clear model for how digital stories, as media artifacts, and Digital Storytelling, as a process, can impact Sonke's work at the individual, community, service provider, and policy levels. We have framed many of the Sonke Digital Storytelling workshops as collaborative ventures involving storytellers and facilitators in a joint process of creating useful public health education and advocacy media – as a way of avoiding confusion about story ownership, project purpose, and considerations of story distribution. And yet in spite of this clarity, storytellers have disagreed about who has "the right" to share particular stories, within close-knit communities, where story subjects may be known even if names are changed and images are blurred. And Sonke staff have struggled to feel comfortable sharing the stories, because of the profound reactions they inspire in viewers. To address these issues, we have worked together to create story discussion guides which lay out in detail the steps involved in ethically sharing stories, and we have trained Sonke staff on how to effectively use the stories in their ongoing work to promote gender equality and address gender-based violence and its linkages to HIV and AIDS. As we move forward, I want to find a way to use the work in a broader context of community organizing, and to develop more consistent follow-up with the agencies we partner with so we can better support them in sharing the stories in meaningful ways. Above all, a key part of our work lies in creating beauty out of situations that are not at all beautiful, in a way that touches people at a core emotional level and, hopefully, encourages critical thought and action against violence and oppression. And to be honest, many of the stories created in our workshops would absolutely not have been made in other community production environments which are still quite often excessively focused on technology tools and skills rather than on offering a safe and open space for reflection.

Joe: Somewhere there is a core theory in this work, related to the larger cultural democracy and arts and social change movements, in which there is an understanding that when people experience trauma, violence, oppression, what happens is a de-signification of their lives. The loss of power in being brutalized reflects itself in people feeling invisible. Cultural work is about re-signifying people, giving them tools to declare the value of their existence and insist on being heard. For better or worse, in our culture, there is a hierarchy of signifying presentations. At the top of that hierarchy is the screen; computer, television, and film. What I have seen is the actual lifting of spirit that occurs as people see their own images, hear their voices, and connect their stories to the medium of film and video. It is a particular dynamic that I don't believe is achieved in dance, music, theater, writing, or visual arts presentations. It is perhaps regrettable that these historic forms have been diminished in their significance as communications media in our culture. But, as my friend Guillermo Gomez Peña has jokingly suggested, the new existential question is "TV or not TV?" There have always been people that recognized this – filmmakers and video artists who have gone up the training and technical ladder and found the large financial resources to express themselves in media. But the idea that filmmaking can be a general literacy, available to a greater mass of people, which is becoming more and more possible with the advent of the digital and social media toolset, is profoundly different.

Amy: What you say points to why many self-identified professional filmmakers and multimedia journalists don't really know what to make of Digital Storytelling and in my experience are threatened by it, because it really breaks down the distinction between "creative professionals/artists" and the rest of us.

Joe: Again we are talking about a relationship between the lay practitioner and a priesthood. The priesthood is very aware that its power is predicated on the obfuscation of the knowledge possessed by priests.

Amy: Popular education theory and practice is relevant here, and has been instrumental to me in developing Silence Speaks. In sharing their own stories and listening to others, people can begin to make links between their personal struggles and the larger social struggles within their communities. Individual stories add up to the larger socio-political story. By starting with an analysis of how structural power informs your own problems, a particular kind of engaged political consciousness becomes possible.

Joe: But in doing Digital Storytelling we are saddled with an inelegant, feature ridden tool set that is regrettably laden with the dominant cultural male attitude of the more toys, the more bells and whistles, the more value is invested in the tools and gadgets …

Amy: Which is why Digital Storytelling work, Silence Speaks work, is so important with those who have been left out – poor people, people of color, women, LGBT and indigenous communities, immigrants and refugees – not only because of the enduring digital divide but because of the awareness that technology has evolved largely as the domain of privileged white males and has in fact been used specifically to categorize and scrutinize and "represent" marginalized groups in ways that are completely voyeuristic, disempowering, and exploitive.

Joe: Final thoughts?

Amy: I really do feel that the work Silence Speaks is doing in helping to provide a transformative experience for survivors of violence and other human rights abuses links us to a continuum of movements for health, economic, social, and political justice. Violence in all its forms – whether in the context of families, neighborhoods, institutions, or nation-states – is fundamentally a human rights violation. Allowing survivors to speak and insisting that their stories be truly heard heals all of us. And this may seem wildly optimistic, but I believe that as we are healed, we can perhaps heal our increasingly ailing world.

Author's Note: In the years since this interview was recorded, Silence Speaks has shifted primarily to an international program that positions personal narrative, in the form of digital stories, as a fundamental and strategic ingredient of education, training, community organizing, and policy advocacy work to promote gender equality and human rights. For more information: www.silencespeaks.org.

13

Stories from Fishing Lake, Alberta

Interview with Yvonne Pratt

When we met Yvonne Poitras Pratt, she was a PhD candidate with the Faculty of Communication and Culture, University of Calgary. She became a collaborator as part of our implementations around Alberta. She has since finished her PhD having completed her dissertation, "Meaningful Media: An Ethnography of a Digital Strategy within a Metis Community" (2011) We spoke in February, 2012.

Joe Lambert: How you were introduced to Digital Storytelling?

Yvonne Pratt: I encountered Digital Storytelling for the first time in my graduate studies program at the University of Calgary. I had been working on a large multi-institutional research project looking at broadband technologies in Alberta, Canada. Our provincial government had recently built a large broadband network called the Alberta SuperNet. I was part of the research team that was traveling across Alberta and looking at the ways that people were using this high bandwidth technology within their communities, within their everyday lives. We were looking at how this new technology allowed for multimodal forms of communication. This research moved beyond the original emphasis of the Alberta government who were initially focused on bringing the information and communication technology (ICT) services into public service buildings and not extending the signal out to the wider community.

So within that research project, I focused my work on the Aboriginal communities in Alberta. Aboriginal communities in Canada encompass the First Nations, the Métis – a people of mixed First Nation and European heritage – and the Inuit people. Through my community research, I found that the Aboriginal people were either having access issues based on a lack of affordability or that there was a general lack of awareness of the potential use for broadband in these communities.

Moreover, I found that there was a lack of culturally relevant and therefore meaningful use of the technology. The notion of "build it and they will come" was not what was needed in our communities especially given the history of colonization in our country. Sadly, our people have been severed from their cultures, through processes like the residential school system that was imposed on our people. Many Aboriginal people in Canada experienced a profound separation from their sense of cultural belongingness and roots. Families, in many cases, have been broken apart.

Yet, I also know from my own personal background that there is a real longing to reconnect with cultural traditions. Part of my Master's work was looking at the implementation of telecommunication technologies, like VoiceIP and videoconferencing and other broadband-assisted technologies, to help in cultural revitalization.

With these several interests in mind as well as my background research in broadband communications, I heard about a Digital Storytelling workshop that was being hosted by the Faculty of Social Work. I had a few acquaintances who had taken Digital Storytelling workshops. They suggested that I try a workshop. The work was led by CDS staff members Rob Kershaw from California and Michelle Spencer, from the Pincher Creek, Alberta area.

As it happened, my mother was in town at the time of the workshop, and it occurred to me that it would be really exciting to try to do an inter-generational story around my grandmother, my mother's mother. So I convinced her to come along with me and we embarked on pulling together a collaborative story.

Joe: Why was it important for you to create a story with your mother?

Yvonne: In thinking about the workshop, I felt a need to find a story that would be culturally relevant, something that could be used within our Aboriginal communities to affect positive social change. I thought to myself, wouldn't this be an absolutely wonderful way to pull together a story that would honor my grandmother, my mother's mother. My grandmother was a well-known community leader in the Fishing Lake community, and I felt this was a once in a lifetime opportunity to capture that legacy, and to do something that would speak to the community at a wider level than just simply an individual story. So with my mother in town and the workshop taking place, it was one of those things where the stars all aligned.

The individual story didn't have the same draw to me, and I think that speaks to the collective orientation of our people – an orientation drawn from our traditional lifestyle – where it's a very collective orientation. I recognized that the reclamation of that collective spirit is threatened in our communities. Part of the reason that we're struggling is we have the legacy of colonization impacting our people at a very deep level, at a very dysfunctional level, and many people in our communities are suffering.

Storytelling is a powerful way to reunite people and to get people talking again. Having my mom come that first day with me and to sit down and to go through the process took a lot of courage for my mother – courage to even enter that realm. It was in the university at the Faculty of Social Work, so I had to convince her that it was OK to enter that space, and to enter this unknown realm of Digital Storytelling. It was also a matter of convincing each other that the story of my grandmother would be for the greater good. There was that sense of responsibility, perhaps unique to our culture, that stories need to serve communities.

After this workshop, I watched a story by Jennifer LaFontaine (a former CDS staff member with Métis Heritage from southern British Columbia), and she had also taken a multi-generational perspective. And there was another young Métis woman here in Calgary who had made a digital story on her own for an Aboriginal literature class. She intuitively went to an inter-generational story format told about her father.

It spanned time. She had her voice as a child talking to herself as a young person, but all the time she's telling a story about her father. So this was fascinating to me. This need to connect across generations, this is a current that underlies our worldview, our orientation to the world.

Joe: What was unique for you in the workshop process?

Yvonne: In this first workshop, my Mom and I were the only partnered story in our workshop. Not too surprisingly, we went into the story circle with two different stories. I started off with one story, but my mother had her own version of it. We walked away from that first day saying, "OK, we're seeing two different sides of the box, and we've got to create one single story."

Once we got to the gist of the story and found a perspective that we were both comfortable with, I actually thought that we were better off by going through the partnered process. I find that by not being individual-focused you can get to a deeper level of meaning. So for us, it was like the story circle didn't end, we were able to continue the dialogue over the first two days.

That struggle revolved around how do we present on the one hand a very public story, but at the same time, a very private one. It took a lot of emotional work to get to a place where we both were happy with the way that the story worked. The story hid parts of the message, but at the same time honored that person that was our relative.

I think reconciling that story about our grandmother has shifted some of the ways our family is now telling stories. Everybody seems to be more interested now in pulling out their old photos, and everybody's coming together and trying to reconstruct that path to our history, a history that was taken away from us or silenced.

Joe: I find that the role of memory given a history of colonization, of rupture caused by history, makes inter-generational discussion difficult for many communities. Different generations don't have the same perspective about the need to uncover the pain that exists in community memory. And the younger generation finds itself negotiating their perceptions of why revisiting the story necessary, whereas the older generation might feel like they want to protect the younger generation from all that misery, precisely because it was very sad and very painful.

Yvonne: I absolutely agree, definitely. You can multiply that understanding, when you look at the specific history of colonization within our Métis community. Our leader, Louis Riel, was hung by the Canadian government in the late 1800s. Our people were pushed out of their homelands. The Canadian government essentially waged a civil war against the Métis people. They shot their own people.

The tragedy of colonization in Canada tends to be the elephant in the room that nobody wants to acknowledge. When I teach this history, my non-Aboriginal students tend to feel a lot of discomfort in addressing these issues. In Canada, we like to perceive ourselves as this peaceful, tolerant, multi-cultural nation, but the truth of the matter is that we colonized, and continue to colonize, our own people. That history has not been fully understood, fully made evident, and the silence about that history only deepens the pain.

So what drives me in my work is my belief that we need to acknowledge this history. In many cases, the Métis are written out of Canadian history. We cannot let that happen. My mom grew up with the derogatory term "half breed." Her family had stones thrown at them by the newcomers that came into our ancestral homelands. So she built up a protective layer. And that layer creates gaps in memory, silences about the specifics of how our Métis communities experienced colonization. The thrust of my life's work is to address how we can close those gaps.

That is why it occurred to me, as my mom and I made our story, that we were engaged in a process of healing. We were doing more than just creating a story. And I could see the potential of this work being applied across communities such as ours. I recognized that Digital Storytelling was a very powerful and meaningful way to use technology in Aboriginal communities.

Joe: How did you feel this related to the broadband implementations and other efforts connected to your research?

Yvonne: Our research team had a whole suite of equipment and we were hooking up through video-conferencing across the province. Working with academics in British Columbia as well as Alberta, we had a dog and pony show where we travelled around and set up video conferencing systems in local communities. As part of the work, we were bringing scholars in from all over the western provinces to engage in discussions with community people. We were actively using the technologies, and I was also working in website development related to the project. These systems acted as a collaborative tool, connecting a team of forty or so researchers. So I, along with my colleagues, were actively trying to realize the full potential of appropriate ICT for community empowerment, across non-Aboriginal and Aboriginal communities. So I was already searching for best practices and methods that might be applied to these efforts.

And in that context I began to look at some of the UNESCO materials that addressed the importance of the cultural element within development work. In too many projects, I believe that the essential cultural element is missing. Vast amounts of money are invested every year into international development programs, and people were left shaking their heads, wondering why certain projects failed. What I was seeing at least from an Indigenous perspective was that cultural element was missing. You could come in and teach all the Microsoft applications you want, but if you didn't get the people excited about the technology, and have them see themselves within the technology, then these projects are simply not sustainable.

Pushing technology simply for technology's sake, does not excite our communities. It does not lead to community members talking to each other. I believe Digital Storytelling engages people in talking about their own stories. And as people get really excited about their stories, the technology fades to the background and the personal relationships come to the forefront.

Joe: So your interest in Digital Storytelling was part of your own reclaiming of connection to the historical community of your grandmother, in Fishing Lake, Alberta. This led to the project where CDS worked with you to implement a Digital Storytelling program within this community. Tell us the story of how this came about?

Yvonne: I was working as a consultant for the Alberta government doing a technology assessment within the different communities. I knew that I had a treasure with the digital stories, and by that time I had completed a second workshop on my return to school in conjunction with the Native Centre based at the University of Calgary. Once again, I witnessed the power of digital stories.

Through the workshop experience I saw the wealth of feelings and emotions that emerged from those stories. And I realized what people can uncover when they dig deep enough, supported by the appropriate facilitators.

There is history, there is healing – you have seen some of the stories about incidents with the Catholic Church in Fishing Lake's history, where there was abuse of some of the community members up there by church authorities. At times the soul of stories that arise are shameful stories. These are stories that have been hidden, or stuffed away, and sort of silenced. Yet I also believed that if we showed, or if I showed, the stories to the right group of people, they would get it, and that was certainly my experience.

This was incredibly powerful, and I felt Digital Storytelling was the missing piece to the technology puzzle of the Alberta SuperNet. Why weren't community members excited about the Alberta SuperNet? Why was uptake so low? Because, I argued, the community members do not have anything driving them. We needed passion – passion that comes with the power of reclamation, the cultural renewal, that is an essential part of the storytelling process, before we would get meaningful use of this technology.

So when I met up with Susie Barthel, the Fishing Lake Education, Employment and Training Director, and Rick Chalifoux then chair of Fishing Lake – at a government meeting, I pulled them aside and said – "I'd really like to show you these two stories." I shared the stories and they were both taken. Right away they said "We'll, we've gotta do this!" That began our journey of trying to get our Fishing Lake project up and running.

Fishing Lake had already undergone an in-depth quantitative assessment of technology in their community. So they had visual diagnostic material that showed that they had skills in their community to succeed with a larger technology program, but the local people just didn't seem that excited about its use since utilization scores were low. Susie and Rick, however, bought into the idea that technology could be useful in their communities.

I knew that my timing had to be just right. I stepped in, I showed them my stories and the dialogues started and we began working hard to try to find funding. It was also at this point that I started collaborating with Rob Kershaw from CDS, and his support and encouragement were critical to keeping our dreams alive.

It did not start easily, during the two-year development period, we were turned down by both the federal and the provincial government, which was very disheartening. But at the very end of our timeline for development, I got a last-minute invitation to come up to Fishing Lake to show our stories to a group of our elders. I sat there and watched them, excited, anxious but still with a smile hidden inside. I could tell they were engaged as they saw familiar faces and voices up on the wall of the seniors' lodge. The looked at me expectantly after the showing, "Is that all there is?"

And I said, "Well, now it's your turn. Literally, it's your turn. You get to tell the stories." That got them revved up about the project, I knew there was no doubt in their minds that Fishing Lake should have a Digital Storytelling program. And once the elders were convinced, then the political people knew that they would need to find a way to make it happen.

Joe: As I understand it, the essence of the proposal was economic development, right?

Yvonne: Yes, but we knew what we really wanted was the cultural revitalization. We knew we wanted the storytelling. We knew we wanted community members to feel empowered by this media. But we had to pitch it as economic development. Both the federal and provincial government saw technological skills development as critical to economic development. So we knew that we needed the storywork to make the technology engagement process work, and all of this would assist in the larger resiliency of Fishing Lake and its economic future.

As it happened, the community had just gone through a tough few years, where we had lost thirteen of our elders. And we knew that we had lost the wealth of their knowledge. We needed to view this as an urgent moment, to begin to capture the stories of elders. So people in the community, leaders in the community felt that we had had enough rejection from the government. They decided then and there that a portion of their settlement budget would be put aside to make sure this project happened.

Joe: We know that in many of these projects, there tends to be a grand inversion of the priorities for successful development work, from our perspective. The focus on the number of software programs learned, and certificates in specific technical skill sets, precede the analysis of who people are, what communities need, and what options will exist for people to use the acquired skills in ways that both serve and develop community wellbeing. Community cultural development, as a first step to healthy economic development, is still considered a marginal perspective in development planning. We have to convince people that having a computer lab available is not in itself of value. We use the metaphor of story – of the importance of capturing stories as oral history, as community memory – as a sense of the healthy root to the tree of community development. The growth and expansion, much less the eventual flowering and fruit of the tree, can only happen if the roots are healthy, if the roots are always tended and supported. But we still recognize that story work is viewed as "softer", or less tangible in terms of metrics, than checking the box that says a person just passed a proficiency test in a given version of a word processor or spreadsheet software. Not that we do not see these a critical life skills, it is just that you should believe your story counts for something as the basis for learning a writing tool and a way to process numbers. For me, the cultural implications of data-centric development is just an extension of the Western colonial mindset. The insistence on success defined by how well you use the dominant cultures mechanisms of communication outweighs the need for communities to hold on to their sacred, their ancient ways of communicating, of learning, of supporting sustainable life in context of a given environment. Of course our work is much, much more than primary source recordings, or oral history projects, it has at the center a message of reclamation, by each individual, by every community, of what has been forgotten, our essential dignity as beings.

And this idea is an old story. One that is being reclaimed by many communities. People like you and your community leadership are saying, "No actually, story is our learning modality, and story is our cultural archival mechanism, and story is the way we process experience." It seems to me that as you said, your community knew that, and they saw also in the stories you showed them that this would be an appropriate mechanism for engaging the community in a thoughtful way about the use of technology.

Yvonne: Yes, absolutely. Once people heard these voices, the stories from their own community, it just energized them. Fishing Lake, like many Aboriginal communities, is quite isolated and remote. People can be shy, but we sit close to the tradition of oral story telling, and it's not been that long since we've relied on these multi-sensory storytelling learning experiences. To me, those are peak learning experiences, and those are lifetime lessons. There is so much more than sitting and reading. My dissertation uses the phrase "meaningful media," a phrase I chose carefully, because Digital Storytelling is built on elements of a participatory approach to media, where there is agency for the learners, for the users of a new communication technology. The heart of this work is to allow the community to seize hold of media practices, so that they see and hear themselves within the media. Digital Storytelling was an absolute natural fit for what I wanted to do as an academic, for what I thought my community really needed.

Joe: Share the project experience, not only what worked, but also some of the challenges of implementing a workshop like this in a Métis community in rural Alberta.

Yvonne: You want the low-down? You want the real story? [laughs]

Joe: To the degree to which you feel that you have the responsibility to protect names and defend the innocent, you can leave that out.

Yvonne: I knew darn well that the standard workshop format was not going to fly in Fishing Lake Métis Settlement. I knew it. Why? Because I know my people. On the one hand there was Rob, representing CDS, trying to be professional, organized, and have everything in place, and Susie at the other end going, "Listen, girlfriend, if I can get people in the room we're going to be happy."

So I knew we would have to adapt the model. Starting with outreach and participation. The workshop was for eight to ten people, that was ideal. But I spoke with Susie, and she said, "The folks in the community are scared. They are absolutely scared. If I can pull this off, it'll be a miracle." She said, "so don't be pushing me for lists."

I have found this is normal, people in a community are curious about a process, but that does not mean they will stop their lives to participate in something new. But we also had the elders' blessing, and more importantly their support, and that helped enormously.

But people still really had no idea what to expect, despite our attempts at providing descriptions of the process. People may think of a workshop as software training, or learning how to use cameras, or just dropping in to be interviewed. Susie had not taken a workshop, so it was not easy for her to describe how powerful the experience would be. She knew how a story looked, but not how an individual, with no prior training could make it. I, on the other hand, knew how much work was involved and I knew how much effort it was going to take.

Rob and I were chatting, and he was looking for those hard numbers of participants and details of outreach and follow-up, and a discussion of how the stories would be used, and project outcomes. I wasn't giving them to him, because I didn't have them.

Then, I had Susie calling me up and saying, "If I get another request for project outcomes,….listen, we just want you guys here, that's all we know."

I picked Rob up at the airport. I didn't know what to expect, and he didn't know what to expect. So when Rob asked me what I thought would take place, and knowing that Fishing Lake had zero idea of what was going to happen in the next few days, I said, "Chaos. Absolute chaos. Mayhem." That's precisely what we entered.

Rob, to his credit, looked at me and said, "OK." It is my belief that once you give up control of the process, and give in to the faith that surrounds storytelling, you enter a different realm.

It's not a very organized or even giving realm. It takes a lot out of you. You have to give everything you have in you. On Tuesday, after being in the community for two days, and we'd encountered everything from snakes entering the community building to elders being afraid to enter the story telling circle to … all kinds of things going on like community people, coming in and coming out … peering over shoulders, giving their own directions. I had a little red book where I was trying to keep track of my pairings of youth and elder, and it was continually getting changed.

I could see, by Tuesday, that Rob was aware that this was not going to roll out as neatly, as nicely as a standard workshop. He looked over at me after everybody left and said, "You know this is crazy, Yvonne, we're not going to get through it."

Quite frankly I was feeling much the same way at that moment. It took all the resources I had to keep the faith going but I knew we could do it – in fact, we had to do it. I focused on the achievement of one youth, one of our young male members who worked with a man named old Joe on the first day. That Tuesday morning the young man hadn't come in. We had made it clear that he was to be working with Joe. He came in around lunch time, I said to him, "Gee, Matt, where have you been?" Teasing him, thinking maybe he had slept in. He gave me this look. And Matt said, "I just sat for the last four hours with Old Joe listening to his stories." He held up the recorder and said "I've got them all here!"

At the end of that day, when Rob was on the ground, and I was almost there with him, I said, "You know what? Matt talked to Old Joe for four hours today, and quite frankly I'm happy. We got that, and that's good enough." And that was a pivotal moment. That's when the energy changed and we had to grab up the reins and save it and march forward. And it did, it changed the energy of the workshop because we knew that what we were trying to do is a very difficult thing.

So even the slightest evidence of hope of some kind of healing between those generations meant something. We had to hang on to the smallest connection with both hands and place our faith there. It's amazing because you're a facilitator, and you know this better than anybody, that a lot hinges on the way that you're in that room, in that space. To me, just finding that tiniest particle of hope allowed us to move forward. I can't even describe the mayhem that happened for the next few days. But we kept faith.

You simply had to be in the moment and create as you went. We had people bringing in guitars and trapping equipment. And we had, in some cases, a glut of information, a boxful of photos and memorabilia. In other cases, we had people that simply didn't show up. And so you were trying to create something out of nothing.

It was an incredibly intense experience.

Joe: All I can say is every one of those stories exist in various parts of the aches and pains in my body. I'm an old theater producer, so the idea of a train wreck just before you get the show up is an old tradition for me. And I'm sure part of the form, for better or worse, reflects, a poor theater approach to getting things done. You invent a lot, and you don't throw money at the problem, because you don't have the money to throw at the problem. You invent out of the process. And because it's community-engaged, of course you know the conditions of the community. Their oppression exists as instability. And that means you are working in the fluidity of whatever little pieces of stability that you're buying through the process, meaning you're giving them a moment to step out of what may be a daily chaos. Not to overstate this idea, because there are certainly people who sit in communities very strongly and hold center the communities. But for many members of communities that are living the legacy of colonialism, it is, in fact, still actively manifests as constant chaos and constant inability to hold center long enough to take a step forward.

Yvonne: That is exactly what we were experiencing. And to try to wrap that in a strict structure, felt to me almost like an act of re-colonization.

Joe: In the way that you told the story, there is an enormous amount of learning. We discuss issues of context and adjustments in perspective based on context. What you described is an ideological gulf. On the one hand some of us, coming from the Western perspective, hear that a level of what is perceived as disorganization is a form of moral failure. We have a controlling mentality. It is part of the air I breathe. It is what I am asked to do everyday. I am supposed to operate within those contexts, just as you have learned in an academic context. To then put on a perspective of relaxed awareness in the moment and vast flexibility, is amazingly difficult.

Growing up with two parents who were political organizers in the South, I was given that idea of patience. This isn't going to happen in 50 years, it's not going to happen in 100 years, we're undoing a great damage, and it will take many, many generations of good work. It seems to me, our ability to hold this awareness while we negotiate between these different modalities, government regulatory bodies, funding outcomes, expectations of visible results, that are both useful mechanisms of accountability, but also ideologies, mythic perspectives about how one "fixes" certain social problems, in many ways, this is the trick of story work, of community cultural development. It is as if we are working on vastly different time scales. And obviously the best and most aware work is done by people from a community, in their community, for their community.

While it may be good that professionals engage to initiate the process, in the end, it is best for people that live and work within those communities and understand the rhythms of those communities to lead a process. I have learned the hard way that the rhythm of the schedule I bring from the outside, has nothing to do with the rhythm of the schedule inside a community.

But negotiating this awareness, these unconscious ideologies, is about living in a spirit of gentle diplomacy as much as learning the ethics and refinements of cultural competency in social work. I'm fascinated by the negotiative role that the Métis played within the Canadian culture, and how this informs your view of the world.

There is a new negotiation with a culture of making media, for example. As the stories are shown outside the community with community involvement there's a new negotiation between what is sacred inside that community as it engages the mainstream. And then there is the negotiation as a lever through story to talk about how we not only redress the historic inequities, but that we forge a new model of respect and dignity in our future.

Joe: Do you think story and story work play a big role in these contemporary negotiations between the historically colonizing populations and the colonized?

Yvonne: For those of us who have a degree of distance from the colonial factor, I believe the notion of giving back to our communities is front and center for many of us. Our work tends to be more intuitive, than analytical. It's innate in our being as Indigenous people, and I think one of the more reassuring things is that I have found fellow Indigenous scholars who spoke about that imperative to work with the communities, our own communities, and to effect some kind of social change, positive social change. That's not always celebrated within an academic environment. So I may be painted as a radical because I profess to do this type of work, but I do not apologize for it.

In fact, when I entered the doctoral program and had this opportunity, I knew my approach was going to make a lot of people uncomfortable, not only the academics, but also the community members. But I thought it just wasn't right. It wasn't right that I had to either apologize for my cultural heritage or I had to hide it. Having gone through the rigours of graduate school and being introduced to many Western notions and theoretical models that didn't fit me, I finally realized that I did not need to be apologetic. I needed to say, these models, of the dispassionate researcher, as the objective analyst, as someone more concerned about neutrality than the needs of my community, these models don't fit me.

After all these years of learning, probably the biggest lesson for me is that you have to be who you are, and where who you are, and do what feels right. That's precisely what I was finally getting empowered to do. Part of what I had to do throughout my training as an academic was decolonize myself and quit feeling bad that certain Western theoretical models, that certain theory, was not suiting my purposes in life. Instead, I really wanted to make a difference.

As I went through this process, I realized that there also had to be some sense made out of my past. There had to be reasons why things happened the way they did. Those stories had to come out, in order for me to see who I was as an individual. I was being very selfish in this work, which was difficult, because who doesn't want to be portrayed as selfless in a process, but I understood that this is what I needed to do – I needed to heal myself as part of my journey. It was what I needed to do to understand the relations of my own family, to encompass what was going on in my extended family, my historical community, and within the larger histories of colonization. There was a selfish purpose because decolonization of myself had to occur first.

That is something that I felt very strongly about, and if I couldn't do it, I was not willing to engage anymore with academia. There were several points where I thought, if I can't do this, then I'm not continuing. Because if I could not look at my own story, my family's story, as part of my research perspective, then the work didn't have the same purpose, the same meaning to it. I simply would not have the same drive.

Joe: In my own journey, I have come to trust the engine of my faith in my work lives in my ancestral past, good and bad. I believe the voices of the ancestral past actually drive us in ways that we do not always know. While Western science may not know what that looks like, in terms of biochemistry or genetic predispositions to avoid the tragedies of human folly, I have learned, as much from my privilege of work with Indigenous communities as any other, that ancestors speak through you. In a workshop I just experienced, I could almost feel, and I think others did as well, that there in the room, the ancestor was speaking through a person and asking them to do things. You hear it as an echo of a voice that is not just the voice of the storyteller.

But of course it's an echo. It's the echo of your grandmother's song in your two-year-old bedroom. It's the echo of what your mother said to you at nine about something that happened at school. It's an echo in all these voices. It is a knowing, a certainty you feel inside yourself, that eventually dignity will be reclaimed. That the shame that was caused by the oppression will be overcome, in time, through the multi-generational process of remembrance. And understanding this is not just a cognitive event. I am willing to just leave it as a mystery – a mystery that most rooted cultures hold as cosmology.

Yvonne: Agreed. After I wrote a particularly hard chapter in my dissertation, where I had to bare my soul and be more vulnerable than I care to be, I had such vivid dreams. And dreams are part of how I set my course. I've been lucky enough to have some spiritual experiences. These things drive me. I allude to them. I don't make them too public. But definitely, there is something driving me. I've felt that throughout my life. Even with my upbringing, it was always, "Why is this going on? This shouldn't be going on."

In the academic world, some of my advisors would ask, "What are your plans?" and I'd say, "You probably don't want to hear this, but I will pray. I will pray every morning, and the answer will come." That's how I set my life course. I realize that makes many academics uncomfortable... When everything falls into place, even though it might be very unnerving, then it just makes sense to me.

With Fishing Lake, I am sitting back and waiting because that's what needs to be done. I need to be respectful of the time they need. At the same time, a fire's been lit in that community, and there's a lot of talk around these stories. There is an incredible power of those stories right now in the community. They are sitting at a cusp and incredible things can happen for them.

At the same time, it might be a double-edged sword. Things could go very wrong. There is fear. The support we have could change. We are reminded that the provincial and federal authorities did not originally support this work

The stories have incredible power. We presented the work last week in Vancouver. There were people openly sobbing in the room. Men, openly sobbing. People that you have no connection to walk into a room and view the stories and hear us talking about the process of the story project and they were so moved.

Joe: It is very humbling to know you were part of that, as a facilitator you are often speechless. What are your aspirations about how this work can make a difference for the communities you work with, but also in the broadest sense for other communities who have faced the historical trauma of colonization. Do you think this is helping?

Yvonne: That's a big question. What I do is driven by the community, and I absolutely allow them to lead the way with what they want to do. I know the potential of the stories. I have my own aspirations, but they are not what will drive what happens to those stories, or to the larger storytelling process. The stories are alive again, and so we have to treat them with deep respect. In my ideal world, those stories would be protected, and the community would have no fear about how and when the stories would be used for healing and connection.

But you can do all the healing you want within a community, but as a nation, as a country, if we want to heal our aboriginal, and our non-aboriginal groups, we have to share these types of stories. I feel it is important that the people of Fishing Lake hear and see the external world's reactions to their stories. Just as it fed my soul, I am sure it would be helpful for others.

I have this wonderful opportunity to project these stories, but I also have to respect that the community is at a place where they need to just sit with them. I have to be respectful.

I look forward to the community members presenting those stories and sparking dialogue between our various indigenous groups. There is so much racism in our northern parts of our province. These stories could start the dialogue, could start the healing. I have included N. Scott Momaday and Gerald Vizenor's work in my dissertation, because they talk about sacred space. When you share those stories, there is a sacred space that is created. That was my approach when I presented the stories in Fishing Lake. I set the context as a sacred space. What was beautiful to me that it felt like the only time I've seen the community that quiet at a public event. That room was hushed as those stories played, as we showed the power and the sacredness of the stories.

At day's end, I often say if I don't wake up tomorrow morning I feel like I've done something that has set my soul free. I absolutely feel I could leave this earth and be quite content because of the work that we did in Fishing Lake. Honestly, I have no idea where it's going but those stories have a life of their own. I am going to do everything possible to protect them and to make sure that they grow and that they are shared in a respectful way.

I am appreciative of having worked with CDS staff. I have seen how they give of themselves. They give fully to these story tellers which in turn enables them to have their stories told in a beautiful, a meaningful way.

Joe: We stand on the shoulders of people who gave of themselves and taught us that story. We learned to hold that center. And we are trying to stay true to those who came before us. I am deeply gratified that you feel that it has been useful to your community. And I am excited about our continuing collaboration in the future.

14

Humanizing Healthcare

A Conversation with Pip Hardy and Tony Sumner, Pilgrim Projects/Patient Voices

Along our journey into Digital Storytelling, we have never been far from issues of health and wellbeing. Since our earliest workshops, stories of people's confrontation with severe illness, the journey through the healthcare system, and recovery, have emerged. And given the call to meaning within our work, many stories have dealt with the loss of someone to illness, and have included narratives about the experience within different healthcare settings.

In the late 1990s, we began to see initiatives in the healthcare field – organizations interested in stories of cancer survivors, the celebration of successful healthcare practices, disability, hospice care, and public health issues. In 2006, we learned of the Patient Voices program of Pilgrim Projects, an organization based in Cambridge, England, that had begun to develop extensive healthcare work in Digital Storytelling. The deeply committed work of Pip Hardy and Tony Sumner has become an inspiration to all of us in the field.

Joe Lambert: How did you get involved in Digital Storytelling?

Pip Hardy and Tony Sumner: We have always used stories as an important element of the text-based and online education programs and learning materials we've developed over the last twenty-five years. In 2003, we were trying to bring the patient's voice into e-learning materials about healthcare quality improvement, and we stumbled across a community history digital story. It seemed to us that this digital technique of telling and sharing stories was the perfect way to convey the important stories of healthcare in a digital medium.

Our hope was that by bringing the very human element of stories back into healthcare education and service improvement programs, we could contribute to the huge task of humanizing a healthcare system that was increasingly characterized by targets and checkboxes, audits and statistics. We often have said that statistics tell us the system's experience of the individual, whereas stories tell us the individual's experience of the system.

Joe: How did your work in Digital Storytelling evolve?

Pip and Tony: The main emphasis of our work has always been on the facilitation of others to tell their stories and share them digitally. We began working with individual patients and care-providers in late 2003, adopting a home-grown approach, and using very open questions to elicit a story about healthcare in relation to values such as equity, dignity, respect, trust, etc. At that point, it would be a further two years before we learned about CDS.

Joe: So can you tell me something about making your own first digital stories?

Pip and Tony: Actually, our very first story was a collaborative effort between the two of us, facilitated by our friend Brendan Routledge in late 2003. It was a little piece, created in order to investigate the technology. It was a community history piece, but the community in question was the flock of doves in our back garden. It was driven by the images, which Pip assembled into a visual story using Windows MovieMaker. When the time came for recording, Tony ad libbed the voiceover and that was "Dove Story."

Eventually Pip discovered the existence of CDS as part of her research for her master's program and came to California to attend an introductory workshop in March 2006.

Pip: It happened to be a facilitator-training workshop (although I was attending as a first-timer). My story was about my relationship with my father, who had died the previous year. Tony had found a picture of the house where I was born in an old Sunset magazine and that provided the prompt for the story.

I remember being incredibly impressed with your comments when I sat with you, Joe. You seemed to understand exactly what I was trying to say.

As someone with a degree in English who has earned a living by writing for many years, developing the script wasn't too difficult for me, although the input from you, Emily, and others in the story circle was invaluable. But I did need a lot of help with Premiere and Photoshop – the use of layers still eludes me today – but was, of course, really pleased with the way the story came out. I learned a lot about my father – and myself – through making the story, and the real power of the Digital Storytelling workshop became apparent to me.

When I showed my story to my half-sister, Lucia, she decided she had to make one as well. She attended a workshop in June and then we both attended the next workshop designed especially for facilitators. My second story turned out to be a much darker piece than I had anticipated. I remember having heart palpitations for a couple of weeks before the workshop and I could barely breathe on the story circle day, but miraculously, since completing that story, there have been no more palpitations and I feel that creating that story helped me to walk past a particular dragon that prevailed over much of my life.

Tony: My first story emerged from a master class held here in Cambridge with you and Emily in April of 2007. One of the reasons Pip and I work in concert together so well is the complementary and mutually supportive nature of our respective skills. As someone who has been involved in software industries since 1981, the technology is not a problem for me, but instead, an entertaining and intellectual puzzle or challenge.

As a sometime-physics graduate, creative writing has never figured obviously in my career path, although I have spent many years developing learning materials with Pip. So, for me the challenge and the benefit lies in the creation and perfection of the story script. Despite that, several of my stories have come, like the first one did, as one of those eureka moments at four in the morning.

Having worked on a story during the first day of the "scar" prompt in the workshop, I found the space to reflect on scars and healing, and what they meant in my recent experience. When this reflection was combined with the catalytic and sharing input of other storytellers – some of whom were friends and colleagues – seeded and brought to life within me a story about how I had felt regarding my mother's very recent treatment for breast cancer.

I woke up early on the second morning scrabbling for a pencil and paper, wanting to write a story in which the language mirrored my experience of the inhuman, unfamiliar, specialized Latinate argot – mastectomy, unilateral, biopsy, etc. – that characterized for me the way that the medical establishment had used language to protect and distance itself whilst interacting with my mother.

I deliberately wrote the story using as few words as possible, to be delivered in a staccato and mechanical fashion because that was how I felt my mother's care had been, despite being clinically effective and, indeed, successful.

Although the story was still very present in my mind when I read it in the story circle on that second day, it was still a deeply reflective and affecting experience.

I've written several other stories since, but for me, the most enjoyable part of Digital Storytelling is actually in facilitating others in coming to terms (as I did) with their own experiences and emotions.

Joe: In your own experience, why do you think Digital Storytelling is useful as a reflective practice?

Pip and Tony: For us there are three sides to the reflective prism that Digital Storytelling provides. First, there is the opportunity afforded to the viewer of a digital story to reflect on his or her own practice (and the practice of others). Sometimes seeing someone else's story about how they made a decision they might now regret can open the viewer's eyes to assess their own practice. This can be especially helpful for nurses, doctors and other people involved in healthcare. Second, there is the opportunity for storytellers to reflect on life experiences and consider the most effective and affective way of conveying their stories. Storytellers tell us that the process changes them. One initially quiet, even reticent, storyteller says, "I feel as though I could talk to anyone now." And we now have people coming back to make stories that are reflections of the impact that going through the Digital Storytelling process has had on their lives. And third, there is the opportunity for us as Digital Storytelling facilitators to reflect on our practice of DS facilitation and our own life experiences.

Also, our own reflective process has two main strands: The first strand is that our post-workshop wash-up meetings always reveal some small way in which we can better meet the needs of storytellers, whether through some smoothing of the technological first steps that they face, or through some refinements of the range of interpersonal skills and approaches that we use to engage storytellers and help them find the heart of their stories. The second strand of our program includes six weeks of once-weekly supervised meetings with an experienced counseling supervisor. It is in these reflective meetings that we are often able to identify issues of transference, and recognize where our own issues and experiences may be affecting our ability to be clear and available for storytellers. We feel these meetings are essential in maintaining our own psychological and emotional well-being, and the safety of the storytellers with whom we work.

As to why DS is so useful, we think it's a combination of things. First, it's a bit like having three days – or twenty-four hours – of individual and group therapy! If we do our job right, people have the experience of being listened to and having their stories heard, often for the first time.

Digital Storytelling and the rigorous process of script revision offers a wonderful opportunity to reflect on our own experiences, and those of others. Delving deeply into the meaning of a story, refining it, and distilling it to reveal its essence can help us to see it differently. Thich Nhat Hanh expresses it nicely: "According to the law of reflection, the perceiver and the perceived have a very close link. When the angle of incidence changes, the angle of reflection will change immediately."

This process of distillation is a gradual process, with the story getting a bit stronger and then a bit stronger again until there is what one of our colleagues describes as a story characterized by "purity, clarity and potency" – the characteristics of any good distillation! There is something about getting rid of much of the substance in order to get to the essence and people can then see the experiences of their lives with a new clarity.

Or put another way, stories spring from, and are linked to, people's past and current life experiences. Inevitably then, within the process of reflecting upon and distilling their digital story, storytellers are given the opportunity, space, and tools with, and within which, to reflect upon their own life stories. If they get to the essence of their story they usually have a better grasp of the essence of the experience.

There is also something about seeing the final story on the big screen at the end of the workshop – things hitherto buried are now out in the open and outside of the storyteller, creating a new kind of freedom. As one storyteller has said, "When you've made your digital story, you don't have to hold it in your head any more. You can put it behind you and it doesn't take up any more space, so you can move on. You've named the beast."

Joe: What is unique to your approach to Digital Storytelling?

Pip and Tony: We have tried to take our original open and facilitative approach to education and blend it with the very best elements of CDS' approach, and with our particular mix of personal and professional skills and life experiences from counseling and group work, teaching, writing and editing, software development, educational materials design and project management to develop our own subtle variant of the process. We feel this is well suited to the vulnerable people with whom we work in health and social care – patients, service users, care-providers (and even clinicians and educators!).

As our original intention was always to create an educational resource, we have come at DS slightly differently, but because we also know that healing and learning are closely connected, we are able to combine the various elements that will, hopefully, contribute to both.

People have described our approach as caring, nourishing, and mindful, and we try very hard to ensure that those qualities are always present in every encounter.

Joe: Pip, can you tell us more about your background and how it has shaped your work?

Pip: Well, my background has been more in education than in therapy, although, as I said earlier, I think the two are closely linked. I've always been interested in non-traditional forms of education, those approaches that really help people to learn, rather than just pouring in information. So I trained as a Montessori teacher and eventually ended up in adult education, working first with unemployed and homeless people and then moving on to teach communication and what was once known in the UK as "liberal studies" – an opportunity for people training to be hairdressers and bricklayers and carpenters to engage with movies and books and discussions about what makes us human. Gradually I moved into writing and editing open learning materials with a real focus always on the learner, and trying to find ways of translating the qualities of a good teacher – someone who motivates and stimulates and informs and encourages and guides and inspires and so on – into written words that would offer people who had missed out on education an opportunity to follow some of their dreams. Of course, I read Carl Rogers, and being a child of the 1960s, I was pretty interested in self development and becoming more aware. I became interested in Buddhism in the late 1970s and that has really underpinned my life and work in different ways.

After working for quite a few years in education, I trained as a psychodynamic counselor and did some group work. I started training as a homoeopath but practicalities meant that I had to return to the world of educational development. But the common themes running through all this have always been around looking at people as a whole – whether you are offering education or healing.

In fact, the dissertation I wrote for the counseling course was an exploration of different ways of viewing and understanding the self – from a Buddhist perspective and a psychodynamic perspective – and an attempt to see whether the two could work in harmony to promote healing. That was some time ago now, and Buddhist approaches are now commonly adopted in the talking therapies – but it wasn't so common back in the dim and distant past of the last century!

Buddhist practice, with its emphasis on being in the present moment and the need to be aware of what's going on in both body and mind, provides the foundation for cultivating understanding and compassion that are all too often missing in both education and healthcare. Such an approach affords an opportunity to link past experiences with current understandings, learning, and healing, and is essential to the functioning of a successful story circle – the core of our practice as DS facilitators. In all of these said traditions, stories play a huge part in leading people to new ways of understanding.

So, as our practice has developed, we have become aware from feedback and responses (and indeed, follow-up stories!), that many people experience the process in ways they describe as "cathartic," "therapeutic," "retreat-like," "transformative," and even "spiritual." Whether this is partly due to the aspects of counseling, group work, and Buddhist practice that I bring to our work, or whether it's inherent in the DS process is debatable. I think that having an awareness of what may be going on for people is an important part of the role of any DS facilitator. If nothing else, it seems to make people feel safe to know that there is this strong ethical and therapeutic underpinning to our work. And, of course, if they feel safe, they are more likely to tell truly authentic stories.

Joe: In healthcare, there are many concerns about patient's rights; protecting people's anonymity; not exploiting the suffering of others as part of the promotional efforts of healthcare agencies. How have you addressed these concerns?

Pip and Tony: Because of the area in which we work, and the nature of our storytellers, one of our key concerns has always been to wrap an appropriate and open ethical consent and release process around the Digital Storytelling experience which would protect and empower the storytellers, ensuring that they are able to give fully informed consent at every stage of the process. So we have a three-stage consent and release process, which gives people plenty of time to think about whether they want to take part in a workshop, whether to release their story and whether to participate in the Patient Voices program.

In our experience, storytellers have almost always been very enthusiastic about their stories being given a wider audience. Objections to this have usually come from educational institutions and the medical establishment. People from these areas have often been concerned that what we were doing was "research" and the stories should therefore be made anonymous. But the desire to be heard is very strong, and in the end, "our hearts rebel against the heartlessness" of the researchers and the statisticians who would anonymise the stories of those who wish to tell them. Repeatedly, people choose voice over silence, and the heartfulness of a personal story over the heartlessness of a randomized control trial.

Joe: As you mentioned, our healthcare systems – while seeking to heal and support others – often leave people feeling dehumanized and disempowered. Can you expand upon the issues of how storytelling helps to humanize healthcare?

Pip and Tony: Dehumanization takes many shapes, including restriction of access to health and social care services, poor quality care, inhumane care as well as terrible violence done to the human spirit by crushing a voice that wishes to be heard. We are fond of quoting James Earl Jones who says, "One of the hardest things in life is having words in your heart that you can't utter."

The majority of our storytellers are patients, professionals, or those involved in family care, and as such, a great many of them have stories of experiences that have been damaging to them or their loved ones. What they all have in common is a desire that, through the telling and sharing and dissemination of their stories, they can make a contribution towards the cessation of those experiences.

Storytellers certainly tell us that they are happy if, by sharing their story, someone else may be spared a similar experience. In that sense, I think people do feel they are contributing to the struggle to create a more humane and compassionate society. The notion of Ubuntu sums up pretty well what we are trying to do and why we are trying to do it:

> When I dehumanize you, I inexorably dehumanize myself. The solitary human being is a contradiction in terms and therefore you seek to work for the common good because your humanity comes into its own in belonging.'
> (Bishop Desmond Tutu)

Joe: Even in our public workshops, people are willing to take risks with emotional material, and ordinarily they are prepared for the emotional impact of this work, but sometimes they are not. How do you address people's potential for going into crisis as part of the workshop experience?

Pip and Tony: Our primary concern is to ensure a place of safety for storytellers. We always have at least two facilitators, one of whom is a trained counselor (and the other makes sure the technology is always working!). In the event of a crisis, one person can stay with the group while the other supports the person in crisis.

We try to make the whole process a caring one, and where possible, that process begins several weeks before the actual workshop with an introductory briefing day for potential storytellers. We take this opportunity to show some stories, describe the process, explain the Patient Voices program, and do a little bit of story work. It gives people a chance to meet us and other storytellers, and to ask questions and make a well-informed decision about whether to attend the workshop. It also gives us a chance to assess things like literacy levels, technical ability, and emotional and mental states. This means that people who don't feel comfortable with any aspect of the process we've outlined need go no further while we, as facilitators, can make suitable preparations to ensure that the workshop is as comfortable and safe as possible for the participants.

We prefer to keep the groups small – usually six to eight storytellers – as we think this helps to create a comfortable, safe space in which to share personal stories.

We ensure that our facilitators are kept emotionally and psychologically fit through having supervision as well as through their own spiritual practices, including meditation, walking, motorcycle maintenance and other Zen-like and mindfulness-based activities.

Aided by our consent and release procedures, we strive to set clear guidelines for the group. We aim to provide a comfortable, holding and nourishing environment (physically, emotionally, and spiritually), and to make a safe place or *temenos* (the Greek concept of a sacred place for telling stories) within which storytellers can explore a range of feelings.

One of the things we do customarily is have dinner with storytellers on the night before a workshop begins. This offers an opportunity for us to break bread and drink wine (literally!), and to get to know one another. After dinner, we go through the program for the workshop and invite people to ask questions and air concerns so that they can begin the next morning with clear hearts and heads. We have observed that a well-formed group is very supportive of its members and this initial process of sharing seems to be quite important in helping the group to bond.

We may also invite people to share dinner with us on the second night if they wish to do so. It's an opportunity to relax a bit and we often take this time to show people more cheerful stories than those they are likely to have heard and seen – stories of joy and celebration, including some that we have made ourselves – and that's a way of letting people know us a little better. They can be reassured that we have walked the same road they are now walking.

We hope that our attempts to create this environment of safety reduces the risk of people going into crisis and, if they do, we make sure that one facilitator is available solely for that person.

We also keep in touch with people after the workshop ends. We let them know that they are now a part of the growing Patient Voices community of storytellers and that we will be contacting them. We always send out an email to everyone after a workshop, and we let them know in advance that we are going to do that. Sometimes that's enough to help people to feel reassured and safe. We thank them for their time and their stories and let them know roughly when we will be doing the post-production – this also links people up with one another, which most groups want. Sometimes people reply and let us know that they have been a bit shaky or wobbly in the first days after a workshop, so then we keep an extra eye on them (usually via email). We contact them again when the tidied versions of their stories are ready for their final approval.

If someone has told a particularly hard or painful story, we usually give them a call after a week or so to make sure they are OK. Some storytellers are keen to stay in touch, and we fall into an email correspondence. Several have joined in to become enthusiastic supporters of our humanizing healthcare initiative.

If we feel that someone is particularly vulnerable, we make an extra effort to maintain reasonably regular contact. Often the people who want to keep in touch are those who have experienced a real sense of transformation. They often make good use of their stories in their own work, want to go on to make other stories, and are great at spreading the word!

Joe: Do you have an intuitive assessment of how your experience of working in these therapeutic contexts might be relevant to other areas of the health professions?

Pip and Tony: Our work was not originally intended to be therapeutic, nor were we working with storytellers for whom that was the main objective. Our intention was always to embed the stories in educational – and quality – improvement programs, conferences, and e-learning, in order to further our aim of humanizing healthcare through highlighting the human side of experience of health, illness, healthcare and the lack of it.

However, it becomes clearer with every workshop and from every storyteller's feedback that the process is inherently therapeutic. We know that Digital Storytelling is a powerful process and that digital stories can be powerful tools for learning and change. Like most powerful tools, we believe that DS needs to be used with care and knowledge, and understanding, and as you remind us, Joe, with love.

We find that people are quite creative in devising new uses for the stories. We have also noticed the wide relevance of any one story to other areas of the health service. Jimmy's story [www.patientvoices.org.uk/nhstay.htm], for example, is used by one lecturer we know to highlight deficiencies in record keeping, patient safety, health inequalities, unnecessary transfers, professional behavior, and corporate liability – she can engage students in five or six lectures through the use of that one story!

The process of creating and sharing a digital story is definitely being taken up in a number of different areas of the health professions in the UK at least. So, for example, we have had junior doctors telling stories about clinical placements as a means of reflecting on their experiences. Newly qualified mental health nurses have told stories intended to be used in training their preceptors and for preparing future students for the reality of life after graduation.

Stories are being used to inform the design of services and devices for people with rheumatoid arthritis, and to share knowledge within and between organizations. Our sense is that people are slowly beginning to recognize the links between learning and healing. As more and more educators and clinicians come to make their stories, understanding is growing about the importance of careful reflection on experience and of listening and attending to patients as one human being to another – and that is the really therapeutic element for any of us.

Joe: In the UK, and much of the world, "complementary" or alternative therapies have gained greater acceptance. How would you position your work in the context of "complementary" medical work?

Pip and Tony: Good question. We have neither tried to position ourselves as an opposition nor as an alternative to anything, but rather have tried to help all stakeholders in health and social care heal the system from within. We want to build bridges rather than tear them down by recognizing that, as Tony has said, "the ability to tell, hear and share stories of experience and aspiration is a prerequisite for the development of a learning organization of reflective individuals."

We want to promote thoughtful use of language and mindful sharing of experiences. We seek to help people tell their stories not in an angry or aggressive way, but rather, in a way that will attract and hold the attention of those who devise and deliver healthcare without antagonizing them, while still retaining the integrity of the story and the storyteller.

Within the context of this question therefore, if DS is therapeutic, then it must be considered as a complementary therapy and a key component to the holistic approach to the patient, rather than an alternative one.

It is our strong view that facilitators need to be well-trained and experienced not just in Digital Storytelling, but in a range of other skills and knowledge bases, and in life experience and self-awareness – otherwise the wonderful alchemy that is Digital Storytelling at its best is likely to be diminished to little more than a PowerPoint presentation – as we've seen happen – where a formulaic use of digital technology takes precedence over the "analog" storytelling and the distillation that results in something that is clear, pure, and potent.

Joe: The issue of access to healthcare in the UK and much of the developed world is quite different than it is here in the United States or in the developing world. We have attempted to link the struggle for voice of recipients of healthcare within our system, to expanded healthcare access. Do you have any thoughts about how the UK system is still challenged by issues of access, and how your work could be instrumental in bringing about change?

Pip and Tony: There is a universal health service in the UK, free for all at the point of need. But inevitably, given the social and economic variations across the country, health inequality remains an important issue. Health inequality for us encompasses not only inequality in access to or quality of healthcare services, but also inequality of voice and influence in the shaping and improvement of those services.

One of our original intentions with the Patient Voices program, and one of the reasons for its name, was to give a voice to those people who have waited patiently to be heard: those "ordinary" people who come from all walks of life. We have worked with people from across the resource spectrum as well as with those on the edges of society and in "hard-to-reach" communities including ethnic minorities, refugees, and economic migrants, people disabled as a result of stroke or other cataclysmic events, people with mental health disorders and those who have been impoverished by disease or economic deprivation as well as the family members and friends who care for them.

By offering a voice to people who are seldom heard, and by distributing their stories as widely as possible, we are able to ensure that the stories are as widely heard as possible. It's really a kind of guerrilla advocacy, whereby the voices of ordinary people can be heard at the highest levels in the National Health Service and beyond.

From our monitoring of the website, we know that the stories are being widely used with the NHS as well as in medical schools and schools of nursing in many UK universities, which means that storytellers have a voice in the education of the next generation of healthcare professionals.

We are really pleased that some of the stories have been used, and hence given a platform, by the Chief Medical Officer and Chief Nursing Officer, and as well as the health minister, Lord Darzi. We have also worked on several projects with the National Audit Office, a body charged with auditing value for money in public sector spending. Their reports, and hence any accompanying Patient Voices stories, go directly to the Parliamentary Accounts Committee.

This means that the stories, and hence the storytellers, have the potential to affect healthcare policy. It may be coincidence, but we have noticed a greater emphasis on words like dignity, respect, and even humanity in policy documents. Patient involvement is now a statutory duty of healthcare organizations in the UK and several recent projects have focused on the benefits of patient involvement.

From a slightly different perspective, in our workshops we try to model the kind of ethos we would like to see in the health service, i.e., where everyone has an equal voice, and people are treated with respect and dignity.

We really do try to do it together, as part of the move toward patient empowerment, our own personal commitment to facilitative and participatory learning, and facilitative and participatory healthcare. Storytellers often remark on the novelty of being treated as equals – as people with something worthwhile to say; people worthy of respect, and they tell us that this experience of having their voices heard and valued gives them greater confidence and, perhaps, a new voice with which they can engage more effectively with healthcare providers and the system.

Joe: In thinking about this discussion for the book, it seemed that the lessons of this work would be relevant to discussions about doing work in the context of disability, life threatening disease, hospice care, etc. What are your thoughts on how this relates?

Pip and Tony: Well, yes. That was the starting prompt in the small story circle of our Digital Storytelling work. Many of our friends, family members, and colleagues have had really terrible experiences of illness, disease, and care. Working within the health sector and trying to ensure that patients really were at "the heart of healthcare" as the UK Department of Health said they should be, presented us with the challenge that resulted in the Patient Voices program. We've now worked on projects covering all the areas that you mention. Stories of health, life, death, and disease can offer us deep insights into not only the storyteller, but the storytellers' family and cultural traditions – if only we are prepared to listen.

Our experience and observations are that, given the opportunity to reflect on, craft and shape their stories, storytellers feel empowered and enthusiastic about telling and sharing their stories. When given the opportunity to see and reflect on the stories, policy makers, deliverers and providers of care are deeply affected by them. In addition, it is particularly important to offer medical, nursing, and other healthcare students the opportunity to see, and where possible, create, their own stories of healthcare so that they begin to develop greater empathy for one another. When a group of final-year medical students made stories, they commented on the powerfully reflective nature of the process and how it enabled them to see their patients more as human beings and less as opportunities for practicing new skills.

Our goal is to facilitate the telling and sharing of stories that are effective, affective, and reflective (EAR) in that they are short, transmissible, and distributable; compelling, honest, and human; provocative, challenging, and mindful.

Joe: Final thoughts?

Pip and Tony: A couple of things. It has come to our attention that many individuals and groups feel that they have the monopoly on suffering. People who have lost someone dear to them, people who are caring for a relative with a life-threatening disease, people with psychosis, people who have been discriminated against, people who have been uprooted from their home; they think their situation is worse than someone else's.

But when you get a group of people together to share stories, there is a realization that we all suffer – it is just a part of the human condition; it is what we do with that suffering that is the really important thing.

And people realize that they can begin to transform their suffering by sharing it – first by articulating it to themselves, then to the small group, and perhaps, to the world. Then the sense of isolation and hopelessness begins to diminish, and a new hope is found in the community and communion of storytellers.

The next thing has to do with different kinds of knowledge. Here in the West we specialize in knowing stuff, learning things, analyzing, criticizing, and acquiring more knowledge. That's the knowledge of the intellect.

Gradually we are recognizing, with the help of people like Daniel Goleman, the Dalai Lama, and other Buddhist teachers, that it's important to balance intellectual knowledge with emotional knowledge. Indeed, as Gandhi said, "the culture of the mind must be subservient to the culture of the heart."

Going one step further, Parker Palmer, and doubtless many others, feel that there is a spiritual knowledge which informs the way we are in the world, and that is also crucial to our understanding of ourselves and others.

Finally, there is what we might call physical knowledge – knowledge of our bodies and how they work (or don't work) and why. There is much to be learned from our bodies.

Together, these four kinds of knowledge represent a holistic approach to knowing and might be called wisdom. We feel that the Patient Voices stories offer the opportunity to learn in these four different ways and have the capacity to contribute to a wiser, deeper, and more loving knowledge of humanity.

Joe: And the third and final thing?

Pip and Tony: One of our most common observations and greatest joys over these years has been of the universality of stories and the commonality of shared experiences across, and within, workshop groups. We constantly see common themes – the themes of humanity – emerging.

> Each affects the other and the other affects the next, and the world is full of stories – and the stories are all one.
>
>   Mitch Albom, *The Five People You Meet in Heaven*

Thanks, Joe, for showing us the way.

15

Digital Storytelling in Higher Education

Conversations with
William Shewbridge, University of Maryland Baltimore County,
Liv Gjestvang, The Ohio State University,
Walt Jacobs, University of Minnesota, and
Cheryl Diermyer, University of Wisconsin (Madison)

CDS has a long history in higher education, with visits to more than one hundred universities around the world. Our work has taken many forms on campuses, but several campuses, including the ones represented here, have created their own capacities for ongoing Digital Storytelling work. This conversation explores those areas. We spoke in February, 2012.

Joe Lambert: When we began back in 1994, it was only about six months before somebody tied to a university asked us to come talk about Digital Storytelling. By 1996, 1997, we were in active process through the New Media Consortium, where I've met many of you, where we were more actively figuring out how our little method fit into the myriad of things that universities were trying to do with new technologies.

What's been interesting is that a community of practice has evolved inside higher education institutions in this country and outside this country, some of which has stayed more or less true to a model that CDS evolved, some of which that have taken that model in countless other directions. Digital Storytelling has become a useful form inside the higher educational process.

So, I want to start with each of you talking a little bit about kind of what led you in this direction.

Bill Shewbridge: I'm the director of the New Media Studio here at the University of Maryland, Baltimore County. We are essentially an institutional support unit. I will start with a little background about what we were doing here at UMBC. I became aware of Digital Storytelling through our participation in the New Media Consortium. If we go back twenty years, our work in new media came out of the TV studio here at UMBC. We had an institutional facility, so we were already active as producers of media. As the do-it-yourself movement was taking hold in the late 1990s I saw that we would be moving from the role of producers to the role of facilitators.

In the 1990s, we became more involved in doing web and multi-media work, mainly supporting grant work that was done here on campus. We're totally cost recovery in my unit. I don't really have a budget from the university. We piggy-back on grants for dissemination and other components.

Digital Storytelling has been very instrumental in one of the changes on our campus. The New Media Studio has actually become much more active on the academic side. This gives us an entrée into working with departments with curriculum matters as well as teaching a number of classes.

Joe: Why don't we jump over to you, Cheryl, and talk about the Wisconsin experience.

Cheryl Diermyer: Sure. I'm at the University of Wisconsin-Madison in the Division of Information Technology. I'm a senior learning consultant here. And, what drew me to start with Digital Storytelling was that I really have just always had a passion for using the still or moving image to communicate and connect people through this sharing of information. And my first career was as a CBS News video journalist. So, as a learning technology consultant, I'm always looking for ways to get students jazzed and engaged about their learning. And I think a media-based assignment, such as Digital Storytelling, is one way to do this.

I'll just tell you a little bit about my first experience with CDS because it relates to why I decided to bring this to campus. As a former news journalist, I was able to easily tell stories. They were objective stories, of course. Stories based on fact. And so, telling stories from a more subjective space, which is what CDS tends to concentrate on, required a lot more work on my part, and the benefits were more far-reaching. In my case, it really helped me to get clear on who I am in this moment and to tell a story about how I can be intentional about moving forward in my own life.

I thought, if we can give our students this opportunity, we are setting them up for success.

Joe: That's great. Thanks. Walt, do you want to talk about what led you in this direction?

Walt Jacobs: I'm an associate professor at the University of Minnesota. I'm also the department chair of the department of African American and African Studies. My entrée into Digital Storytelling was very personal. In the spring of 2007, I had published a memoir called *Ghostbox*, which is essentially about trying to recover from a life with a stepmother who cancelled Christmas when I was 13 years old, among other things. I was enrolled in a class about shooting short films in the fall of 2007 that was taught by a graduate student here at the University of Minnesota. And as we were talking about my ideas for possibly trying to turn the memoir into a short film, she said, "You know what? What you're interested in is really all about Digital Storytelling, and you should go take a class out at the Center for Digital Storytelling." I decided to go out and take the standard workshop as a fortieth birthday present to myself. Loved the workshop. Made my very first digital story. And then, that summer, came back here to Minnesota, got together with Rachel Raimist, a graduate student, and said, "Hey, we should do a class together about Digital Storytelling."

As Cheryl mentioned earlier, I thought this would be a great way to get students to think about who they are as students. To rethink their identities.

So we designed a course and we taught it in the fall of 2008 and I've been doing it ever since.

Joe: Fabulous. Liv, do you want to introduce yourself?

Liv Gjestvang: Sure. I am in Learning Technology, which is in the Office of the Chief Information Officer at Ohio State University. I come from the background of documentary and community media, so prior to coming to Ohio State, I was running the Columbus Jewish Film Festival and had worked with a PBS affiliate in New York doing youth media work. I had done a documentary project with nine gay high school students about being gay and out in high school. So I had come from a long history of work helping facilitate storytelling and helping people learn the tools to share their voice in ways that maybe more mainstream media wasn't capturing.

I was invited to participate in a Digital Storytelling committee meeting at the very beginning of the movement at Ohio State. On my first day there. That was in 2006. Two librarians, Karen Diaz and Anne Fields, had gone to a workshop CDS offered and became really excited about Digital Storytelling. They brought Joe to OSU to offer a workshop to librarians and other staff and faculty at the university.

We have built a program that's a collaboration between the Office of the Chief Information Officer, the University Center for the Advancement of Teaching and the university libraries. Our program has been focused almost exclusively on faculty Digital Storytelling, with some staff, and we focus less on students in terms of our approach. We've been helping faculty think about ways to share the academic work that they do through digital stories, which has been, at times, very challenging, and also really exciting.

I think we've made quite a progression. Historically, we hit some stumbling blocks and then worked through those and came to a program that's been very successful. I want to say we have had more than 100 participants come through intensive workshops to learn to do storytelling. And for me, what's exciting is thinking about the storytelling aspect, particularly for faculty who are doing research but perhaps haven't been connected to ways to communicate about the work they do, how to be engaging to a broad audience – perhaps beyond academia to the communities that they live in, too.

Joe: What is clear to me, is that your entry into Digital Storytelling involved re-thinking some part of the way you had approached your work, and that the challenge was to take aspects of the CDS model, and find a way to apply it within the academic context. Each of you comes with a slightly different perspective about what this means for curriculum, in terms of serving faculty, staff and students, but also the issues of how this connects universities to communities.

Could you provide us with some specifics about your various implementations.

Walt: I have done two semester-long courses. The first one was in the fall of 2008 with Rachel Raimist, now an assistant professor at the University of Alabama. The course that was called Digital Storytelling In and With Communities of Color. We definitely wanted to have students of all races and ethnicities, but about half of the students were of color, to think about the ways that the media had represented them and their communities. The course was offered as a way that they could speak back to those representations, to make their own representations about themselves and their communities. The students had a number of readings that they did about the history of the media and its effects. Then they did a personal digital story.

One innovation from the CDS model was to add an additional ground rule for the approach to giving feedback in the story circles. We let the students know that it was appropriate that some of the stories may appear to be more serious than others, but that they were all valid and to show respect to the speaker's truths. That was the first one, that particular class. I was there to tell my own story and to use my examples to help the students explore their own experiences. Rachel focused more on the technical aspects.

Then, three years later, in the Spring of 2011, I led a course again. One of the students in the first class, Syressa Lewis, who became my teaching assistant acted as my co-instructor.

I've also helped out some folks who were doing their own digital stories as part of their own projects. For instance, I worked with a group of Somali students. Minneapolis has a huge Somali population. One of the other professors organized an oral history project so that Somali students could tell their stories. They wanted to add a Digital Storytelling component, so I conducted a workshop for them.

I am hopeful to start a project with a group of African-American women athletes who played Division I sports back in the 1970s. Another professor had completed a research project with them and they wanted me to do a workshop to turn their experiences, about women athletes in the period before Title IX, into digital stories. Hopefully, we'll be able to do that before the current semester is over.

Joe: What strikes me is that you saw the importance of this work in both oral history and identity, in essence, at two ends of the life process. Bill, oral history is certainly some you have experience with your work at Charlestown, but perhaps you could talk first about your work in faculty development.

Bill: We've been doing faculty development workshops annually for six years, starting with the workshops CDS supported. Eventually, it became a peer-to-peer community of support with a list of over 170 members many of which are continuing in the classroom today.

One example is a class I team-taught with history professor Kriste Lindenmeyer, a class in youth activism from the 1960s. A group of graduate students developed stories early in the semester about their coming to awareness in political issues, focusing on that personal narrative aspect. Then they developed traditional, scholarly papers about a topic about activism, usually from the 1960s.

Finally, they took their Digital Storytelling skills and create mini-documentaries based on their scholarly papers. They came full circle.

Also in history, Constantine Vaporis is using Digital Storytelling to explore Samurai culture. He has students develop visual essays that they share as a class, looking at one aspect of the course content. We use the process in our Media and Communications Studies program to look at media theory. Students prepare visual essays deconstructing a media theorist based on their writings.

Again, all this work emerges from the faculty workshops, where faculty immerse into their own personal narratives. This idea of knowing your own story becomes a point of departure for them. They have this "aha" moment where they see other ways they can apply it in their class. In many cases, they move away from the personal narrative aspect in the classroom approach, but the power of the form is always rooted back to that initial experience that they had in the workshop.

But you are right, Joe, I think probably the most rewarding, long-term project we've done has been the Charlestown digital story project. Six years ago, we started a partnership with Retirement Living Television here on campus. Initially they funded us to allow us to take our students, train them in Digital Storytelling, and take them out to retirement communities in the area to make stories with the residents there. Eventually, this project has been sustained by being integrated into a number of classes that we're doing, so we return to Charlestown twice a year.

Joe: We have pointed to the Charlestown project many times as an example of multigenerational learning, a way to make the idea that every time a person dies, a library burns down, tangible to students. The experience is meaningful, and powerful for everyone involved. Cheryl, you have not just dealt with your own campus, but tried to extend this work throughout the many campuses of the University of Wisconsin system. Tell us about this process.

Cheryl: In 2008, I was lucky enough to receive a University of Wisconsin System grant. This grant allowed us to explore the use of Digital Storytelling in higher education, across the state, on fifteen different campuses. Every campus received train-the-trainer training, and by the end of 2009 all fifteen campuses across the state offered at least one Digital Storytelling workshop. Several campuses remain active with their use of Digital Storytelling. As part of the grant we had a big kickoff, a two-day conference, with Joe, Liv and cognitive scientist/educator Roger Schank and Greek shipowner, Dimtris Lyras, as keynotes. This helped the campuses to bring storytelling onto their own campuses. At Madison we've held workshops and received positive feedback and interest across campus.

We also did two informal classroom pilots that used Digital Storytelling as a final assignment for their students. This actually gave us more material to show other faculty and so once more faculty were able to see the stories that students and faculty were producing, they had a better understanding of the process and how it aligns with the elements of a quality education, or what's known on many campuses as the essential learning outcomes. That helped to get buy-in and increased interest.

Within a couple of years, Digital Storytelling became part of the focus of our Engaged Faculty Award program, where we had a faculty Digital Media Assignment award. Forty-four faculty received the award which comes with a small financial award and a whole lot of consultative support. The award is given to faculty from across disciplines, the hard sciences to the humanities. Classes included hundreds of students to just twelve students. All of which helped us to further explore and shape Digital Storytelling as a learning tool.

Through the Engage program, we were able to invite wider campus involvement. For example, by involving the libraries and our tech partners across campus, we were able to do more assessment of the learning affordances of Digital Storytelling. Through this cross-campus collaborative effort, UW-Madison was been able to create a process for digital media assignments that is quite sustainable.

We're now moving into using stories with some of our open source tools such as Case Scenario Builder and ARIS, our mobile application. We also have another Engage grant that's coming up that's based on case, place, and stories in situated learning, so much of the work from the Digital Storytelling initiative will transfer over into the next Engage faculty award.

Joe: I am always enormously impressed with the adaptations that people make with a model of the digital story, and with the various processes of engaging students. Liv, you had a similar experience as Bill and Cheryl, in planting a seed through personal story, that grows into numerous other processes at Ohio State.

Liv: Yes. I mentioned initially we had some issues, which I will address when we talk about challenges, but we eventually came to run our program on the model that's very similar to the CDS a three-day intensive workshop. We request applications from around the campus, thirty or so applicants apply, and twelve are chosen for the program, almost all faculty. We hold these during spring break or winter break.

We have faculty from all different disciplines working together. This became an interesting experience for them to be thinking about, talking about, the work that they were doing in veterinary medicine, physics, food, and agricultural science, et cetera.

Talking across those lines to each other, some great partnerships and friendships came out of those programs that have been sustained. The community that we have of people who have been involved with Digital Storytelling stretches across almost all disciplines at the university and they're a group of people who continue to work really closely together.

We did a partnership with the Asian-American Studies Consortium within the Committee on Institutional Cooperation (CIC) and brought in faculty, students, and staff participants from across most of the CIC institutions. That was an interesting exercise in having people who were working in very different roles but all in the same field. So that was a great collaborative group.

We had another experience with Peter M. Shane, a faculty member from the Moritz College of Law. He had received a grant from the Knight Foundation about information needs in a democracy and had been conducting town meetings across the country. He was really interested in capturing the stories that he'd been hearing across these town meetings and asked me if I would help him make a documentary.

He started telling me more about what he was trying to do. It became clear to me that what he actually wanted was to capture the voices of the people that he was hearing in communities across the country, and that Digital Storytelling would be a great way to accomplish his goals.

So rather than having him pay a documentary team and try and send them all over the country, he wrote a grant that was funded to bring twelve people from across the country from diverse backgrounds to do a three-day program where they produced twelve stories that are now on a website at www.informationstories.org. They also were able learn the tools to tell their own stories, and brought some of that capacity back to their communities.

In addition, the Information Stories Project produced hundreds of DVDs that were distributed for free in every community that wanted to use them. This led to a number of public access TV broadcasts as well.

Our most recent project is student-based as a partnership with the Disability Studies Program and Asynchronous Line Signal (ASL) at Ohio State. We're putting together a Digital Storytelling program for deaf high school students that we'll be offering this summer.

As you can see, we work as a partnership across different parts of the university. And I would have to say that Digital Storytelling is one of the strongest examples of cross-organizational collaboration at the university, not just as a technology process, but of all of the coordinating bodies I have participated. Coming from the administrative and development side, we've had a huge success in building relationships across those organizations through this work.

Joe: That's tremendous work, Liv. When you think of an institution as vast as Ohio State, not only the largest public university in the country in terms of students, but with one of the largest library systems in the world, one of the largest research capacities, the idea that Digital Storytelling, that stories, becomes one of the threads that humanizes such a massive machinery of education, is quite wonderful. But I know it has not all been a straight line, talk a bit about the challenges. Some of it started with you experimenting with the model of faculty engagement.

Liv: Yeah, so we actually initially thought that because we were working with faculty that there was no way we were going to get people to commit to a three-day program. A, they were going to be teaching, or B, when they weren't teaching they didn't really want to be on campus for three whole days at a workshop. So we tried to set up our program over the course of the quarter; initially I think it was every other week on Fridays. We were trying to get people together for two or three hours, for several weeks in a row. We had a lot of interest and success in the first, probably, month and a half. We were running it as a three month, every other week meeting and as you can imagine, people kind of dropped off over time when they had to actually start producing and bringing things in, they would go away for a week and not necessarily get it all together. The attrition rate was pretty high.

Ironically, we found that switching to a model that was a three-day immersion program was actually exactly what we needed to do to keep people involved and to kind of push them through to the point where they felt the concept, and parts of the process, stuck with them. The immersion also helped people who felt like they didn't know what story to tell, or they didn't have a story, or it simply wasn't going to work for them as a process. Actually having to come back those next two mornings helped to push people past their barriers.

I know you see this all the time, Joe, that point where people think "Oh my God, this is never going to happen," and then they come out the other side of it. One thing that helped us was we made a slight amendment to the model. When we accepted people for the program, we also offered a half-day story circle workshop that would happen six weeks prior to the three-day session.

People who were trying to tell a story about their academic work often started out talking in the third person or doing sort of a report version. It was really helpful to get them in and give feedback about how to think about using a personal voice. Then give them a little bit of time to rethink everything they thought they were going to do before they had to show up and push their way through three intensive days. That was all helpful.

We found an interesting partnership, too, around Digital Storytelling and the whole issue of fair use and copyright-free media. We have a really great resource on our website that is just a huge list of image and audio and video clips that are copyright-free and it's helped us to get faculty thinking about how they can encourage their students to make work and think about Creative Commons licensing and that whole idea of sharing and collaborating and co-producing.

Joe: Many Digital Storytelling projects end up with issues around copyright, and about the ease of the shortcut of using copyrighted material, but the shortsightedness that keeps the stories from having long-term value to the organizations and communities where the stories have been made. Great to see solutions coming out of that dilemma. Bill, your issues have much more to do with providing direct support to classroom implementation, why don't you talk about that.

Bill: Once the faculty go through the workshops, they're inspired and they want to do something. But everybody seems to have different sets of needs as to how that can be facilitated by our staff. In many cases, we provide research assistants. We have a great graduate program in imaging and digital arts here. We take students from that program and send them into the classroom, so the faculty have some support in getting the basic software, hardware, and media skills training aspects of the process.

In some cases, as with our Linehan Scholars Program right now, we go in one day a week and facilitate the whole process.

Another model that we've been having a lot of success with is we've created a one-credit lab course called Multimedia Literacy Lab in our Media and Communications Studies program. It is like a science lab in that it is attached to another course in the curriculum. The students can take this one-credit lab while they're taking MCS 333, which is a media theory course.

The instructor is freed up from having to teach the skills side of the process. However, they can have the expectation that the students know what they're doing as far as production is concerned. So they're integrating those assignments much more in the classroom.

One of the great things about the work here is that it unexpectedly has become a gateway to talk about media literacies throughout the curriculum, and how we support that here on campus. Digital Storytelling has been a catalyst for some working groups examining digital humanities overall and coming up with the long-term strategies. These broader conversations are exciting for all of us.

Joe: It sounds like the challenges just have presented other opportunities, and that while each discipline, each faculty member in each classroom, will continue to face specific hurdles in implementing this work, the campus wide conversation gives them a number of resources to turn to, and a number of options to consider in addressing their application. Walt, you were one of those faculty members, leading a class, what did you face in implementing the project?

Walt: With my two classes I did not face that many challenges. I think one of the advantages that I have as a department chair is that I control the curriculum so it was like "I know I want to do these classes, so I'm just going to schedule them. Who is going to come and take them?" In the first one with Rachel, we did a lot of reading and a story circle, they made a digital story, then some more reading. Rachel is a documentary filmmaker, so for the second big project she wanted the students to do mini-documentaries. When I did the course the second time with Syressa Lewis, I really was not as interested in the mini-documentaries, I had them do three digital stories. We focused the entire class on doing those there, story circles, extensive feedback and screening the stories in class. They were really great experiences.

I think the challenge now with Digital Storytelling is in how to approach the content. What content is the most powerful. For me, the real power of Digital Storytelling in higher education is by having students make digital stories where they think about who they are as students, they rethink their identity, their purpose here in the classroom, what they want to do with their lives, reflecting on past experiences.

One of the students in my first class said "Wow, I really wish I had had this class as a freshman. It might have changed how I have thought about myself or the type of things that I would have given myself permission to go into."

I've been using Digital Storytelling in more, shorter workshops in which students get the entire process over a day or two. Workshops where they can really think about, now, what do they really want to do with their time at the University of Minnesota going forward.

For example, there is a program called Access to Success, for students who have potential, but they either lack the grades or the test scores to go directly into one of our degree granting colleges. Once admitted to UM, they use Access to Success to prepare them for successful integration into the university.

We would like to incorporate a Digital Storytelling component into this program. Where students can reflect on the challenges that they faced in the past, and the strengths that they bring to the University of Minnesota – strengths that might not have been valued by the institution as a whole. Having this critical reflection process also helps them make more informed choices going forward.

Joe: Walt, the image you are creating has been discussed as a portfolio process in education, but in your case, it is a portfolio of the student's identity as a learner, as much as what has been learned that is the basis of the reflection. Many students go through dramatic changes in their approach to learning in the first years in college, but they are rarely asked to look at one has changed in themselves, that made this possible, and many powerful stories are inside those very personal shifts in identity. Cheryl, Walt suggests that there may be a sweet spot for Digital Storytelling, but in your work, defining what we mean by Digital Storytelling is perhaps the largest challenge.

Cheryl: There have been a lot of misperceptions or misunderstandings of what Digital Storytelling is or isn't. We had the same experience with the games and simulation initiative that we had on our campus in 2007 and 2009. Many thought games don't belong in higher education and didn't see the value of games in teaching and learning, didn't think that games aligned with these defined learning outcomes in higher education. Now we see games being very prevalent at several campuses across the nation. I think Digital Storytelling fell into these same footprints.

We had to work hard to show the academic rigor of the process of Digital Storytelling so that many of these misperceptions are no longer an issue. But again it took developing partnerships across campus, including our faculty, to help us explore these academic affordances, then share that information out across campus so faculty were sharing it with other faculty.

The first hurdle was to inform the campus on the process. The Digital Storytelling process includes many of these essential learning outcomes which our campus leadership, specifically the Vice Provost for Teaching and Learning, have been supporting. Outcomes like inquiry and analysis. And Walt mentioned critical thinking. Visual literacy, written and oral communication, team work, and global and civic knowledge.

How would one know Digital Storytelling addressed these issues unless they have been exposed to it in this way? The first challenge was buy-in; educating people on how Digital Storytelling can align with the same academic rigor that this institution values.

The second challenge, the larger challenge, is in simply recognizing that when we allow our students time for reflection and expression of emotion, it enriches the learning process. While there is ample research on reflective teaching and emotional intelligence, it remains a challenge to bring this practice into a higher education classroom. The value of integrating reflection and emotion in our teaching and learning is sometimes hard to recognize and even harder to practice. Surprisingly, when we started working with the hard sciences, it seemed to open more doors and raise the awareness of the value of using stories in higher education for teaching and learning.

I do remember trying to fit the three-day workshop process into a semester timeline as being a challenge, but we seem to have worked that out well. And one final challenge is, how can our students and our faculty work collaboratively online with these types of assignments and where can these digital assignments be stored?

Joe: Of course as more and more students create video files, the storage and file management issues become enormous.

Cheryl, you make several important points about learning outcomes, and the way affective learning can be promoted through this work. I have come to believe emotional health should be much further up the outcome considerations of educational leadership. We are preparing people for a vastly complex world, with endless serious and intractable issues, likely economic instability, and dramatic structural shifts in society, and yet we treat the emotional preparation as either an ancillary support issue for "struggling" students, or a deeply secondary issue of general physical health and well being. As much as imagination is a twenty-first-century skill, so is mental health maintenance. There needs to be more open discussion about these issues.

But healthy thinking starts with remembering to celebrate the stories of when we are succeeding. Share with me a moment, a story, about when the work on your campus felt successful, felt as if you were making a difference. Let's start with you, Bill.

Bill: We've had so many great ones. But I always go back to the story that Jesse Poole made, called "Missing in Action." It was something that came out of the Charlestown project. We've gone back to Charlestown several times. We have a lot of repeat participants in the workshops. And Jesse, she did maybe four of them with us. But the first time I met her, she came to me with twenty pages of written material, this story about her husband during World War II who was shot down over Burma. He was missing in action. She didn't really realize what had happened to him. Her son had essentially unearthed the story.

It was a great story. Very moving. But it was also twenty pages. Jesse wanted me to see it and read it, but she just wasn't ready to do that story at that point in time. She had done two very nice stories. One was quite funny. But on the third year, when she came back, she took me aside and she said, "I think I'm ready to do this one now." We worked with her for three days to get it down to something that was just, for me, one of the most moving stories that I've ever seen.

What struck me was the idea that we had to go through a three-year process of building trust, for her to feel comfortable enough to share that story. I know that she took a lot out of the process, as well.

Joe: Part of the strength of the project is the longitudinal consistency, everyone becomes familiar with the approach, and the depth of trust. Liv, I remember your wonderful story about a chemistry professor, could you share that story?

Liv: With our focus on faculty and academic stories, it's a bit challenging sometimes to find a strong emotional storyline, but I think Terry's is a great example. Terry Gustafson, a chemistry professor who was also an associate dean and returned to teaching. He really wanted to connect more to students. At Ohio State, we have some really huge classes and he lectures in front of large groups of students, and he had talked about his yearning to connect with students and be able to communicate his passion for his own research to them, but had struggled with trying to find a way to do that.

He produced an absolutely beautiful story called, "Why I Love Research." And it's about his early fascination, as a little boy, with lasers on the Death Star and with James Bond and then with this combination of pretty colors and science and how his personal connection to those pieces brought him into a really successful career as a researcher and a professor and then a dean.

Terry plays the story at the very beginning of class. He has spoken about power, of being able to call a group of 175 students together without having to stand at the front of the room and wave his arms or say, "We're about to get started here." But to just play this piece that speaks eloquently and from the heart about why he does the work that he does. The story is also about trying to find answers for questions that we don't understand, a great metaphor for the scientific process. The story changed the tenor of an entire classroom through his telling a very personal story.

As a result, Professor Gustafson is interested in bringing together a collection of his colleagues from the department to produce a body of similar work that could rotate through at the beginning of classes.

Joe: Again the idea of a chemistry professor leading a department in exploring powerful personal stories is inspiring, and suggests many parts of your institutions could make room for storytelling processes. Cheryl, you said you had someone from outside the humanities as well.

Cheryl: I always think of a faculty member, Margaret Nellis, who was from human ecology. A very courageous woman. Margaret would tell you that she is not a technology person. She had never done a PowerPoint before, but she was adamant about whatever she assigned to her students, she would have to do first. She wrote and produced her own story. She took some hand holding, but she got through the process. She is a good role model for faculty, for anybody that might be stuck on the idea that this takes a lot of knowledge in technology. One can start at very basic level. Her class won the Hirsh award that year for innovative work by students and faculty who explore the University's diversity and excellence.

When I run into Margaret today on campus, still she'll tell me that she still thinks about the story she produced. It has made an everlasting imprint on her understanding of who she is today.

I get such great feedback from faculty who are attending. Sheila Reeves, from college of agriculture and life science, has said, "I feel so empowered and reconnected with my love for teaching."

The Digital Storytelling workshops have inspired our faculty. This is one instance when I feel like I'm contributing to quality education.

Joe: I believe it is true that the workshop model not only gives a mechanism for surfacing story, but it also models an approach to teaching that can inspire educators to think differently about the way they teach, and the way that classroom engagement can happen. It is always exciting to hear back from educators, in K-12 and higher education, and here them say, "you changed the way I teach, and my classroom is the better for it." I also think the idea that instructor takes on the task of making something that they are asking their students to make is vital, you have to know yourself as a learner in the same process.

Walt: I just agree with that 100 percent. It's so important for the professors to model their own process before we ask the students to do it for themselves. So in both of the classes, the students read my memoir. They read the entire thing, and then I answered questions that they had about the memoir. Very personal questions. Then they watched the digital story that I made at CDS called "Letter to My Mother," to get a sense of how it's done. And then my co-instructors, deconstructed my story, changed the pacing, changed the music, to show the students that the same stories can be told and re-interpreted in many different ways..

This creates an open environment. When we do our story circles, students share very personal aspects of their lives. There's a lot of crying. Tears. The students support each other. I find myself as facilitator stepping back and let the students kind of give guidance and support for other students.

One student told a beautiful story about coming to terms with the death of his little brother. And he said he shared this digital story with his family, and the family had basically their first in-depth catharsis about the death. It was made possible by the digital story.

Another student told me she wished she had made a story as a freshman. She came back from a Study Abroad session, and asked her advisor if she could make a digital story to reflect on her experience. The advisor approved, and it turned out well. Now she says that because of the story from my class, and her reflection on her Study Abroad, she is re-framing her plans for graduate school.

Joe: Those are all great stories. It is clear there are countless, an infinite number, of applications for this work. But I feel that sometimes certain applications are just so. Walt brought one up, the closing report of an important experience of learning. That is an example we are hearing about throughout education, a big moment of change being reflected on that sets the stage for the next decisions by the student. The process for the story accomplishes so many things, it forces a person to examine themselves in a time of change, and perhaps duress, to look at how their expectations either were met or challenged, to assess how the resources they had within them to survive, to thrive. The classic narrative arc. But that is just one example.

Liv, start off with that thought. What is your gut telling you? What is the sweet spot for educational Digital Storytelling in five years?

Liv: What I see more and more broadly across the entire campus is this understanding of the power of stories.

I feel like there's an increasing awareness that the ways that we connect to each other and to the world around us is through stories and that I see an increasing openness to that in higher education. Even just five or six years ago, I think there was much more reluctance to use the word "storytelling." We've gone back and forth between calling them digital narratives and digital stories precisely because of that struggle.

I see a clear increase in understanding that the world that our students live in, and are going out to become professionals in, is one in which the ability to tell a story, no matter what kind of work you do, or where you find yourself in the world, is extremely important.

As an example, there's a huge bike ride to raise money for cancer here that's a significant initiative at the university. This past year they made a beautiful collection of still photographs that was actually put to music and not to spoken audio. The university president traveled to every county in the state over the course of the summer, and they took recordings of his telling the story of what those travels meant to him along with stories from people across the state and put them into a collection of still photos. At the highest levels of the promotion and marketing of our university, the president demonstrated the idea that sharing stories is how we connect, how we become better citizens, how we make the core value of service visible to a public.

The skills that we can give students, not just in written literacy but in the literacy of finding and accessing and interpreting information and constructing their own stories, as well as creating arguments in writing and in digital media, are incredibly important skills. We do students a service by teaching this and I would say as a land grant institution, we do a service to our state by helping our students learn those skills.

Joe: Bill, do you want to add to that?

Bill: I would agree with the idea of Digital Storytelling as being part of a cumulative evaluation. I'm working with some folks here in the sciences to look at the idea of using the process to gather qualitative data about how students learn and their journey as learners. They want to have students talk about how their perceptions of learning change over the course of a semester, so we would have a reflective component built in to a study.

Joe: That's excellent. Walt, do you have some thoughts about where this is going in terms of sweetness?

Walt: Yeah, I think a couple of things come to mind. One is public relations. Here at the University of Minnesota, we are a huge research institution, but around the country some of the state legislators are questioning what professors do. So we are considering having students make digital stories about what they do here at the University of Minnesota, especially what they've done as researchers. We have a huge undergraduate research program where we encourage students to do their own research alongside professors, so that could be stories to get out to the legislatures.

The second thing as I mentioned earlier, is developing work within the transition programs. We're looking at how digital stories can help the students think about where they've been and where they're going and help them start thinking about some choices they can make. Starting with some of first-year programs, that are acting as a bridge for the incoming students through the freshmen orientation programs.

But this presents the problem of scale. We have 2,500 incoming first-year students each year in my college, and 5,000 first-year students overall on the Twin Cities campus. How can we have a large-scale ramping up of digital stories processes? We can not logistically run them through the lab as was the case in my courses.

So we may take a look at is using iPhones or iPads and doing some workshops that incorporate mobile technologies into making digital stories versus having them all go to the physical labs.

Joe: I have to say that looking five years out the idea that the stories live on the mobile phones and tablets seems obvious. We are approaching the first generation of mobile devices that really can edit video effectively, and the machines already have all the other media tools in place. What we need are more great design examples that inspire incoming students to think about their entrance essay as a digital story as well, something that introduces them to the new community, and acts as a digital calling card with professors and staff. Every Facebook page should have one as far as I am concerned.

Cheryl: When I think of Digital Storytelling the sweet spot is communication, communication, communication. In some of my workshops I define Digital Storytelling as "effective communication with a creative flair." We have also been using Digital Storytelling for university communications. If you go to our home page, we now have a story right up front and center on our university home page. We were working with our former Chief Information Officer on using stories to communicate the Information Technology strategic plan. We've used stories in our first-year program, as a way for students to learn from one another and understand their path to being a successful student. I see more and more embracing of the use of stories. The sweet spot, is that Digital Storytelling is just an excellent tool for community building and communication, both internally and externally.

Liv: Cheryl, I have to say, if you get a good digital story out of your CIO strategic plan, I'd love to see that.

Joe: Yeah, we all would love to see that. On that note, I invite you each to share some closing thoughts.

Walt: This is my fifth year as a department chair. I have found that my deepest passions are actually in academic administration. I'm one of those weird faculty who actually loves administration even more than being a faculty member. So my days of being directly involved in Digital Storytelling facilitation might be coming to an end, but I think that I'll always be a big advocate for digital stories and Digital Storytelling. So as I go to the next level, I'll always try to figure out, how can I encourage others to use the tools of Digital Storytelling to create really powerful and creative learning environments for our students.

Cheryl: I'm in that same boat. My work is shifting, but through the help of many others on campus I think we have a really good structure in place right now that works on campus as well as with the Madison community. There's active participation, so I will definitely be an active advocate for this type of work going forward.

Bill: Well, I'm always constantly amazed at just how far we've gone with this here. When I took that first workshop with Daniel in Vancouver so many years ago, it just never occurred to me that this would actually have inspired so many twists and turns in how we do things here. I'll give you one great example. Two years ago our president, Freeman Hrabowski, did the keynote at EDUCAUSE. So the culmination of his speech there was the whole idea of what we were doing with Digital Storytelling. He argued that despite the perception that we were becoming more isolated through our use of technology, this work was putting a human face on the technology. I think what people grab onto with Digital Storytelling is so much the personal aspect of it, that it really does bring people together in a very fundamental way.

Joe: When I look back to 1997, and the first workshop we created at California Polytechnic University in Pomona with university professionals, this idea seemed so, I would say, revolutionary, and yet here are four major institutions with commitments to this work that are shaping the future of the entire institutions. I am so impressed with all of your work.

So Liv, that leaves you the last word.

Liv: I would just say that one thing that I'd like to see continue to happen is more of a building of community across institutions around this kind of work. It was great to be a part of this, to hear what's happening elsewhere. I think there are so many great applications of this work and overlaps and also really different ways that it's being applied in different institutions that I would really welcome the opportunity to start thinking about how we produce networks to share information and share stories across institutions and think not just about the stories that we tell, but the sharing of those stories.

Addendum

Silence Speaks Digital Storytelling: Guidelines for Ethical Practice

From www.silencespeaks.org

This document was developed in 2011 by Lucy Harding and Amy Hill.

Introduction

We at Silence Speaks believe that Digital Storytelling has the potential to nurture individual and collective healing and justice by facilitating the production of personal media narratives and bringing these into carefully considered public spheres. However, without high ethical standards, there is the potential for Digital Storytelling to result in harm, particularly when processes involve vulnerable individuals.

This document draws on our experiences of working in a variety of settings around the world to outline the principles that we think should guide ethical practice when working with digital stories. The document aims to describe standards for daily practice. It is also intended as a framework for conversations with storytellers and partner organizations about appropriate responses to ethical challenges that may arise in the course of carrying out projects.

Section A details five core principles that are central to Silence Speaks' approach to ethical practice. Section B outlines the key ethical issues that need to be considered in preparation for, during, and following a Silence Speaks Digital Storytelling workshop. Section C focuses on ethical concerns related to the sharing and distribution of finalized digital stories, beyond the workshop setting. Finally, the Appendix, "Digital Storyteller's Bill of Rights," describes for storytellers the rights we believe they are entitled to, in the context of our work.

Note: This document is intended as an evolving set of recommendations for good practice – not a static and rigid set of rules. We recognize that the ethical considerations that arise within each project and storytelling workshop are unique. These guidelines should not act as a substitute for discussions tailored to an individual project/workshop or for on-going critical examination of best practices.

Section A: Core Principles

1 Well-Being. Silence Speaks places storytellers' physical, psychological, and social well being at the center of all phases of a project. Put simply, we believe that the *process* of creating stories within a workshop is as important as the end product (media pieces) resulting from that workshop.

2 Informed Choices. Silence Speaks believes that storytellers' ability to make informed choices about the content, production, and use of their work is crucial. We are committed to providing storytellers with the information they need to make these choices, and we understand that storytellers have the right to withdraw their stories from public circulation at any time.

3 Ownership. Silence Speaks views storytellers' right to represent themselves as a core component of the Digital Storytelling process. Storytellers are provided with the space and flexibility to describe what they have experienced, within the parameters or thematic concerns of a given project. We recognize that preserving storytellers' sense of ownership can be particularly challenging when digital stories are screened outside of a workshop setting. We do our best to engage storytellers in outlining appropriate context and messages for their stories, and, where there is interest, to partner with them on story distribution.

4 Local Relevance. Silence Speaks aims to ensure that its methods are sensitive and appropriate to the local context of a given project. We always work with local partners – and, where possible, we train local facilitators. We adapt our methods to fit local technological resources and capacities, emphasizing always the importance of participatory production.

5 Ethics as Process. Silence Speaks views ethics as a process rather than as a one-off occasion of "gaining consent". We believe that ongoing dialogue between storytellers, staff members, and project partners about the challenges of designing and implementing an ethically responsible project is key to ethical practice.

Section B: Ethics and the Digital Storytelling Workshop

1. Protection

1.1 Readiness. Silence Speaks recognizes that the benefits of producing a digital story can only be realized when an individual is fully prepared and able to tell a story. Potential storytellers must be encouraged to consider whether they feel ready to tell their story in a workshop setting; ultimately, the decision about whether or not to participate is theirs alone. Particular care needs to be taken when a potential storyteller appears to be "in the middle" of the story (e.g. living in an abusive relationship, struggling to meet basic needs). We work closely with local project partners to recruit appropriate storytellers and assess their readiness to participate.

1.2 Expectations. Silence Speaks recognizes that care needs to be taken to ensure that storytellers arrive at and leave the workshop with realistic expectations. The limitations of what the process Silence Speaks and partner organizations can offer needs to be established with potential storytellers prior to a workshop and managed throughout the process. We place particular emphasis on clarifying with storytellers what they can realistically expect to change as a result of a workshop/project and informing them of the project timeline and likely end-point.

1.3 Choice. Silence Speaks workshops often center on broad themes that are intended to provide a framework for discussions by storytellers. Within these themes, storytellers can decide whether or not to reveal private information in words or images, what language to use, and how to represent their experiences in a story. We do our best to make sure that storytellers are aware of the potential social and political implications of their choices and to support them in making decisions that feel right for them.

1.4 Trauma.[1] Silence Speaks understands that many storytellers will have experienced trauma and that it is incumbent upon us to be mindful of how these experiences may impact their participation in a workshop. We ask that our project partners make a support worker well-versed in trauma intervention available to storytellers throughout the workshop process.

1.5 Risk. Silence Speaks recognizes that awareness of potential physical, psychological, and social risks is a key factor in the design and implementation of any project. Storytellers are counseled on the risks and possible emotional challenges involved in creating a digital story, as well as on the ways in which story creation may put the storyteller and/or individuals mentioned in a story at risk for harm. We pay special attention to the need to mitigate risks related to the context in which the workshop is taking place, the composition of the group of storytellers, and the physical space of the workshop. We reserve the right as facilitators to recommend that storytellers remove information/images from their stories that may place themselves or others at risk.

1.6 Confidentiality. Silence Speaks is transparent about its inability to guarantee anonymity to storytellers, given that we cannot control what they reveal outside of a workshop. We work with partners and storytellers to establish clear ground rules for behavior within the workshop, and we stress within these ground rules that workshops must be conducted under an agreement of confidentiality (e.g., everyone present at the workshop agrees that what is said during the session must remain private). We discuss with storytellers whether names, details, or images need to be removed from a story in order to uphold this agreement.

1.7 Copyright. Silence Speaks respects copyright laws globally and works with partners to design processes that ensure that laws pertaining to the use of images and music are adhered to. Where possible, we strive to work within a Creative Commons framework.[2]

1.8 Data Protection. Silence Speaks takes care to ensure that project data (e.g., story source materials, draft and final scripts, etc.) is removed from computers on which stories are produced and archived on hard drives which are stored in a locked cabinet, accessible only to key project staff. Upon request, we also provide partners with source materials on data DVD, and we ask that they establish methods for safely archiving this data.

2. Communication

2.1 Information.[3] Silence Speaks recognizes that information is central to the ability of potential storytellers to make informed choices about their participation in a project. Potential storytellers receive appropriate information prior to deciding whether to attend a workshop as well as during the workshop itself. This includes information about project goals and objectives, their rights within the project, the process of creating a digital story, and the potential ways the digital stories may be used after a workshop.

2.2 Accessibility. Silence Speaks understands that information needs to be provided in an accessible format with consideration of potential barriers to communication, such as language and literacy. Information also needs to be meaningful; for instance, we typically show potential storytellers sample digital stories prior to a workshop, in order to convey what Digital Storytelling is all about.

2.3 Dialogue. Silence Speaks believes that information should be exchanged in the context of discussion with potential/confirmed storytellers. We aim to provide storytellers with the space to ask questions, raise concerns, and reflect on ethical challenges (e.g. risks) associated with a project, in relation to their own lives.

3. Structures

3.1 Equal Opportunities. Silence Speaks knows that in spite of best efforts to assure maximum benefits, projects can contribute to uneven access to resources at a community level. We strive to be thoughtful about who workshops are made available to and how this feeds into, or challenges, pre-existing power structures. We take care to ensure that potential barriers to workshop attendance (e.g. costs of childcare or travel) are minimized, particularly when they disproportionately affect vulnerable groups/individuals. As noted in item 1.5, we also take account of group composition within workshops and how this may affect the ability of all participants to contribute.

3.2 Professional Facilitation. Silence Speaks believes that high standards of facilitation are crucial for the Digital Storytelling process to be beneficial to storytellers. Our facilitators are careful to be respectful and supportive of storytellers while at the same time maintaining clear professional boundaries. Facilitators are competent, versed in the Digital Storytelling process, and committed to high standards of ethical practice.

3.3 Improving Practice. Silence Speaks builds a reflection of ethical practice into project evaluations – and encourages ongoing discussion within Silence Speaks (staff and advisors), with local partners, and with storytellers.

4. Looking Forward

4.1 Thorough Planning.[4] Silence Speaks encourages project partners to be clear prior to the implementation of any workshop processes about the purpose of working with digital stories and their plans for sharing these narratives post-workshop. Knowing the specifics of why local partners are interested in working with digital stories and how project partners plan to distribute digital stories informs all aspects of project design and implementation and has a particularly important impact on informed consent procedures.

4.2 Documentation. Silence Speaks believes that storytellers, project partners and Silence Speaks should be provided with copies of informed consent forms. Informed consent documentation should be clear and legally valid. Further, documenting discussion of consent with a storyteller, stipulations on consent and storytellers' expectations is vital to ensure that the way a digital story is used post-workshop is in line with discussions and the consent provided within the workshop.

4.3 Closure. Silence Speaks believes that the steps of wrapping up a project must be discussed with local partners during the initial planning stages. We and our partners make clear to participants the length and type of engagement they can expect from a given project and follow-up workshops by sending storytellers an appreciation letter or email. We also ensure that storytellers receive copies of their digital stories, in whatever format is determined to be most accessible to them (e.g., CD-Rom, DVD, etc.). If storytellers reside in locations where viewing stories in electronic format is not possible, we provide them with still photographs from stories and/or certificates of completion.

4.4 Sustainability. Silence Speaks understands that one-off workshops do not necessarily provide storytellers or partners with usable media production skills for ongoing story development. As resources allow, we choose to focus on longer-term partnerships that include multiple workshops and training sessions designed to ensure sustainability. We strive to discuss with partners and funders the importance of local capacity building and the realities of the time and resources that it requires.

4.5 Follow-up. Throughout the process, including prior to a workshop, storytellers should be encouraged to think about what support they already have in place (friends, colleagues, family, counselors). Where appropriate storytellers should be counseled as to whether there are ways they can develop their current support network. Where possible, Silence Speaks will direct storytellers to appropriate psychosocial services and/or counseling programs. In the months following a workshop, where the primary engagement is usually with local partners, Silence Speaks encourages these organizations to act as intermediaries and take the time and effort to connect participants to relevant support services. Finally, we ask that local partners commit to debriefing storytellers a couple of weeks after a workshop and maintaining regular contact with storytellers monthly for up to six months following a workshop.

Section C: Ethics When Sharing Digital Stories After a Workshop

5. Protection

5.1 Consent. Silence Speaks stresses that digital stories should only be shared in the specific ways for which consent has been obtained from storytellers. Where possible, we work with partners to develop consent procedures that allow consent to be discussed and re-obtained at various stages of a project, in recognition of the fact that storytellers' feelings about a project and relationship to their narrative may change over time.

5.2 Withdrawing Consent. Silence Speaks strives to employ consent procedures that allow storytellers to withdraw their consent at any stage of project implementation. We are transparent within these procedures about the fact that various methods of distribution may be impossible to control (e.g., web publication, DVD publication), and we therefore counsel storytellers on the limits of withdrawing their consent.

5.3 Expectations. Silence Speaks recognizes that public exposure of digital stories can raise expectations of storytellers. We do our best to manage these in a way that gives the storyteller a realistic sense of the changes they can expect as a result of a given project and/or form of story distribution. We are also sure to be clear with storytellers at all phases of a project, about the degree of involvement they will have in story distribution.

5.4 Counsel. It is important that storytellers understand the public environment in which their work will be shown/incorporated and both the potential positive and negative effects. Storytellers need to be counseled as to the specific challenges associated with presenting work publicly, including potential negative reaction to their work and a loss of privacy. Storytellers should have the opportunity to discuss any questions and concerns. If a storyteller is present at a public screening of their work a trained staff member should be present.

5.5 Risk. The risk to those viewing a digital story should be considered. Viewing digital stories can trigger experiences or emotions for the viewer – this should always be discussed with an individual prior to them watching a story.

5.6 Environment.[5] Silence Speaks believes that careful attention should be paid to the environment in which digital stories are screened. We recommend, within the context of our projects, that story screening organizers consider audience appropriateness of stories to be shown; audience size (we suggest small groups, which are easier to engage with); and the need to set ground rules to ensure that comments about stories are respectful to the storyteller.

5.7 Professional Facilitation. At any story screening professional facilitation is crucial. Professional facilitation includes, but is not limited to, a facilitator: being well versed on the issues raised within a story; understanding the context, audience and available support services where a story is being screened; establishing a safe space for discussion where everyone viewing the story can contribute; guiding and managing difficult discussions.

6. Ownership

6.1 Viewing. Silence Speaks believes that storytellers have a right to view their story, or where this is not possible, to hear/view transcripts or audio recordings, before their stories are distributed or screened publicly.

6.2 Involvement. Silence Speaks believes that storytellers should have meaningful involvement in and/or input into decisions about how, where, and when they wish their stories to be shared. We discuss the importance of this kind of input with partners during planning phases so as to build in opportunities for storytellers to be included in decision making about story distribution and/or in the planning/execution of specific story screenings.

6.3 Context. Silence Speaks recognizes that individual narratives take shape, inform, and are influenced by larger social, historical, and political structures. As such, we consider it important to embed stories within workshops that shed light on these structures. We work closely with partners and storytellers to ensure that context is made clear when stories are shared online, in community settings, as part of curricular materials or advocacy agendas, etc.

6.4 Representation. When using digital stories Silence Speaks considers it important to recognize the nuances and complexities of individuals and their stories. Outputs using digital stories should avoid reducing storytellers to a singular identity or reducing storyteller's narratives to a specific issue. We consider it important to highlight that storytellers are more than their stories. Stories capture a moment in time and cannot claim to be "ultimate truths" about storytellers' lives and identities.

7. Communications and Transparency

7.1 Informed. Silence Speaks believes that whenever possible storytellers should be kept informed about the ways in which their stories are being shared. We urge our partners to stay in contact with storytellers about specific screening events, the impact of story screening, and ways that they may stay connected to a given project.

7.2 Income. Silence Speaks rejects the increasing commodification of story, in the context of human rights journalism and relief work. We do not sell stories for profit, and we do not partner with organizations that wish to do so. We take care to inform and gain consent from storytellers related to any plans for generating income from their stories (e.g., the development and distribution of educational DVDs to generate resources for Silence Speaks or its partners

Appendix: Digital Storyteller's Bill of Rights

The Workshop

- The right to know from the outset *why* a workshop is being carried out.
- The right to assistance in deciding whether you are ready to produce a digital story.
- The right to understand what is involved in the process of producing a digital story.
- The right to know who might view your finished story after the workshop.
- The right to decide for yourself whether or not to participate in a workshop.
- The right to ask questions at any stage of the workshop, before, during, or after.

- The right to ask for teaching instructions to be repeated or made clearer.
- The right to skilled emotional support if your experience of making a story is emotionally challenging.
- The right to tell your story in the way you want, within the limits of the workshop.
- The right to decide whether or not to reveal private or personal information to fellow participants and instructors at the workshop.
- The right to advice about whether revealing your identity or other personal details about your life in your story may place you at risk of harm.
- The right to leave information and/or photographs that identify you or others out of your final story.
- The right to reject story feedback (about words and images) if it is not useful or offered in a spirit of respect/support.
- The right to decide what language to use in telling/creating your story.
- The right to be respected and supported by capable workshop facilitators.
- The right to a written consent form if your story will be shared publicly including a signed copy for your records.
- The right to know what contact and support you can expect after the workshop.

Sharing Your Digital Story After The Workshop

- The right to decide with project partners how your digital story may be shared.
- The right to view and retain a copy of your story before it is shared publicly in any way.
- The right to know who is likely to screen your story and for what purposes.
- The right to know who is likely to watch or read your story and when (e.g. rough timeframe).
- The right to counsel if you are concerned about publicly sharing your story.
- The right to emotional support if you are present when your story is shown in public.
- The right to demand that no one should be able to sell your story for profit.
- The right to know if any money will be made from your story being shared (e.g. to support not-for-profit human rights work).
- The right to withdraw your consent for the use of your story at any time.
- The right to information about the limits of withdrawing consent for your story to be shared, if it has already been circulated online or on CD, DVD, etc.

Notes

1 For further discussion about Digital Storytelling and issues of trauma see: Silence Speaks – Addressing Trauma.
2 For information on the Creative Commons framework see: http://creativecommons.org/.
3 For further discussion of specific questions to pose to potential storytellers/storytellers see: Silence Speaks – Workshop Participant Screening Guidelines.
4 For guidelines on planning and developing a project see: Silence Speaks – Project Development Guidelines.
5 For a more detailed discussion of how to share stories see: Silence Speaks – Workshop Follow-up and Story Sharing Guidelines.

Bibliography

Albom, Mitch, *The Five People You Meet in Heaven.* New York: Hyperion, 2003.
John-Steiner, Vera. *Creative Collaborations.* Oxford: Oxford University Press, 2000.
Miller, Richard K. *Writing at the End of the World.* Pittsburgh: University of Pittsburgh Press, 2005.

Digital Storytelling

Hartley, John and Kelyy McWilliam. *Story Circle: Digital Storytelling Around the World.* New York: Wiley-Blackwell, 2009.
Howell, Dusti and Deanne Howell. *Digital Storytelling: Creating an eStory.* Santa Barbara, CA: Linworth, 2003.
Johnson, Steven. *Interface Culture.* San Francisco: HarperSanFrancisco, 1997.
Lambert, Joe. *Digital Storytelling Cookbook.* Berkeley, CA: Digital Diner Press, 2002.
Laurel, Brenda. *Computers As Theatre.* Menlo Park, CA: Addison-Wesley, 1993.
Lundby, Knut. *Digital Storytelling, Mediatized Stories: Self-representations in New Media.* New York: Peter Lang Publishing, 2008.
Murray, Janet H. *Hamlet on the Holodeck: The Future of Narrative in Cyberspace.* New York: The Free Press, 1997.
Ohler, Jason B. *Digital Storytelling in the Classroom: New Media Pathways to Literacy, Learning, and Creativity.* New York: Corwin Press, 2007.
Porter, Bernajean. *DigiTales: The Art of Digital Storytelling.* Ballston Spa, NY: BP Consulting, 2004.
Sloane, Sarah. *Digital Fictions: Storytelling in a Material World.* New York: Ablex Corp., 2000.
Snyder, Ilana. *Page to Screen: Taking Literacy into the Electronic Age.* London: Routledge, 1998.
Standley, Mark and Skip Via. *Digital Storytelling with iMovie/Powerpoint.* Anchorage, AL: Visions Technology in Education, 2004.

Storytelling, Story Work, and Public Speaking

Birch, Carol L. and Melissa A. Heckler, eds. *Who Says? Essays on Pivotal Issues in Contemporary Storytelling: American Storytelling from August House.* Little Rock, AR: August House Publishers, 1996.
Cassady, Marsh. *The Art of Storytelling: Creative Ideas for Preparation and Performance.* Colorado Springs, CO: Meriwether Publishing, 1994.
Cox, Allison M. and David H. Albert. *The Healing Heart: Storytelling to Build Strong and Healthy Communities.* Gabriola, BC: New Society Publishers, 2003.
Davis, Donald. *Telling Your Own Stories.* Little Rock, AR: August House Publishers, 1993.

Mooney, Bill and David Holt. *The Storyteller's Guide*. Little Rock, AR: August House Publishers, 1996.
Polletta, Francesca. *It Was Like a Fever: Storytelling in Protest and Politics*. Chicago, IL: University of Chicago Press, 2006.
Robbins, Jo. *High Impact Presentations: A Multimedia Approach*. New York: John Wiley and Sons, 1997.
Terkel, Studs. *Working: People Talk About What They Do All Day and How They Feel About What They Do*. Chicago, IL: The New Press, 1972.
Tilly, Charles. *Stories, Identities, and Political Change*. Lanham, MD: Rowman & Littlefield, 2002.

Creative Writing and Autobiography

Atkinson, Robert. *The Gift of Stories: Practical and Spiritual Applications of Autobiography, Life Stories, and Personal Mythmaking*. Westport, CT: Bergin & Garvey, 1995.
Case, Patricia Ann. *How to Write Your Autobiography: Preserving Your Family Heritage*. Santa Barbara, CA: Woodbridge Press, 1995.
Egri, Lajos. *The Art of Dramatic Writing: Its Basis In The Creative Interpretation Of Human Motives*. Rockford, IL: BN Publishing, 2009.
Goldberg, Natalie. *Writing Down the Bones: Freeing the Writer Within*. Boston, MA: Sambala, 1986.
Kunz, John A. and Florence Gray Soltys. *Transformational Reminiscene*. New York, Springer, 2007.
Lamott, Anne. *Bird by Bird: Some Instructions on Writing and Life*. New York: Pantheon Books, 1994.
Maquire, Jack. *The Power of Personal Storytelling*. New York, Tarcher–Putnum, 1998.
Metzger, Deena. *Writing for Your Life: Discovering the Story of Your Life's Journey*. San Francisco, CA: HarperCollins, 1992.
Polking, Kirk. *Writing Family Histories and Memoirs*. Cincinnati, OH: Betterway Books, 1995.
Rainer, Tristine. *Your Life As Story*. New York: G.P. Putnam's Sons, 1997.
Roorbach, Bill. *Writing Life Stories: How To Make Memories Into Memoirs, Ideas Into Essays And Life Into Literature*. 2nd Edition. New York: Writers Digest Books, 2008.
Selling, Bernard. *Writing From Within: A Guide to Creativity and Life Story Writing*. Alameda, CA: Hunter House, 1988.
Stone, Richard. *The Healing Art of Storytelling: A Sacred Journey of Personal Discovery*. New York: Hyperion, 1996.
Strunk, William, Jr. and White, E.B. *The Elements of Style*, (5th edn). Boston. MA: Allyn and Bacon, 2009.
Vogler, Christopher. *The Writer's Journey: Mythic Structure for Writers*. Studio City, CA: Michael Wiese Productions, 2007.

Counseling, Group Process, Facilitation

Cole, Marilyn B. *Group Dynamics in Occupational Therapy: The Theoretical Basis and Practice Application of Group Treatment*. Thorofare, NJ, Slack Incorporated, 1993.
Corey, Gerald, Marianne Corey, and Patrick Callanan. *Issues and Ethics in the Helping Professions*. Pacific Grove, CA: Brooks/Cole Publishing Company, 1993.
Jacobs, Ed E., Robert L. Masson, and Riley L. Harvill. *Group Counseling, Strategies and Skills*. Belmont, CA: Thompson Higher Education, 2007.
Webne-Behrman, Harry. *The Practice of Facilitation*. Westport, CT, 1998.
Yalom, Irvin D. and Molyn Leszcz. *The Theory and Practice of Group Psychotherapy*. New York: Basic Books, 2005.

Design, Media and Applications

Bone, Jan, and Ron Johnson. *Understanding the Film: An Introduction to Film Appreciation*. 4th Edition. Lincolnwood, IL: NTC, 1995.

Coles, Robert. *Doing Documentary Work*. New York: Oxford University Press, 1997.

DuChemin, David. *Within the Frame: The Journey of Photographic Vision*. Berkeley, CA: New Riders Press, 2009.

Horn, Robert. *Visual Language: Global Communication for the 21st Century*. Bainbridge Island, WA: Macrovu Inc., 1999.

McCloud, Scott. *Understanding Comics: The Invisible Art*. New York: Kitchen Sink Press, 1993.

McCloud, Scott. *Reinventing Comics: How Imagination and Technology Are Revolutionizing an Art Form*. New York: Perennial, 2000.

McDonagh, Deana, Paul Hekkert, Jeroen van Erp, and Diane Gyi eds. *Design and Emotion*. Boca Raton, FL: CRC Press, 2003.

McKee, Robert. *Story, Substance, Structure, Style and the Principles of Screenwriting*. New York: It Books (HarperCollins), 1997.

Nichols, Bill. *Introduction to Documentary*. Bloominton, IN: Indiana University Press, 2001.

Powazek, Derek. *Design for Community*. Berkeley, CA: New Riders Press, 2002.

Shedroff, Nathan. *Experience Design*. Berkeley, CA: New Riders Press, 2001.

Withrow, Steven. *Secrets of Digital Animation: A Master Class in Innovative Tools and Techniques*. Hove: RotoVision, 2009.

Storytelling and Education

Alterio, Maxine. *Learning Through Storytelling in Higher Education: Using Reflection and Experience to Improve Learning*. London: RoutledgeFalmer, 2003.

Bell, Lee Anne. *Storytelling for Social Justice: Connecting Narrative and the Arts in Antiracist Teaching*. London: Routledge, 2010.

Bruner, Jerome. *The Culture of Education*. Cambridge, MA: Harvard University Press, 1996.

Egan, Kieran. *Teaching As Story Telling: An Alternative Approach to Teaching and Curriculum in the Elementary School*. Chicago, IL: The University of Chicago Press, 1986.

Egan, Kieran. *The Educated Mind: How Cognitive Tools Shape our Understanding*. Chicago, IL: The University of Chicago Press, 1997.

Fields, Anne M., and Karen R. Diaz. *Fostering Community through Digital Story-telling: A Guide for Academic Libraries*. Santa Barbara, CA: Libraries Unlimited, 2008.

Frazel, Midge. *Digital Storytelling Guide for Educators*. Washington, DC: International Society for Technology in Education, 2010.

Cognitive Theory, Psychology, and Narrative

Carson, Jo. *Spider Speculations: A Physics and Biophysics of Storytelling*. New York: Theatre Communications Group, 2008.

Dennett, Daniel C. *Kinds of Minds: Toward an Understanding of Consciousness*. New York: Basic Books, 1996.

Fireman, Gary D., Ted E. McVay, and Owen J. Flanagan. *Narrative and Consciousness: Literature, Psychology and the Brain*. New York: Oxford University Press, 2003.

Gardner, Howard. *Frames of Mind: The Theory Of Multiple Intelligences*. New York: Basic Books, 1993.

Goleman, Daniel. *Emotional Intelligence: Why It Can Matter More Than IQ*. New York: Bantam Books, 1995.

Gubrium, Jaber F. *Analyzing Narrative Reality*. Thousand Oaks, CA: SAGE, 2009.

Harvey, John H. *Embracing Their Memory: Loss and the Social Psychology of Storytelling*. Needham Heights, MA: Allyn and Bacon, 1996.

Hunt, Celia. *Therapeutic Dimensions of Autobiography in Creative Writing*. London: Jessica Kingsley Publishers, 2000.

Kast, Verena. *Folktales as Therapy*. New York: Fromm International, 1995.

Kurtz, Ernest. *The Spirituality of Imperfection: Storytelling and the Search for Meaning*. New York: Bantam, 1992.

Linde, Charlotte. *Life Stories: The Creation of Coherence*. Oxford: Oxford University Press, 1993.

McAdams, Dan P. *The Stories We Live By: Personal Myths and the Making of the Self*. New York: Guilford Press, 1993.

Ong, Walter J. *Orality and Literacy: The Technologizing of the Word*. London: Routledge, 1982.

Parry, Alan and Robert E. Doan. *Story Re-Visions: Narrative Therapy in the Post-Modern World*. New York: The Guilford Press, 1994.

Schank, Roger C. *Tell Me a Story: Narrative and Intelligence*. Evanston, IL: Northwestern University Press, 1990.

Storytelling in Corporate and Organizational Contexts

Boje, David Michael. *Storytelling Organizations*. Thousand Oaks, CA: SAGE, 2008.

Brown, John Seely, Stephen Denning, Katalina Groh, and Laurence Prusak. *Storytelling in Organizations: Why Storytelling Is Transforming 21st Century Organizations and Management*. Boston, MA: Butterworth-Heinemann, 2004.

Denning, Stephen. *The Springboard: How Storytelling Ignites Action in Knowledge-Era Organizations*. Boston, MA: Butterworth-Heinemann, 2001.

Denning, Stephen. *The Leader's Guide to Storytelling: Mastering the Art and Discipline of Business Narrative*. San Francisco, CA: Jossey Bass, 2005.

Fog, Klaus, Christian Budtz, and Baris Yakaboylu. *Storytelling: Branding in Practice*. New York: Springer, 2005.

Gargiulo, Terrence L. *The Strategic Use of Stories in Organizational Communication and Learning*. Armonk, NY: M.E. Sharpe, 2005.

Gunaratnam, Yasmin and David Oliviere. *Narrative and Stories in Healthcare: Illness, Dying and Bereavement*. New York: Oxford University Press, 2009.

Parkin, Margaret. *Tales for Change: Using Storytelling to Develop People and Organizations*. London: Kogan Page, 2004.

Simmons, Annette. *The Story Factor: Inspiration, Influence, and Persuasion Through the Art of Storytelling*. 2nd Edition. New York: Basic Books, 2006.

Community Arts Practice

Goldbard, Arlene. *New Creative Community: The Art of Cultural Development*. Oakland, CA: New Village Press, 2006.

Goodman, Steven and Maxine Greene. *Teaching Youth Media: A Critical Guide to Literacy, Video Production, and Social Change*. New York: Teachers College Press, 2003.

Graves, James Bau. *Cultural Democracy: The Arts, Community, and the Public Purpose*. Champaign, IL: University of Illinois Press, 2004.

Howley, Kevin. *Community Media: People, Places, and Communication Technologies*. Cambridge: Cambridge University Press, 2005.

Krensky, Beth. *Engaging Classrooms and Communities through Art: A Guide to Designing and Implementing Community-Based Art Education*. Lanham, MD: AltaMira Press, 2008.

Schwarzman, Mat, and Keith Knight. *Beginner's Guide to Community-Based Arts*. Oakland, CA: New Village Press, 2005.

General

Boyd, Brian. *On the Origin of Stories: Evolution, Cognition, and Fiction.* Cambridge, MA: The Belknap Press of Harvard University Press.

Birkerts, Sven. *The Gutenberg Elegies: The Fate of Reading in an Electronic Age.* New York: Ballantine, 1994.

Campbell, Joseph. *The Power of Myth.* New York: Doubleday, 1988.

Carr, Nicholas. *The Shallows: What the Internet is Doing to Our Brain.* New York: W. W. Norton & Company, 2010.

Citron, Michelle. *Home Movies and Other Necessary Fictions.* Minneapolis, MN: University of Minnesota Press, 1999

Fuller, Robert. *All Rise: Somebodies, Nobodies, and the Politics of Dignity.* San Francisco, CA: Berrett-Koehler, 2006.

Gilster, Paul. *Digital Literacy.* New York: John Wiley and Sons, Inc., 1997.

Kandel, Eric R. *In search of Memory: The Emergence of a New Science of Mind.* New York: W. W. Norton; 2006.

Krippner, Stanley. *Dreams as a Mirror of Change in Personal Mythology,* http://education.victoriavesna.com/MFACRIT2010-a/sites/default/files/uploads/u1/Personal_Mythology.pdf, n.d.

McLuhan, Marshall. *Understanding Media: The Extensions of Man.* Cambridge, MA: MIT Press, 1994.

Rappoport, David. *Emotions and Memory.* Whitefish, MT: Kessinger Publishing, 2006.

Rossinow, Doug. *The Politics of Authenticity: Liberalism, Christianity, and the New Left in America.* New York: Columbia University Press, 1998.

Siegel, Daniel J. *The Developing Mind: How Relationships and the Brain Interact to Shape Who We Are.* New York: The Guilford Press, 2012.

Turkle, Sherry. *Alone Together: Why We Expect More from Technology and Less from Each Other.* New York: Basic Books, 2011.

Index

Lightning Source UK Ltd.
Milton Keynes UK
UKOW05f2007080516

273752UK00006B/32/P